IMAGES
of America

VICTORIAN AUGUSTA

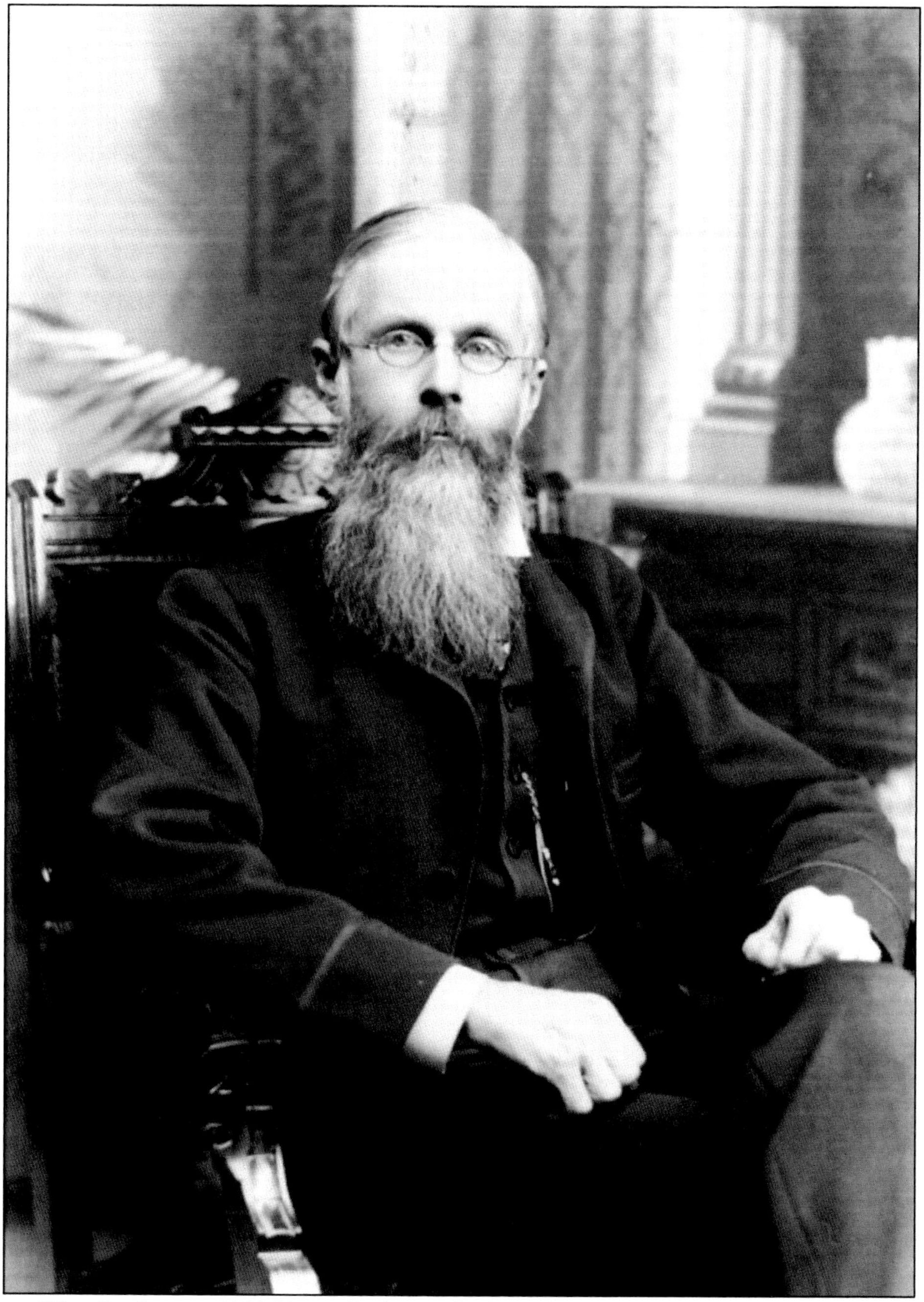

Born in West Gardiner in 1822, Henry Bailey worked as a photographer in Augusta from 1867 to his death in 1894. Three hundred of his stereo views survive to document the appearance of Maine's capital city and its surrounding communities during the Victorian era. (Hawkins collection.)

On the cover: Please see page 61. (Coffin Collection, Maine Historic Preservation Commission.)

IMAGES
of America

VICTORIAN AUGUSTA

Earle G. Shettleworth Jr.

ARCADIA
PUBLISHING

ISBN 978-0-7385-5774-8

Published by Arcadia Publishing
Charleston SC, Chicago IL, Portsmouth NH, San Francisco CA

Printed in the United States of America

Library of Congress Catalog Card Number: 2007936591

For all general information contact Arcadia Publishing at:
Telephone 843-853-2070
Fax 843-853-0044
E-mail sales@arcadiapublishing.com
For customer service and orders:
Toll-Free 1-888-313-2665

Visit us on the Internet at www.arcadiapublishing.com

This book is dedicated to Marion S. Coffin (1909–1995), who preserved the collection of Henry Bailey stereo views that bears her name at the Maine Historic Preservation Commission, and to Col. Richard S. and Marion F. Hawkins, whose generous sharing of family history, research, and pictures has been invaluable in understanding the photographic careers of Bailey and Augustus F. Morse.

Contents

Acknowledgments		6
Introduction		7
1.	Public Buildings	11
2.	Churches	25
3.	North End	33
4.	Water Street	43
5.	Residences	57
6.	Capitol Park	69
7.	Togus	75
8.	Surrounding Towns	87
9.	Summer Retreats	95
10.	Henry Bailey and His Family	117

ACKNOWLEDGMENTS

For more than a decade, I have considered compiling a book of Henry Bailey's photographs of Augusta. Recent significant changes in the city have made me realize the urgency of sharing these remarkable images with the public in the hope of illustrating what a beautiful place Augusta has been.

Any research on Maine's capital city must begin with James W. North's encyclopedic 990-page *History of Augusta.* Although North stopped chronicling the community's history shortly before its 1870 publication date, the book contains a wealth of information found nowhere else. Other useful volumes include *Illustrated History of Kennebec County* (1892), *Augusta Centennial Souvenir* (1897), and Joseph T. Beck's *Historical Notes on Augusta, Maine* in two parts (1962 and 1963).

Augusta newspapers from the 19th century, especially the *Kennebec Journal* and the *Maine Farmer*, provided many period articles upon which the text of this book is based. Likewise, the more recent 10-year run of "Antiquarian Notebook," Anthony Douin's biweekly column in the *Capitol Weekly*, proved a fruitful source. Douin is Augusta's most knowledgeable historian, and he has been of great assistance to me, especially as a reader for this book.

Zachary Violette's architectural and historical overviews of Water Street, Winthrop Street, and Sand Hill are in-depth resources for understanding the development and fabric of these areas of the city. They attest to Violette's skills as an architectural and urban historian.

I also made frequent use of the Maine State Library, the Kennebec Historical Society, the Maine Historical Society, the Maine Historic Preservation Commission, and the Gardiner Public Library. Not to be overlooked are the maps of Augusta, found in the collections of these institutions, that were published in 1838, 1851, 1856, 1862, 1875, 1878, and 1879.

Finally, this book would not have been possible without the help of the Coffin and Hawkins families, who both preserved the legacy of Bailey. As early as 1973, Marion S. Coffin shared with me the extensive collection of Bailey's stereo views, which her family had been given by Bailey's descendents. After her death in 1995, her children gave these images to the Maine Historic Preservation Commission, where they comprise a collection that bears her name. Unless otherwise noted, all photographs in this book are from this collection.

Similarly, Col. Richard S. and Marion F. Hawkins of Augusta made their family history, research, and pictures available, which document the life and work of Bailey and his brother-in-law Augustus F. Morse. The Hawkinses' interest, support, and friendship have been much appreciated.

INTRODUCTION

Of the several hundred Maine photographers who made stereo view cards between 1860 and 1900, few were as prolific in their production as Henry Bailey of Augusta. These cards, featuring two images of the same view placed side by side, were put in stereoscopes with a pair of lenses that merged the pictures into one, creating a three-dimensional effect in the process. Looking at stereo cards was a widespread entertainment in Victorian America, and Bailey and his fellow Maine photographers responded to this popular pastime by marketing large numbers of town and city views. Once common, these now-rare photographs provide the single most comprehensive pictorial record of Maine during the second half of the 19th century. To date, approximately 150 of Bailey's Augusta views have been located along with more than 150 of his pictures of other locations in the central and coastal regions of the state. These stereo views are found at the Maine Historic Preservation Commission, the Maine Historical Society, the Kennebec Historical Society, Historic New England, the American Antiquarian Society, and in private collections.

Born in West Gardiner in 1822, Bailey was the youngest of Timothy and Betsy Bailey's nine children. He grew up on the family farm in a Quaker household, although he became a Methodist in his adulthood. According to his daughter Eunice Bailey Shorey, he devoted his early life to preparing for Bowdoin College, a goal he never reached. During the years he attempted to prepare for college at Litchfield and Bowdoinham Academies, he worked as a cobbler, a peddler, and a jack-of-all-trades. He settled on shoemaking, a trade he pursued from the 1840s through the 1860s. During this period, he lived primarily in Brunswick, but also spent time in Bowdoinham, Richmond, and Yarmouth.

In 1856, at the age of 34, Bailey married Elmyra Gray of Hallowell on her 16th birthday. The couple had two daughters, Etta in 1858 and Eunice in 1864. The marriage ended with Elmyra's death at the age of 27 on March 14, 1867. After his wife was buried in the Friends Cemetery in West Gardiner, Bailey went to Hallowell to live with his wife's sister Sarah Gray Morse and her husband, Augustus F. Morse, who was a portrait, landscape, and stereo view photographer. Bailey's youngest daughter, Eunice, was sent to live with family members at the Bailey homestead in West Gardiner, while Etta stayed with her father and the Morses.

The death of his wife, Elmyra, and his resulting move to Hallowell marked a significant turning point in Bailey's life. As early as 1851, he had written from Bowdoinham to his brother Alvah that he was experimenting with photography, which, at that time, meant he was working with a daguerreotype camera. This latent interest was given expression after his wife's death, when he moved in with Morse, his brother-in-law. Morse offered training in photography, which by then was a wet plate process using glass negatives. Bailey rapidly acquired his photographic education from Morse, and in May 1867, he purchased a photograph saloon on Water Street near Winthrop Street in downtown Augusta and opened his own business.

Conveniently sited adjacent to Augusta's railroad station, Bailey's small wooden one-story building featured a board-and-batten facade with an overhanging gable roof trimmed in bargeboards. This attractive shop contained a display space at the front and a studio with a skylight and a darkroom at the rear. Glass cases of tintypes and framed tintype portraits hung on the exterior at either side of the entrance door. The modest scale of Bailey's building could be found in others along Water Street, where one-story frame structures mingled with more substantial brick blocks in a commercial district still recovering from a devastating fire in 1865.

Bailey conducted business at this location until May 1877, when he received notice that he was being displaced by the construction of North's Hotel. Bailey then moved his saloon to the north end of Water Street near the railroad bridge, where he continued to operate until April 1885. That month, he sold his building to Mr. and Mrs. Frank Gaslin for a millinery and fancy goods store. From that time until his death in 1894, Bailey used the home he had purchased in the 1870s near the foot of Winthrop Street as his studio, spending summers taking tintype portraits in a tent in downtown Bar Harbor, Maine's famous tourist destination. A March 28, 1888, article in the *Kennebec Journal* indicated that he passed the winter in Jacksonville, Florida, where he also may have taken photographs.

Of the more than 300 known stereo views by Bailey, approximately half of them depict Augusta. These photographs capture the look of Maine's capital city in the post–Civil War period. State government is represented in pictures of the statehouse, the Augusta Mental Health Institute, and a militia encampment in Capitol Park. Other local subjects range from panoramic views and street scenes to the exteriors and interiors of public buildings, churches, commercial blocks, and residences. Some 30 cards document the newly established federal veterans' home at Togus in nearby Chelsea. Among the specific events depicted are an 1875 military parade on Water Street and the 1883 train wreck at Riverside. Such topical views of current happenings represent a public demand for journalistic pictures in a time when newspapers and magazines could not reproduce photographs.

Much of the balance of Bailey's stereo views reflects his practice of photographing coastal resorts and religious campgrounds during the summer months. His pictures indicate that he visited such early vacation retreats as Boothbay Harbor, Capitol Island, Harpswell, Monhegan Island, Mouse Island, Ocean Point, Popham Beach, Portland Harbor, Pemaquid, and Squirrel Island. In the major resort towns of Boothbay Harbor and Bar Harbor, Bailey operated his studio from a tent in which he took tintype portraits and sold stereo views

Bailey practiced photography commercially from 1867 until his death in 1894. During the period between 1868 and 1885, when he conducted his photograph saloon in Augusta, 30 Dunn credit reports on Bailey's business were made, indicating that he was engaged in a constant struggle to survive financially. Many of the reports characterize his business as small, and they caution against extending credit to him. However, they also reflect how Bailey benefited from the rapidly expanding coastal tourist trade after the Civil War.

After Bailey closed his studio on Water Street in 1885, his summer excursions to Bar Harbor became even more important as a source of income. Entries from his brother-in-law Morse's diaries for the summers of 1887, 1893, and 1894 reveal that the two veteran photographers worked together in Bailey's tent to take tintype portraits of vacationers. Sometimes Bailey's daughter Etta, who was an accomplished photographer in her own right, assisted them. Daily receipts in 1887 ranged from $1.50 to $25.20. In 1893, Morse noted in his diary that they often worked from 5:00 a.m. until 7:00 p.m. For such extended hours, Bailey paid Morse $2 a day.

During the summer of 1894, Bailey spent only July and August in Bar Harbor, returning to Augusta in the company of his daughter Etta on September 1 and leaving Augustus alone to take pictures for another month. Bailey's health was failing rapidly from tuberculosis, and he died on November 6, 1894, at the age of 71.

Two days later, the *Kennebec Journal* eulogized Bailey as a well-known and respected citizen. Bailey was laid to rest in the Friends Cemetery in West Gardiner next to his wife, Elmyra, who had died 27 years before. On his stone, the following passage is engraved: "I shall be satisfied when I wake to behold his likeness," as though the image of God himself might be captured by the photographer's camera.

An earlier version of this essay first appeared in the Fall/Winter 2002 issue of *Maine History*, a periodical published by the Maine Historical Society.

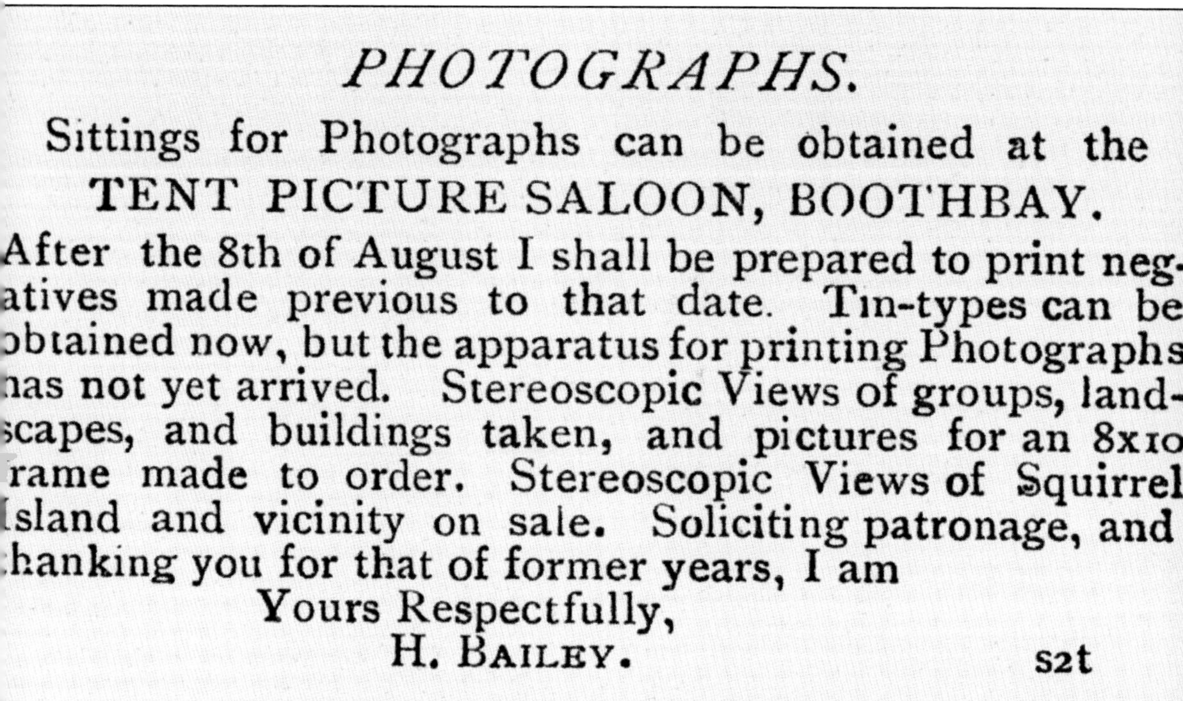

PHOTOGRAPHS.

Sittings for Photographs can be obtained at the

TENT PICTURE SALOON, BOOTHBAY.

After the 8th of August I shall be prepared to print negatives made previous to that date. Tin-types can be obtained now, but the apparatus for printing Photographs has not yet arrived. Stereoscopic Views of groups, landscapes, and buildings taken, and pictures for an 8x10 frame made to order. Stereoscopic Views of Squirrel Island and vicinity on sale. Soliciting patronage, and thanking you for that of former years, I am

Yours Respectfully,

H. BAILEY. s2t

This July 29, 1882, advertisement from the *Squirrel Island Squid* announces Henry Bailey's photographic services in Boothbay Harbor.

One

PUBLIC BUILDINGS

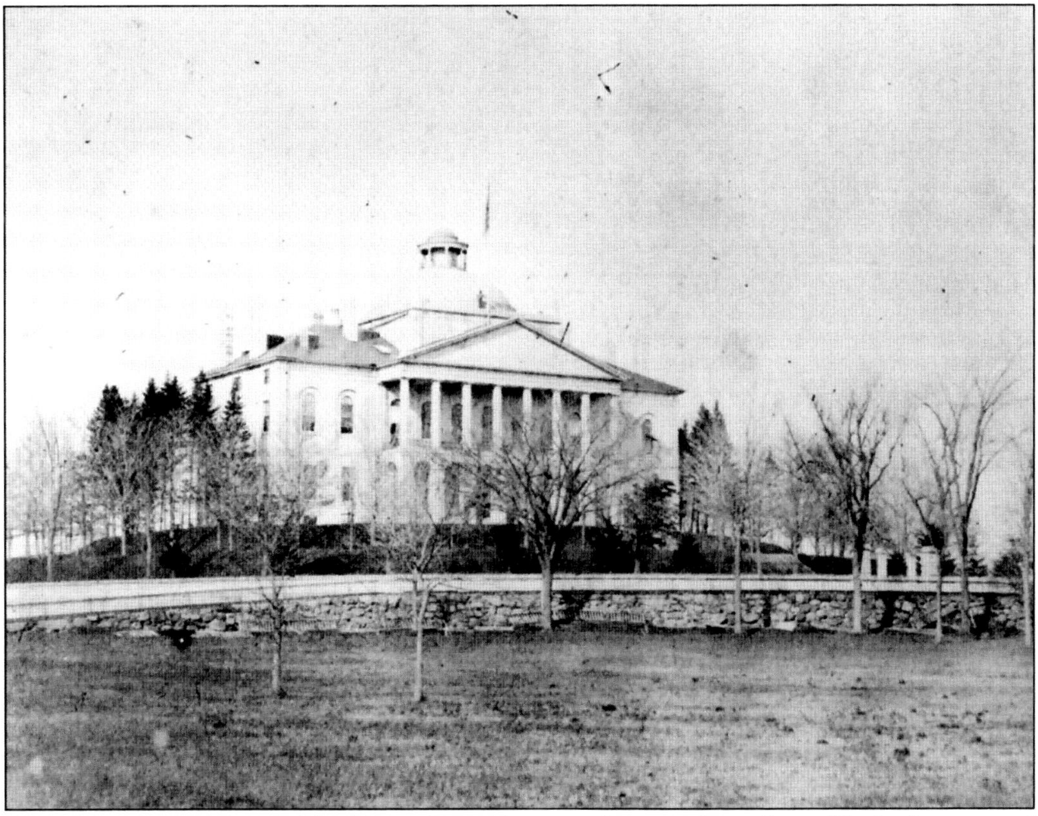

State Street runs in front of the Maine State House in this view from Capitol Park. Constructed of Hallowell granite between 1829 and 1832, the building was designed in the Greek Revival style by the noted Boston architect Charles Bulfinch. An initial cost estimate of $80,000 expanded to a final bill of $145,000 due to changes in plan and construction delays.

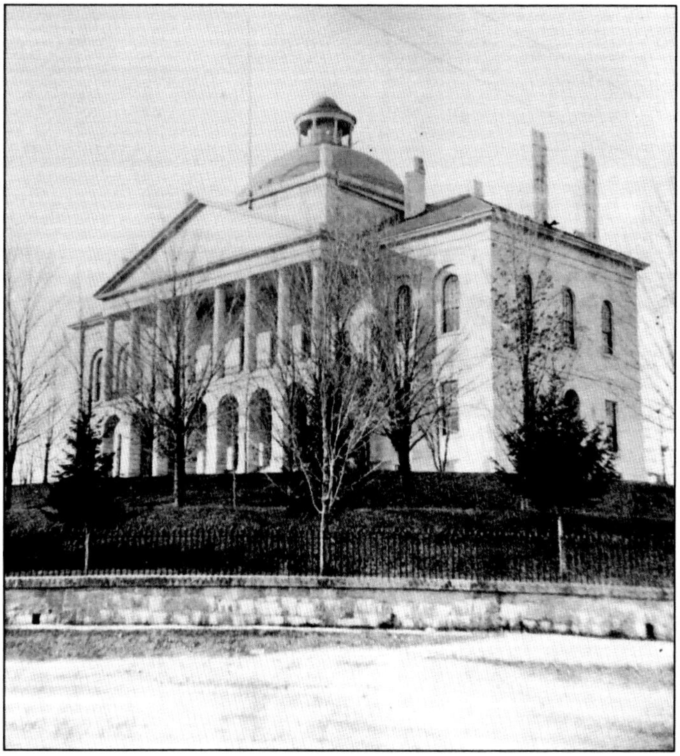

Photographed from the corner of State and Capitol Streets, the Maine State House stands atop Weston's Hill, displaying its monumental Doric portico and saucer dome. From 1832 to 1890, this is how the capitol building looked. In 1890 and 1891, the west wing was added to the rear, followed in 1909 and 1910 by the construction of the north and south wings and a 185-foot dome.

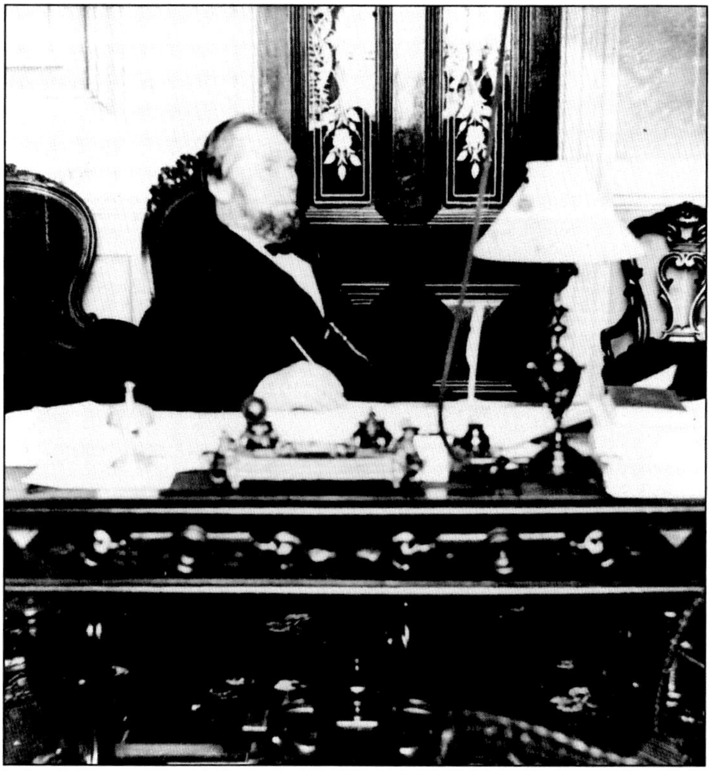

Gov. Sidney Perham is seated at his desk in the statehouse in this photograph taken between 1871 and 1873. Born in Woodstock in 1819, Perham worked as a teacher and a farmer before his election to Congress in 1862, where he represented Maine's Second District for six years. In 1870, he won the first of three one-year terms as governor. In retirement, he divided his time between Paris Hill and Washington, D.C., where he died in 1907.

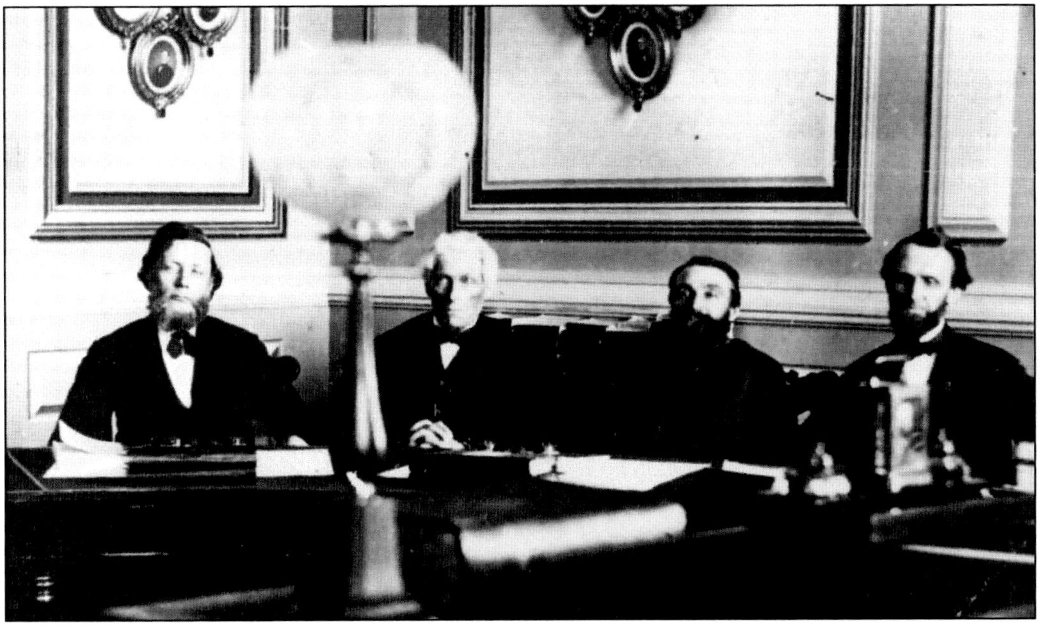

When Maine became a state in 1820, its constitution provided for a seven-member executive council that approved gubernatorial appointments. Taken between 1871 and 1873, this photograph shows four council members seated in their statehouse chamber with the governor's desk in the foreground adorned by a gas lamp. The executive council was a feature of state government until 1977.

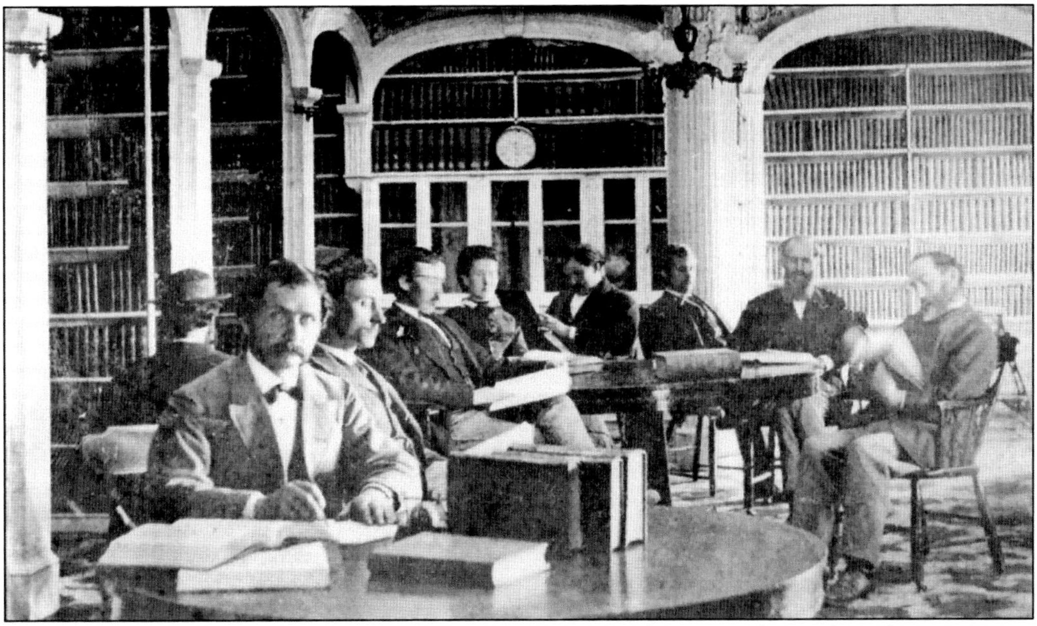

Established by the legislature in 1837, the Maine State Library was located in the statehouse for most of its history. In 1866, the library's modest quarters were transformed into this elegant reading room designed by architect James H. Cochrane to provide arched alcoves of shelving for 14,500 books. This space served the library until 1891 when expanded facilities became available in the new west wing of the statehouse.

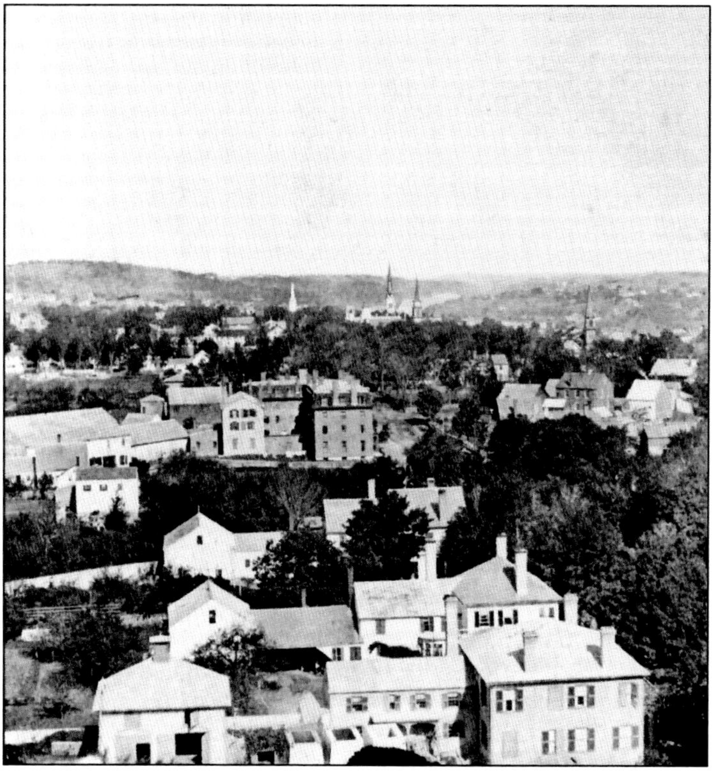

Shown in the foreground, the Blaine House, home of Maine's governors since 1919, was built at State and Capitol Streets in 1833 by Capt. James Hall. In 1862, James G. Blaine gave the house to his wife, Harriet, as a birthday present. The results of the Blaines' first remodeling in 1869 appear here in the form of an ell porch and a hipped roof on the carriage house. At the center of the photograph is a side view of the Augusta House hotel.

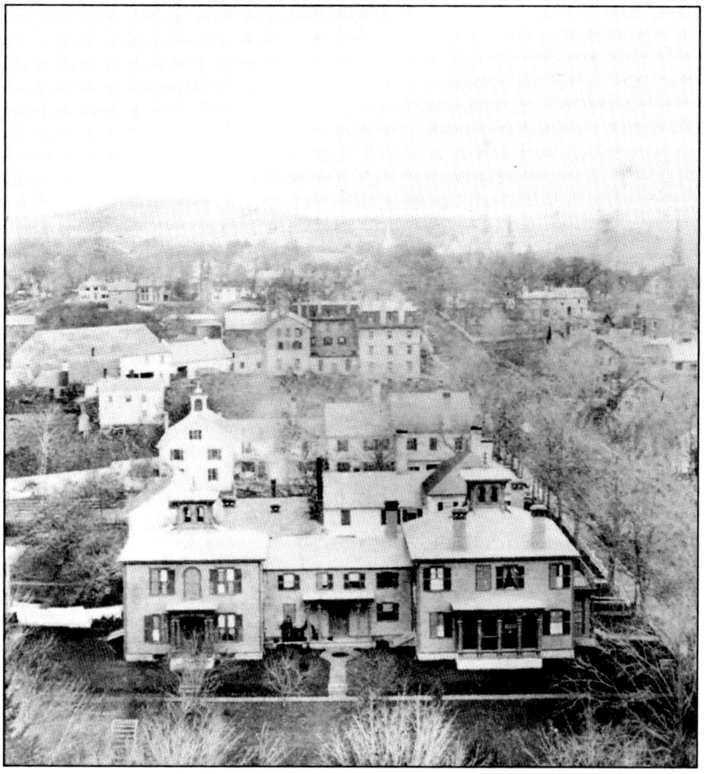

In 1872, the Blaines further remodeled their home by adding a bay window and cupola to the main house and a new wing to the ell for a library, billiard room, and bedrooms. From 1862 to 1892, Blaine dominated the Maine political scene, serving as speaker of the U.S. House of Representatives, U.S. senator, secretary of state, and the Republican Party's 1884 presidential candidate.

A northwest view from the statehouse dome in winter places Capitol Street in the foreground and the neighborhood beyond Western Avenue in the background. The fence running perpendicular from Capitol Street defined Blaine's backyard and that of his neighbors. To its left are houses that were acquired by the state in 1919 to expand the Blaine property to Chamberlain Street for aesthetic and security reasons. The residence at the far left was retained for staff.

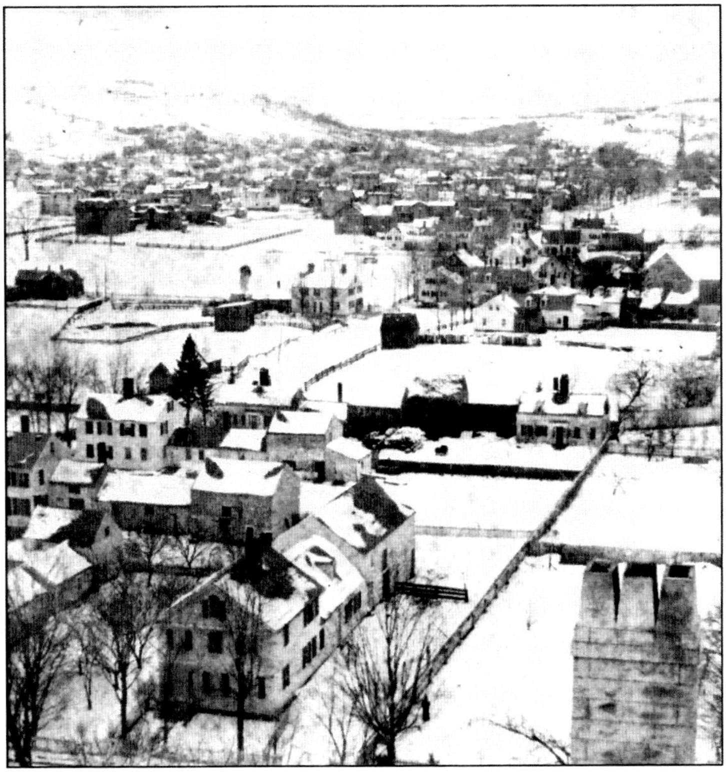

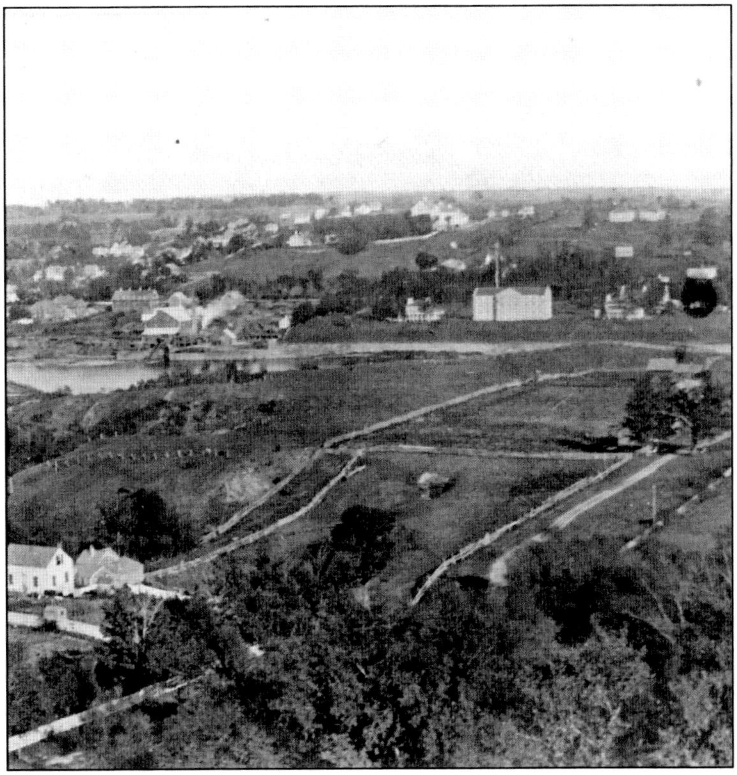

A northeast view from the statehouse dome shows Capitol Park at the far right paralleled by a dirt road that became Capitol Street. Open land extends to the Kennebec River, across which stands the central building of the Kennebec Arsenal, flanked by quarters No. 2 and No. 3. To the left of the arsenal is the sawmill of the Kennebec Land and Lumber Company.

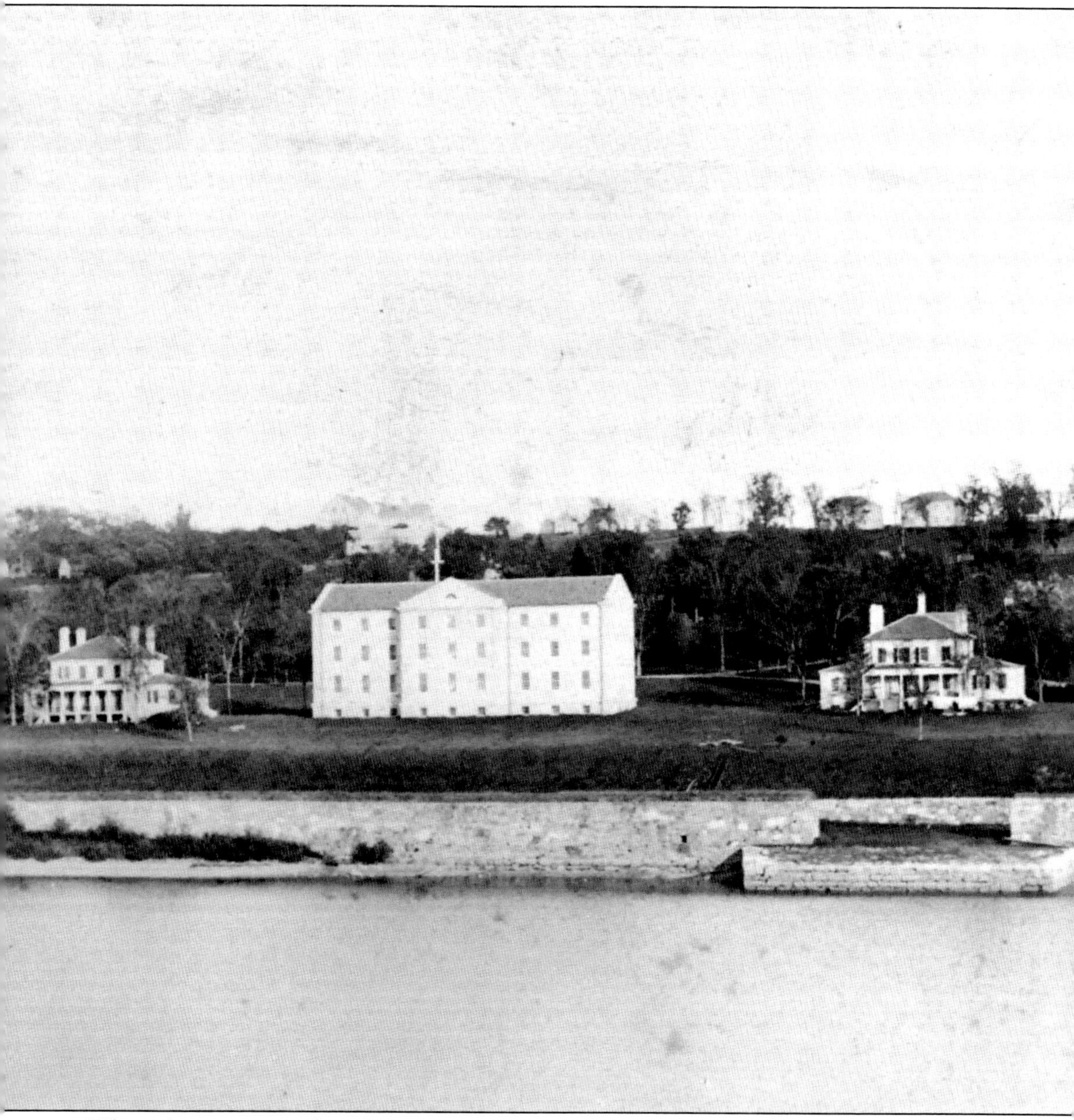

When Augusta was selected as Maine's capital in 1827, the War of 1812 with England was still a vivid memory, and the northeast boundary with British-controlled Canada remained unresolved. Thus the federal government established the Kennebec Arsenal on the east side of the Kennebec River in 1827 to provide military supplies for a "part of the country so much exposed, and liable to become the seat of war."

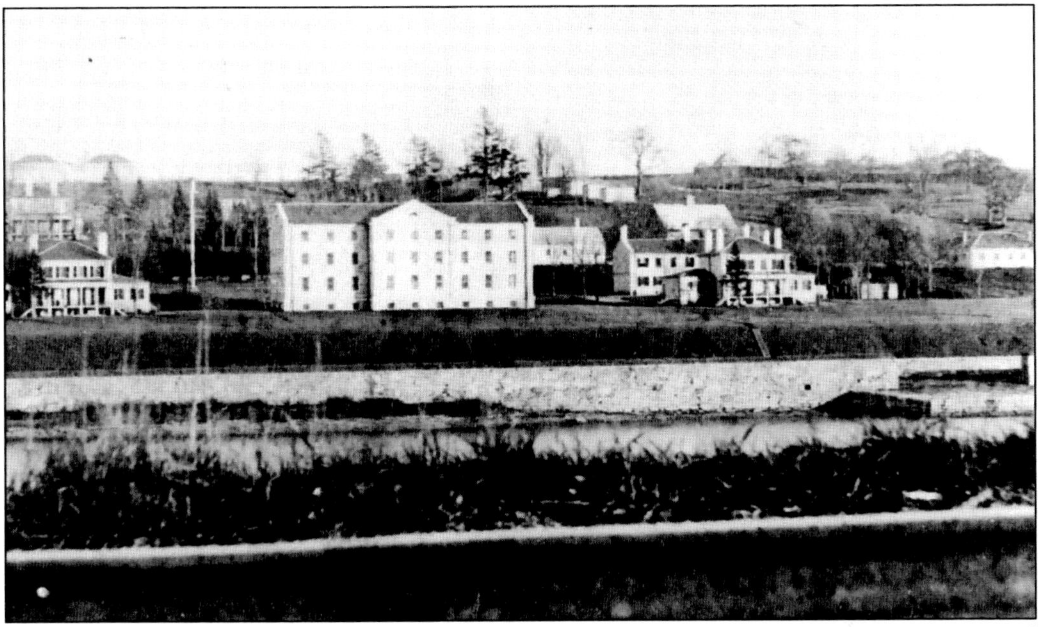

The Kennebec Arsenal was built between 1828 and 1838. Its major buildings were constructed of Hallowell granite in a chaste transitional Federal–Greek Revival style from designs by the U.S. Army. From left to right are the commandant's house, quarters two, the arsenal building, the barracks, and quarters three. The riverfront is lined by a stone retaining wall with a pier at the right.

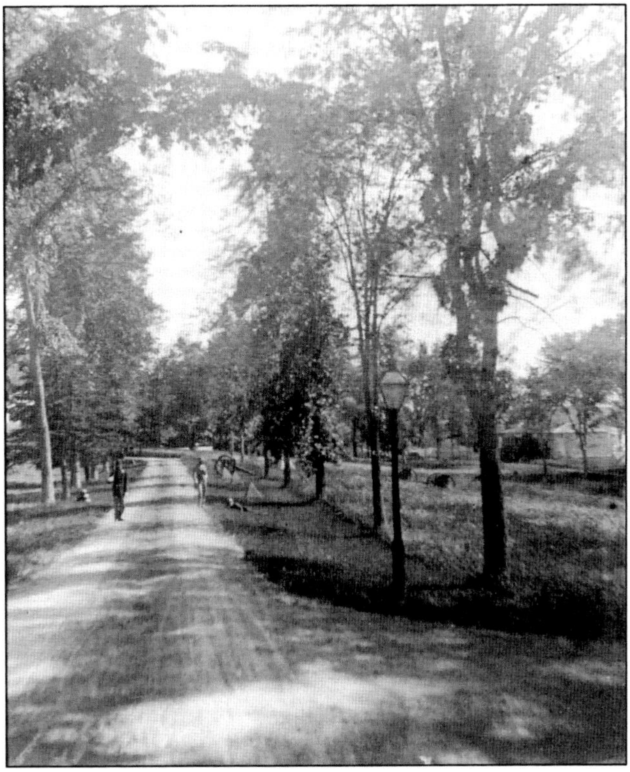

Elms line the Arsenal Street entrance to the Kennebec Arsenal with a sentry on duty at the left and the parade ground at the right. During the Civil War, the arsenal manufactured ammunition for the Union army. Declared obsolete after the Spanish-American War, the installation was closed in 1903 and transferred to the State of Maine in 1905 for use as part of the Augusta Mental Health Institute. This national historic landmark complex now awaits adaptive reuse by a private developer.

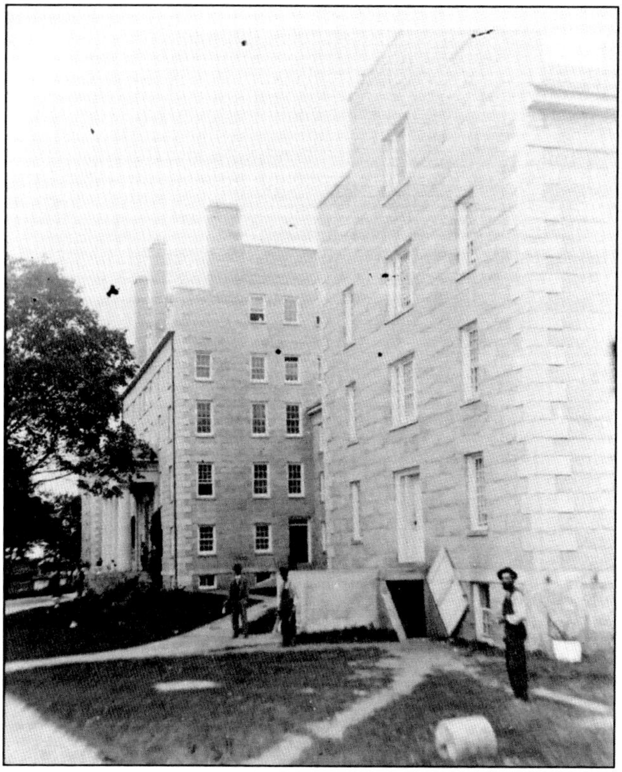

In 1834, the legislature established a state institution for the mentally ill. Sited on the east side of the Kennebec River, the Maine Insane Hospital took form in the stone building made of Hallowell granite between 1836 and 1840. Hallowell architect John D. Lord designed this monumental Greek Revival structure with a central pavilion flanked by matching wings. At the right is the south pavilion added from 1846 to 1848 for male patients.

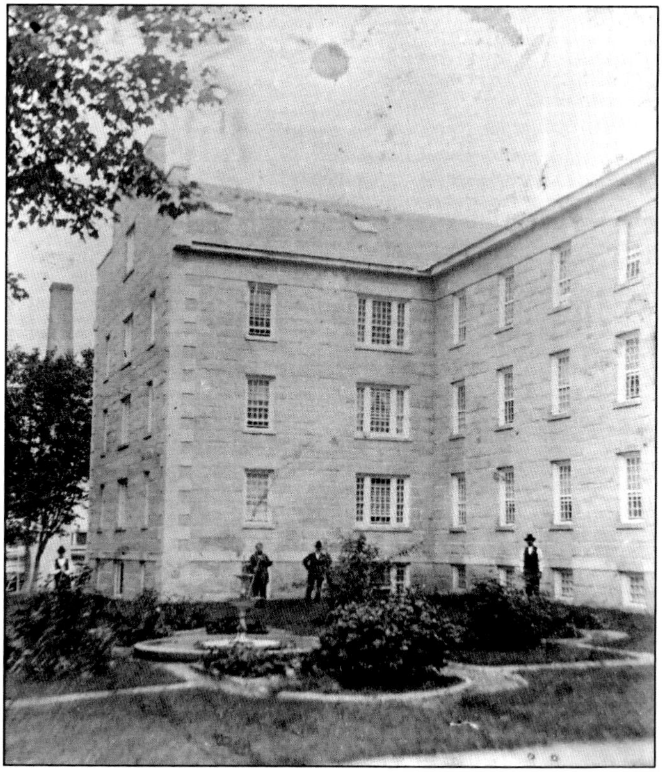

The north pavilion was added to the stone building between 1854 and 1855 for female patients. Both the north and south pavilions were planned by Augusta architect Henry Sawyer to be compatible in style, scale, and materials to the hospital's main section. This photograph provides a glimpse of the Victorian landscaping that once ornamented the hospital grounds.

The entrance hall and main staircase of the stone building appear more residential than institutional. During its first full year of operation in 1841, the Maine Insane Hospital treated 133 patients, which grew to 350 in 1870 and 725 in 1897.

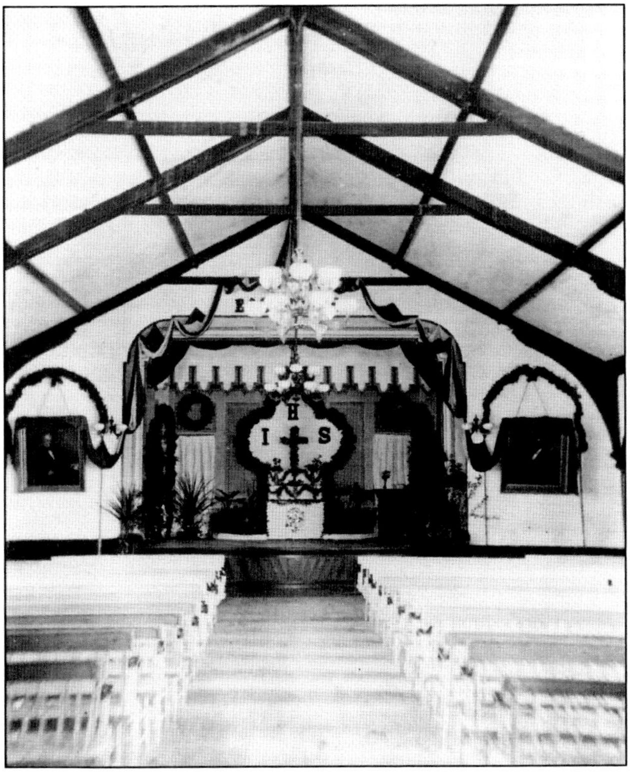

The expanding patient population at the Maine Insane Hospital resulted in the construction of the brick central building behind the stone building in 1875. Designed by Francis H. Fassett of Portland, Coburn Hall (as it was renamed in 1887) contained a first-floor kitchen, a second-floor assembly hall that doubled as a chapel, and an attic with living space for employees. Here the assembly hall–chapel is decorated with greens for Christmas services.

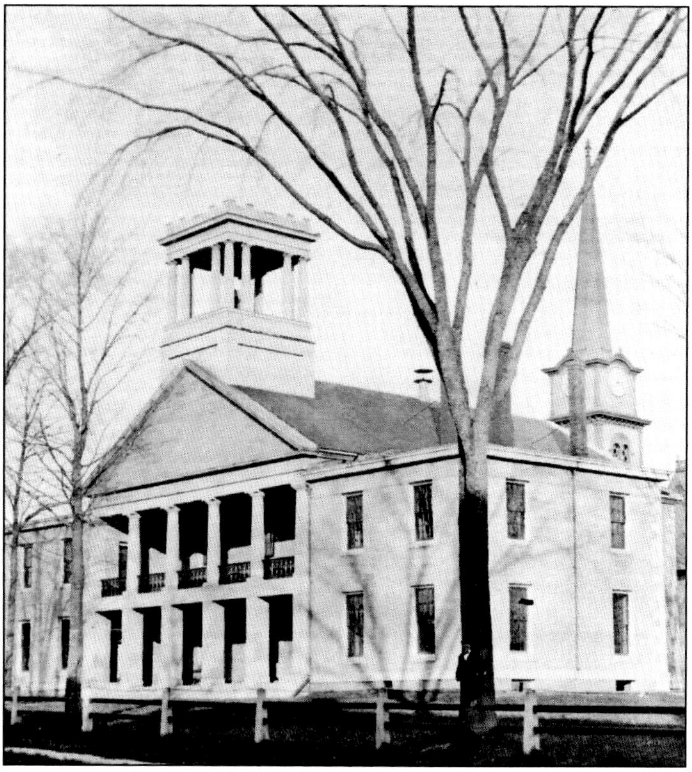

The Kennebec County commissioners voted in December 1827 to erect a courthouse at State and Winthrop Streets. Construction of a 50-by-60-foot Augusta granite building designed by James Cochran occurred from 1829 to 1830. A lack of space necessitated the expansion of the courthouse in 1851 under the direction of A. D. Sawyer. Using Hallowell granite, Sawyer added north and south wings as well as a columned Greek Revival facade and belfry.

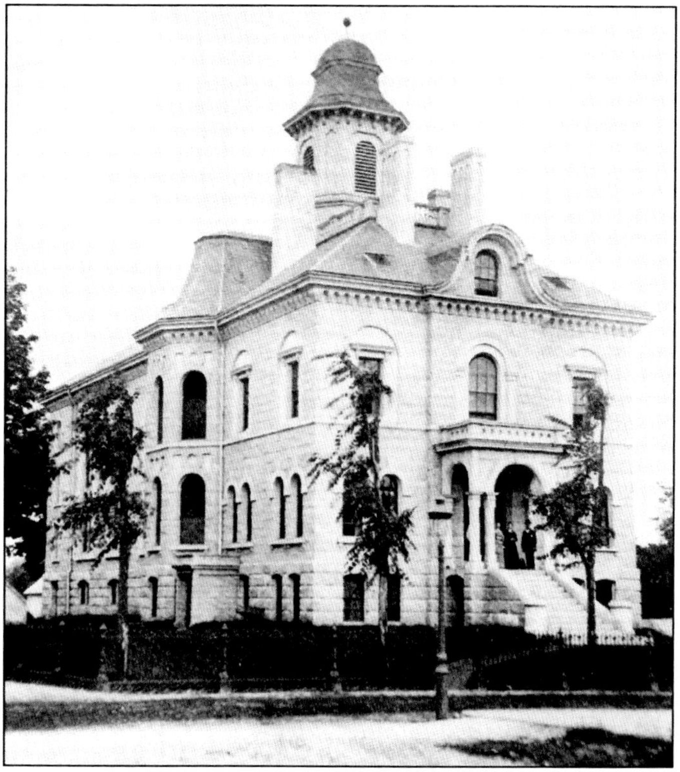

In 1857, the Kennebec County commissioners hired Gridley J. F. Bryant of Boston to plan a new county jail on State Street next to the courthouse. Constructed in 1858 and 1859, this imposing granite prison was designed in the Italianate style with mansard roof features. So elegant in appearance was the building that visitors to Augusta mistook it for the statehouse, a cathedral, or a palatial residence.

In 1869, Augusta affirmed its commitment to educating its youth by issuing bonds to construct a new high school and grammar school at State and Bridge Streets. Opened in 1870, this substantial, brick, mansard-roofed building was designed by Francis H. Fassett and built by John B. Shaw to accommodate a 200-student grammar school on the first floor and a high school of the same number on the second floor.

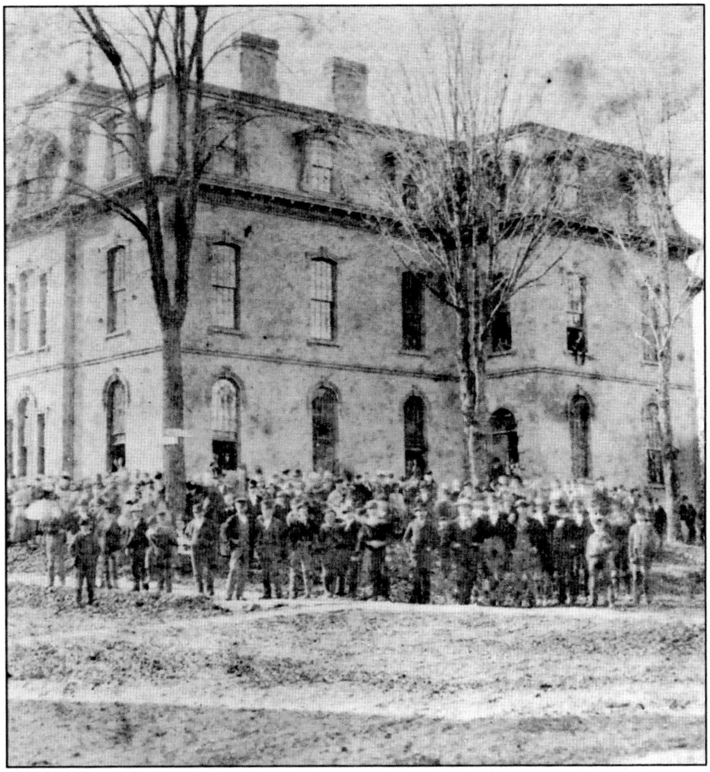

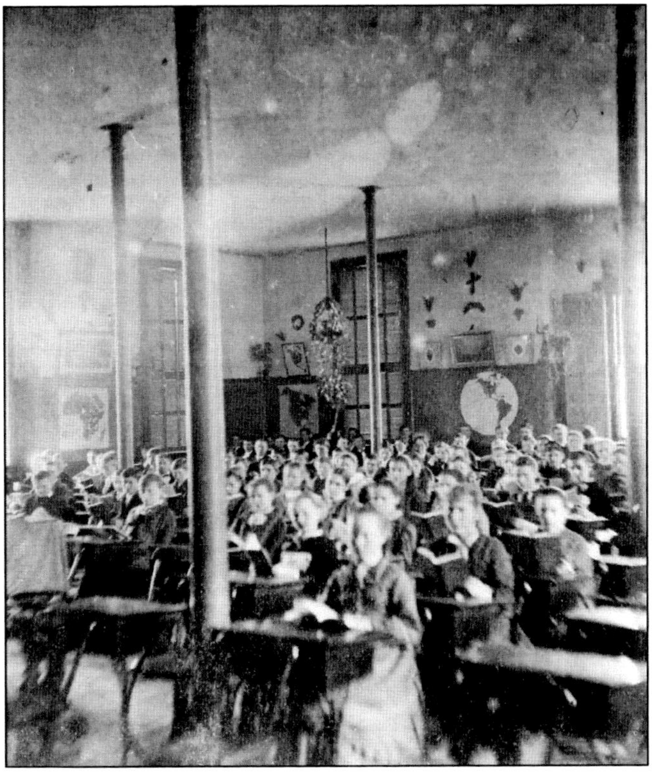

The first and second floors of Augusta's new school each contained a classroom and two recitation rooms. In the large open classrooms, boys sat at desks on one side and girls on the other. With the opening of Cony High School on the east side in 1881, Smith School became solely a grammar school. A recently constructed commercial building now occupies the site.

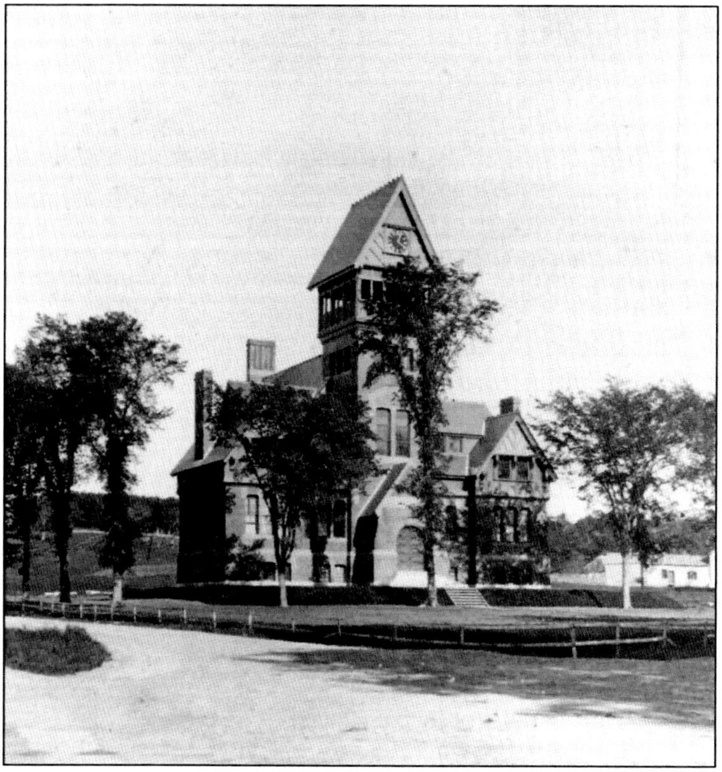

In 1815, Daniel Cony established the Cony Female Academy at Cony and Stone Streets. On that site in 1880, Cony's trustees constructed Cony High School, giving Augusta free use of the new building. Designed by Gridley J. F. Bryant of Boston, the school was expanded in 1909 and replaced by the Flatiron building in 1926.

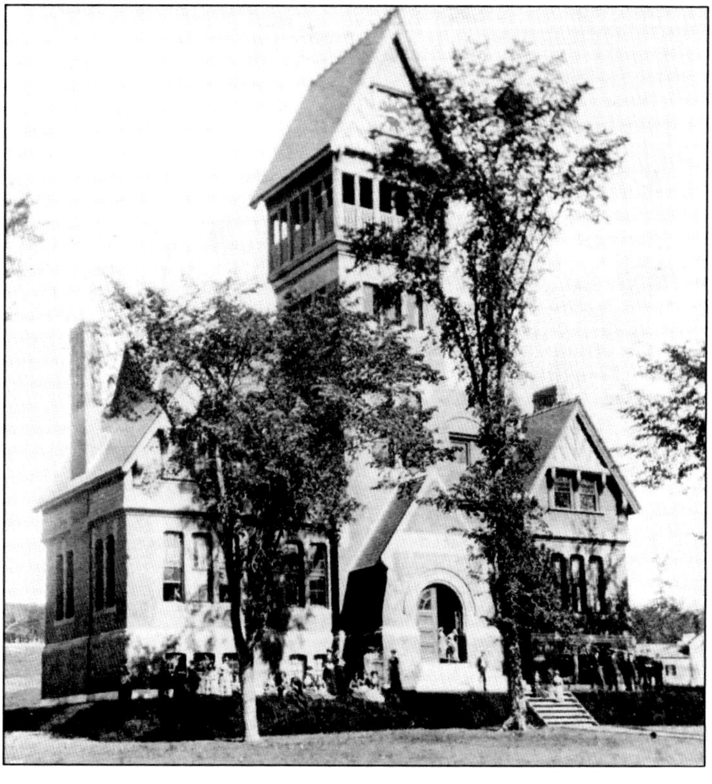

A striking example of Queen Anne architecture, Cony High School featured a brick basement, first story, and tower highlighted by stonework and a half-timbered wooden second story and belfry. According to the April 16, 1881, *Kennebec Journal*, from the tower, Augusta "spreads out at your feet like a great map. We know of no point in the city where a finer view can be had."

Gen. Alfred Redington, a prominent Augusta businessman and the city's first mayor, built this grand Greek Revival mansion in 1837 at Arsenal and East Chestnut Streets. In 1868, the house was enlarged at the rear to accommodate St. Catherine's Hall, an Episcopal girls' school. In 1900, the hall was purchased by the Augusta General Hospital and became the site for today's Maine General Hospital.

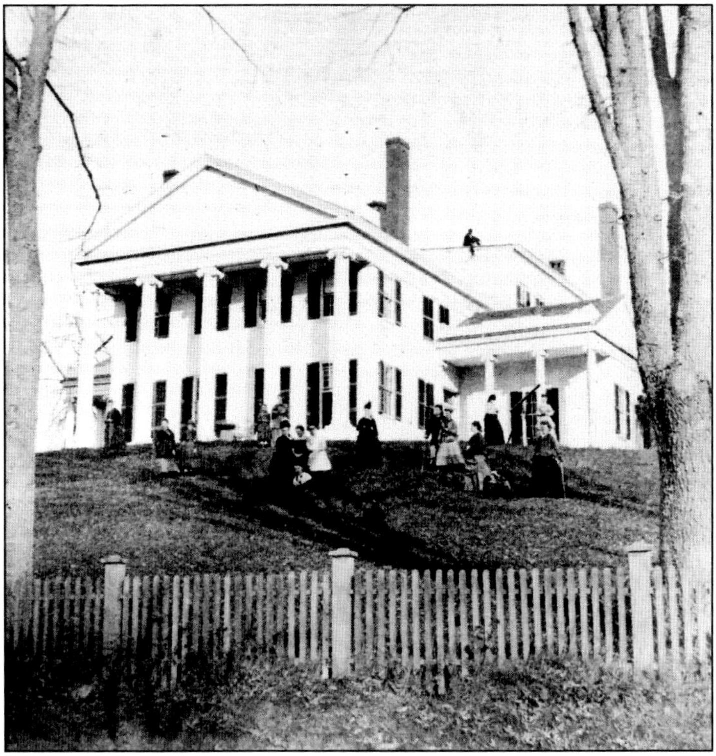

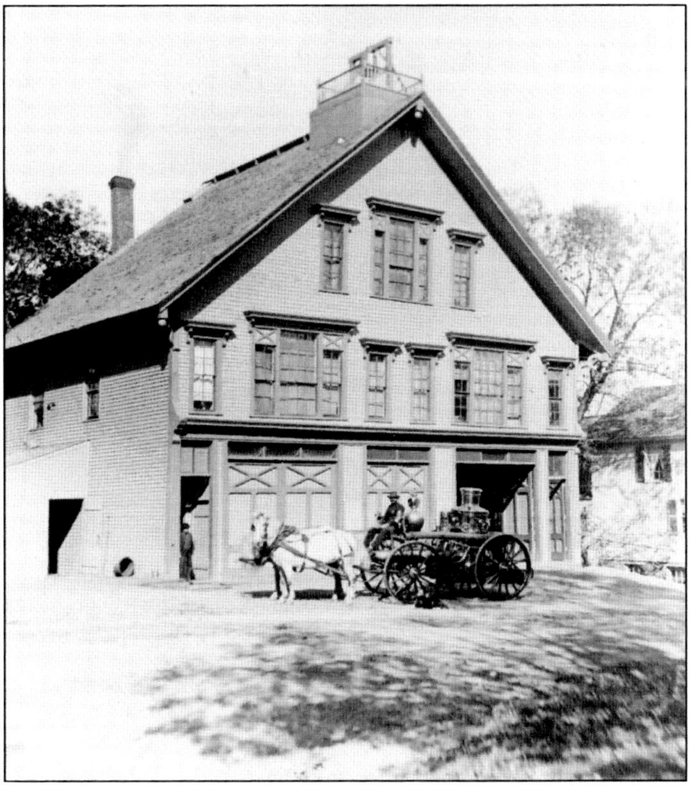

Built in 1851 and remodeled to its Victorian appearance in 1877, the Cushnoc Fire Station on Bridge Street served Augusta until its replacement by the Hartford Fire Station in 1920. In this photograph from about 1880, Alexander McCausland is in command of the horse-drawn Cushnoc steam fire engine. Due to its use until recently as a furniture store, the building survives today.

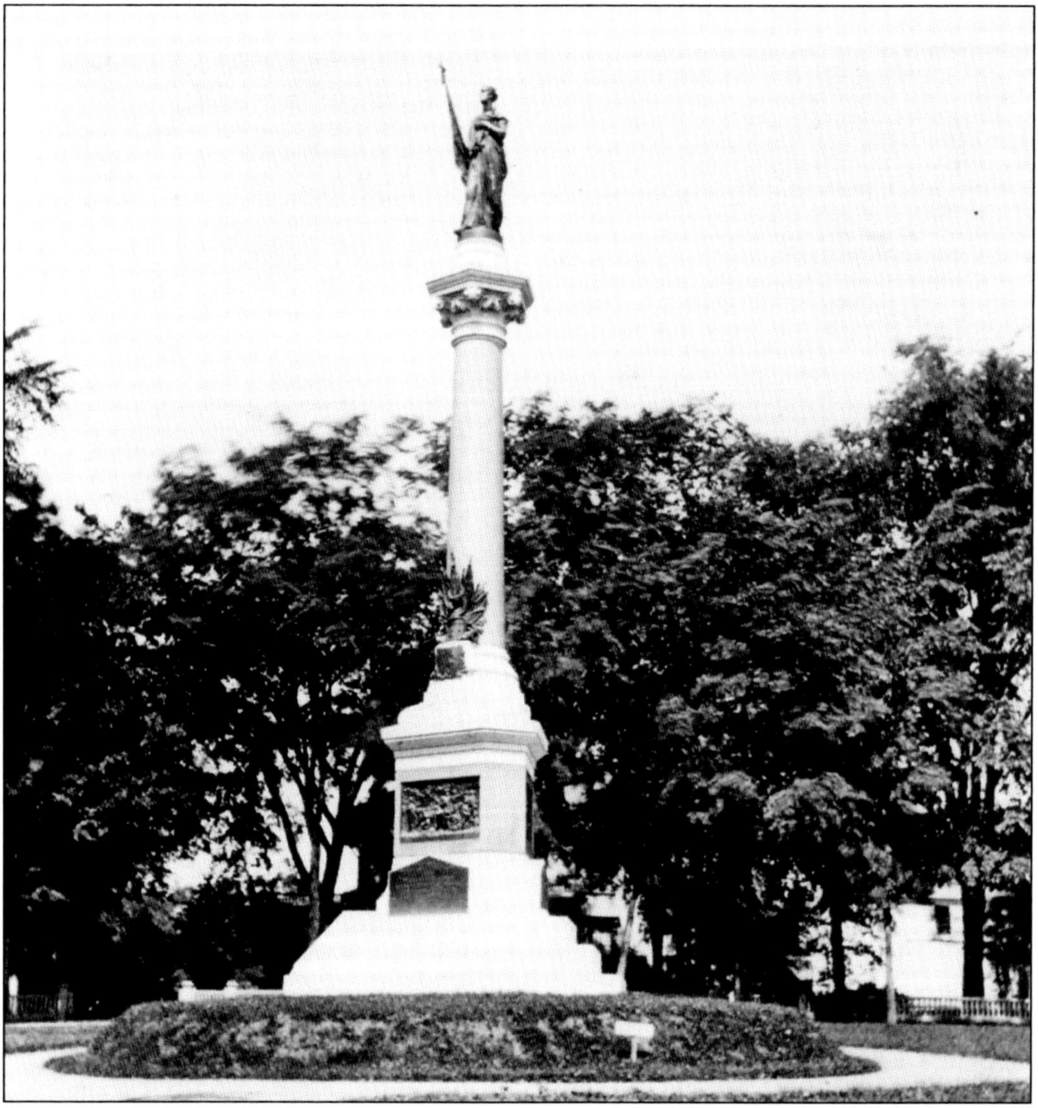

Beginning in 1864, more than 125 Maine communities erected Civil War monuments in the decades following the conflict. Prominent among these is the Augusta Soldiers' Monument, which was built in a small park at State and Grove Streets in 1881 and dedicated in 1882. Designed by Maurice J. Power of New York, the monument consists of a Hallowell granite base and column that provide an ornamental pedestal for a bronze statue of patriotism.

Two

CHURCHES

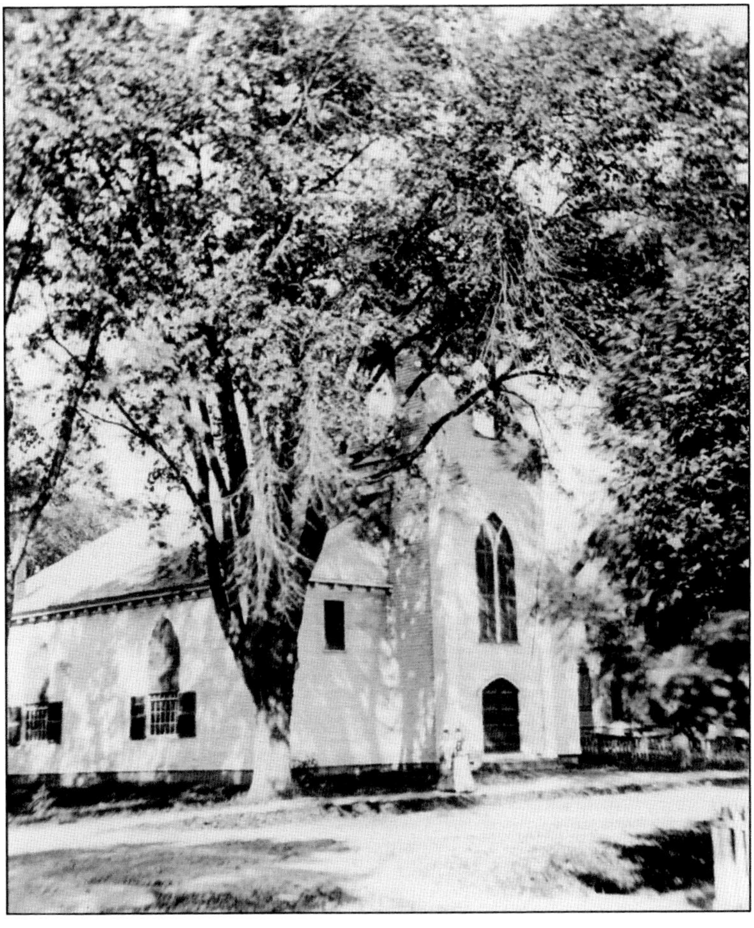

This Gothic Revival church was built at State and Oak Streets in 1833 and served Augusta's Unitarians until its replacement with a larger Unitarian church on the site in 1879. Architecturally, the building belongs to the first period of the Gothic Revival in which the pointed arch features are applied rather than being structural.

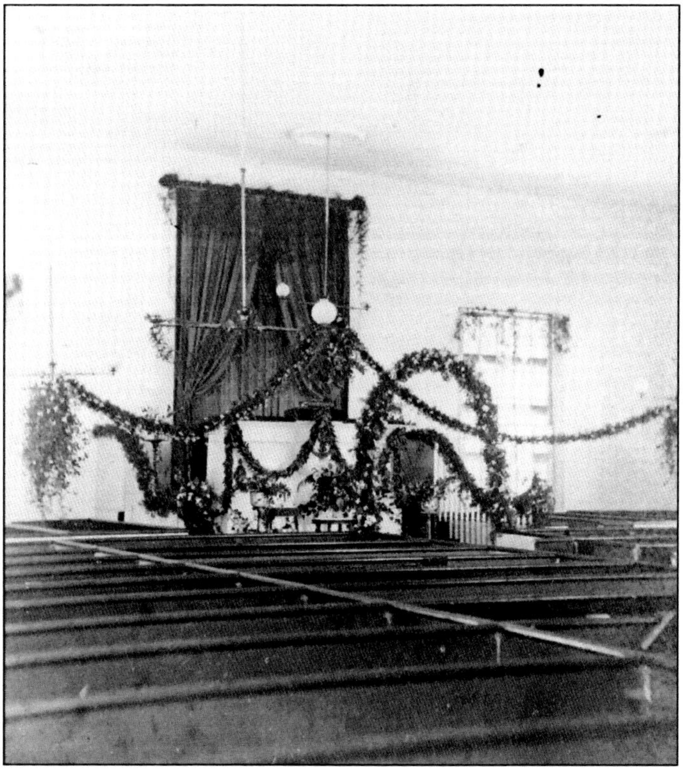

The simplicity of the Unitarian church interior was embellished by ornate Victorian floral decorations. The pulpit shown here was occupied from 1840 until 1853 by Rev. Sylvester Judd (1813–1853), a noted Unitarian minister who authored several novels in the transcendentalist mode and was known widely for his strong positions against war, slavery, and intemperance.

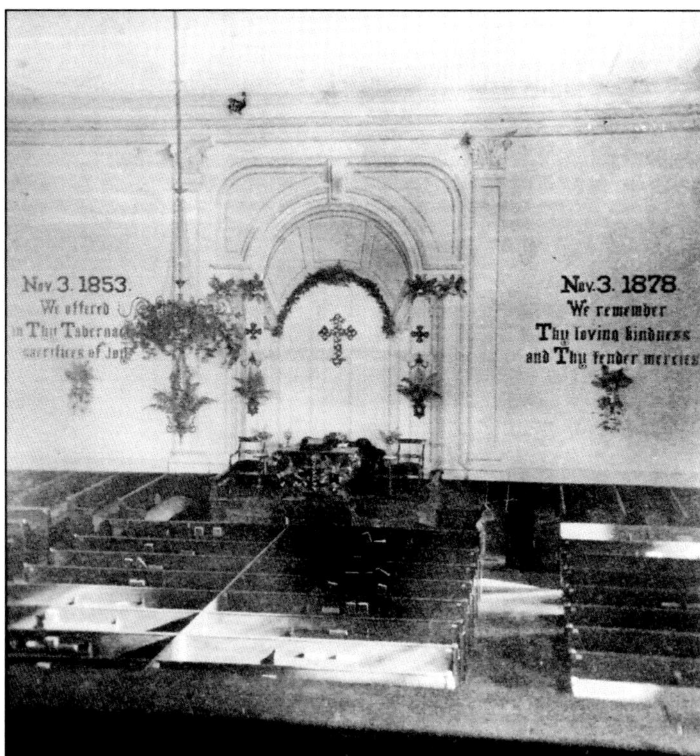

Efforts to found the Free Will Baptist Church began in 1834 and were renewed in 1850, resulting in the construction of a church on State Street in 1853. This view of the auditorium shows an elaborate trompe l'oeil arch behind the pulpit and biblical passages on the front wall with dates commemorating the 25th anniversary of the building in 1878.

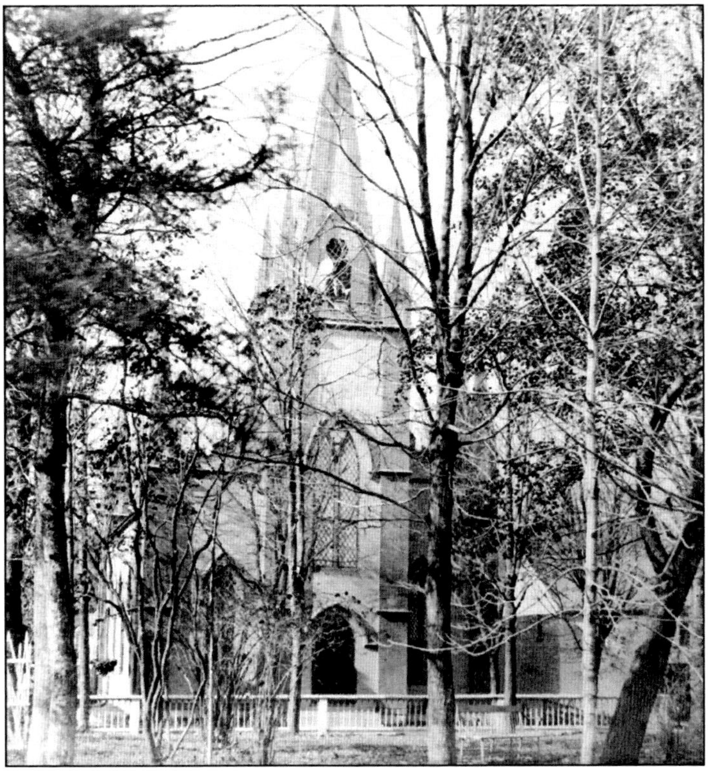

Between 1841 and 1842, St. Mark's Episcopal Church was built on State Street between Winthrop and Oak Streets. This distinctive Gothic Revival structure was erected by carpenter George Freeman of Norridgewock and mason William Wade of Augusta. The building was vacated for the present St. Mark's in 1887, and the site is now a parking lot.

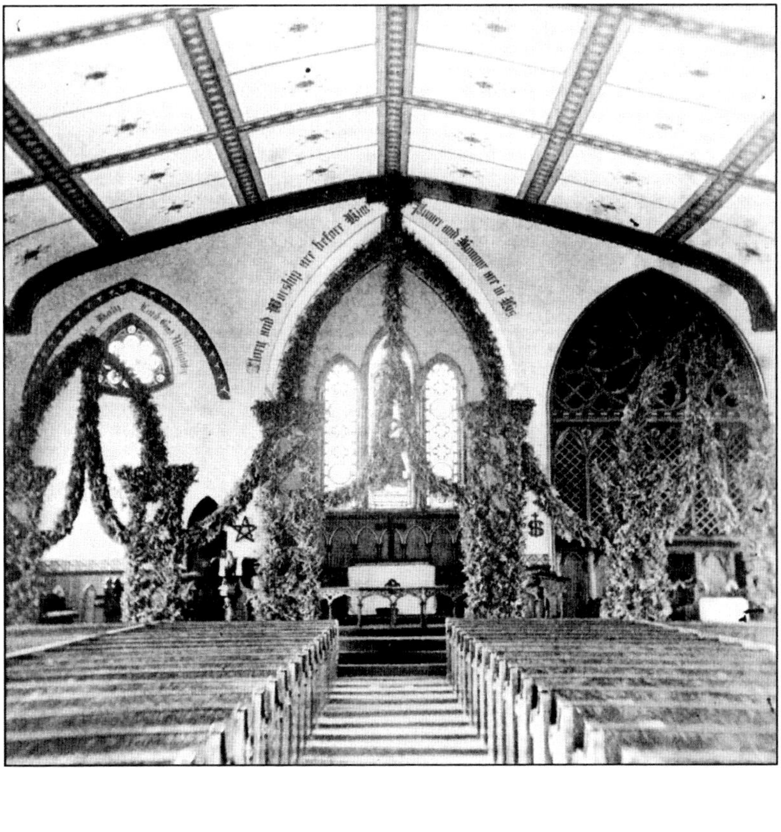

The interior of the first St. Mark's Episcopal Church is shown after its 1873 remodeling in which the seating arrangement was changed and a decorative paint scheme featured scriptural texts on the walls and bands of vine leaves and grapes on the ceiling. This photograph captures the church adorned with Christmas greens.

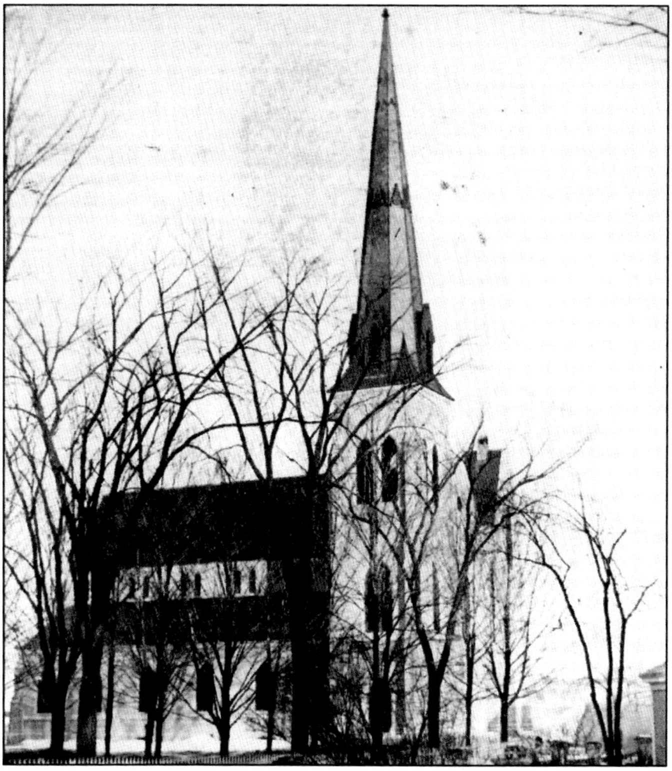

Of the Augusta churches built or remodeled in the 1860s, the South Parish Congregational Church on Church Street is the most elaborate. Erected in 1865 and 1866 to replace an 1809 Federal meetinghouse that burned on the site, South Parish is an impressive English Gothic Revival church constructed of granite from plans by Francis H. Fassett of Portland. His designs follow the medieval form of a nave with clerestory flanked by aisles and crowned at the front corner by a square tower and spire that rises 178 feet.

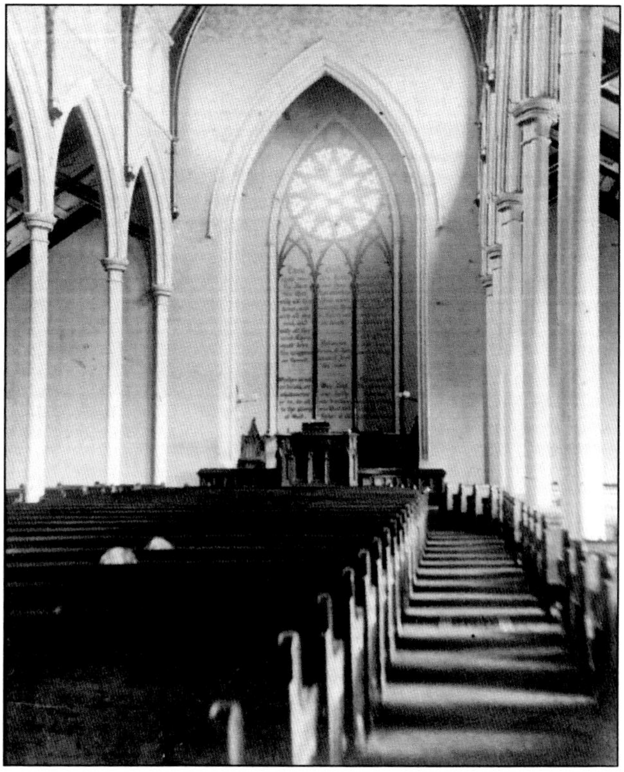

The South Parish Congregational Church contains a grand 57-foot-high interior space. This view looking toward the front of the 750-seat auditorium shows the arches that divide the nave from the aisles as well as support the clerestory. The focal point of the front wall is a monumental recessed arch that provides the setting for a large circular stained-glass window.

The rear wall of South Parish's auditorium is devoted to a gallery that contains the organ as well as seating for the choir and a few church members. As described in James W. North's 1870 *History of Augusta*, "The organ, encased in black walnut, 18 feet broad and 35 feet high in the Gothic style, was made by the Messrs. Hook of Boston." The organ was first played publicly on June 22, 1866, followed by a second performance at the church dedication on July 5, 1866.

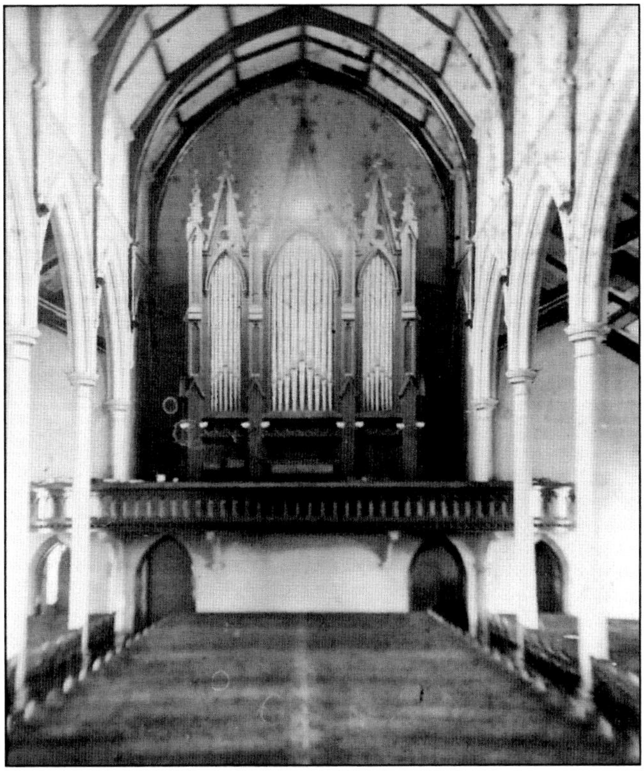

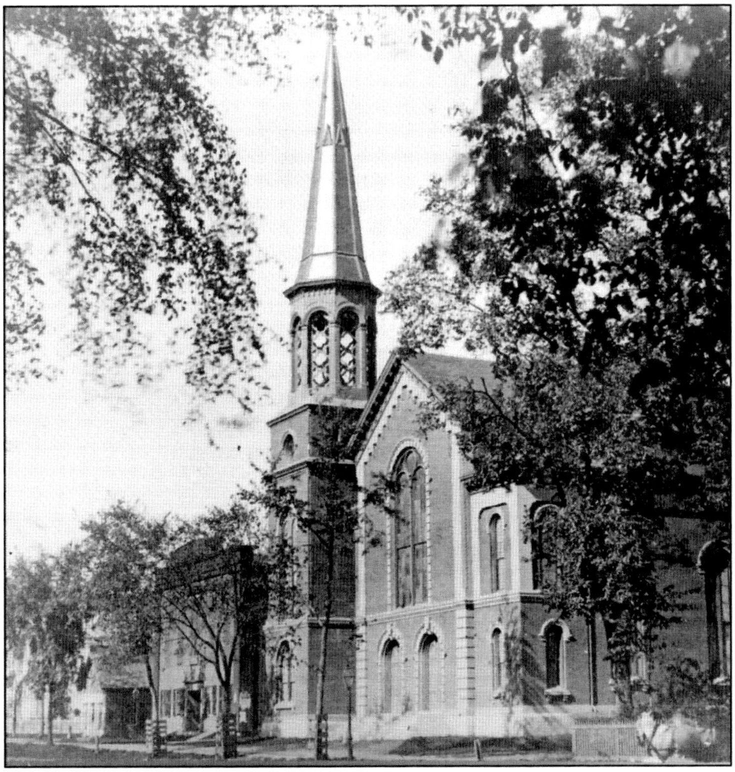

The 131-foot corner tower of the Universalist church rose dramatically above the fashionable Winthrop Street neighborhood. Located at Winthrop and Summer Streets, this 500-seat church was built in 1867 and 1868 from a Romanesque-inspired design by Fassett with Rodney L. Fogg of Augusta as contractor. The building was replaced by the present Unitarian Universalist church in 1981.

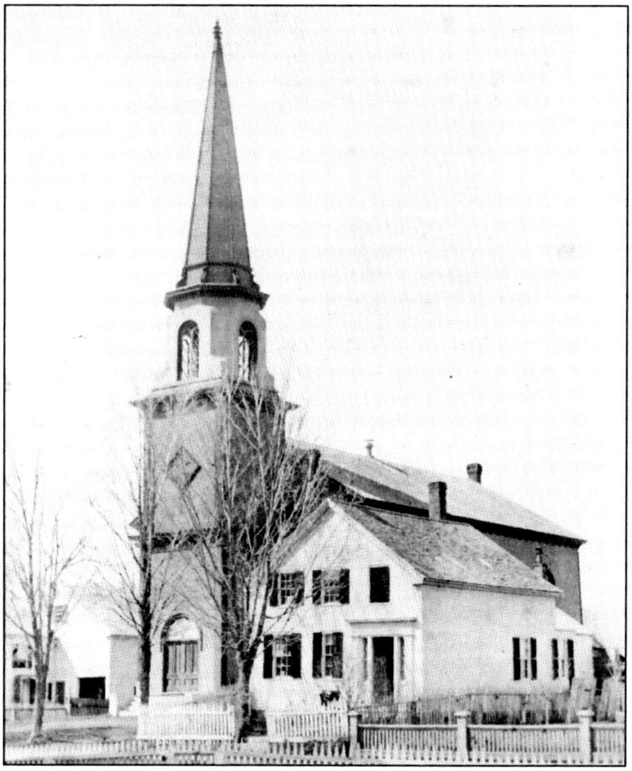

The Green Street United Methodist Church was built in 1828 and assumed its present appearance through remodeling in 1848, 1856, and 1867. That year, Augusta architect John C. Tibbetts designed and George Snow built the distinctive 100-foot Italianate tower and large arched side windows that can be seen today. At the right is the parsonage, a Greek Revival house built in 1847 that was replaced by a larger minister's residence in 1895.

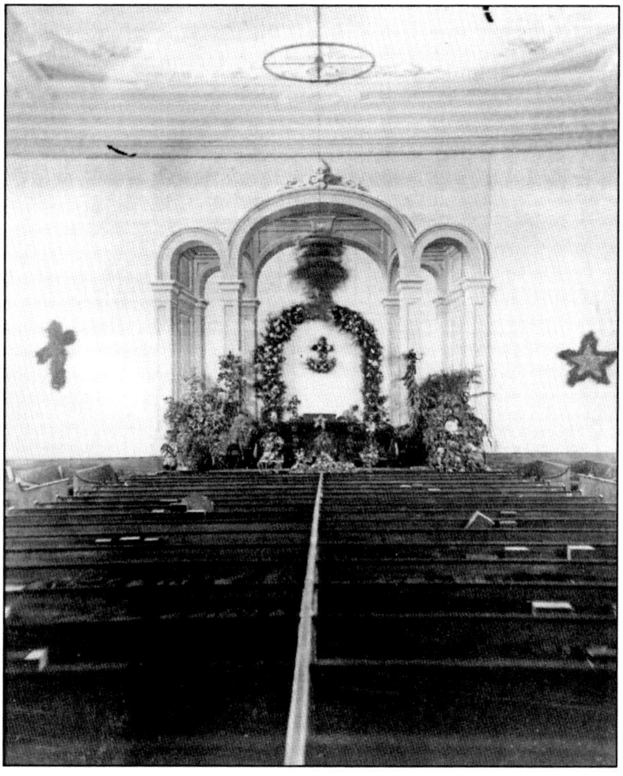

Tibbetts's design for remodeling the Green Street United Methodist Church in 1867 called for interior and exterior transformations. Eighteen pews were added, and the pulpit was framed by an elaborate ensemble of trompe l'oeil arches painted by Charles J. Schumacher of Portland, who also decorated the walls and ceiling. Music was provided by a new organ from Hamill of Cambridge, and members were summoned to worship by a new bell.

When the First Baptist Church was built in 1835, the building faced on Perham Street toward the back of the Kennebec County Courthouse. In February 1868, the Baptists hired Tibbetts to remodel the church in the Italianate style to "face Winthrop Street, raise it seven feet higher, make it twenty feet longer, and surmount it with a handsome spire." Contractors Elisha F. Pinkham and John P. Wyman finished the work in time for a December 15, 1868, dedication.

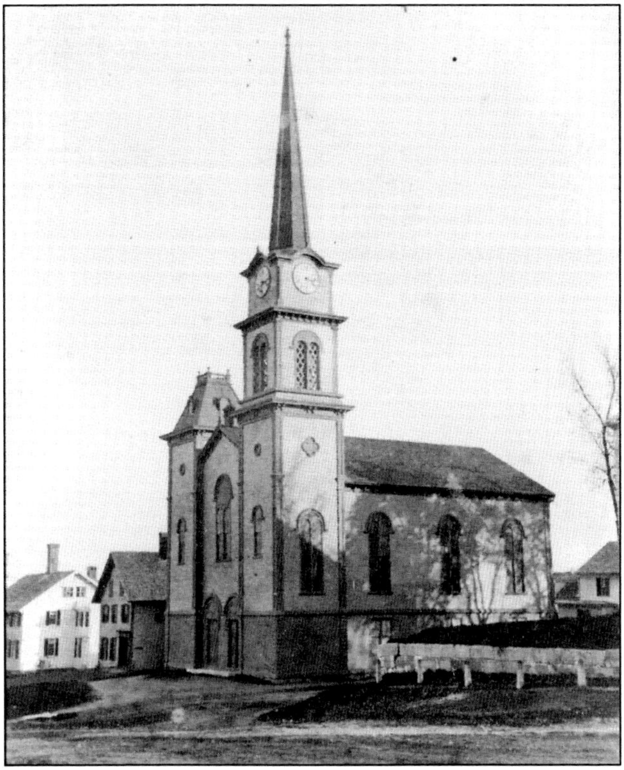

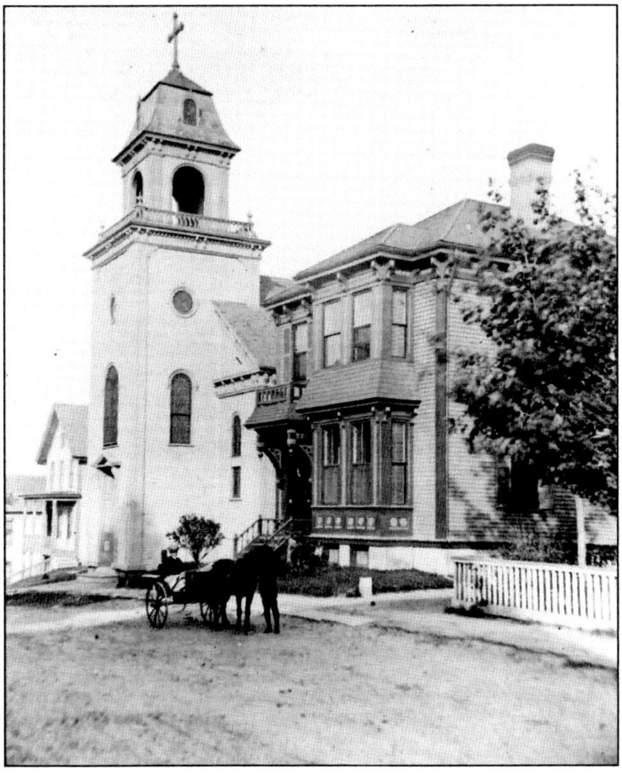

As a result of many Irish laborers coming to Augusta in the 1830s to work on the Kennebec Dam, St. Mary's Catholic Church was built on State Street between Bridge and Laurel Streets. Opened in 1846, St. Mary's served the parish until its replacement by the present stone church on Western Avenue in 1927. At right is the church rectory.

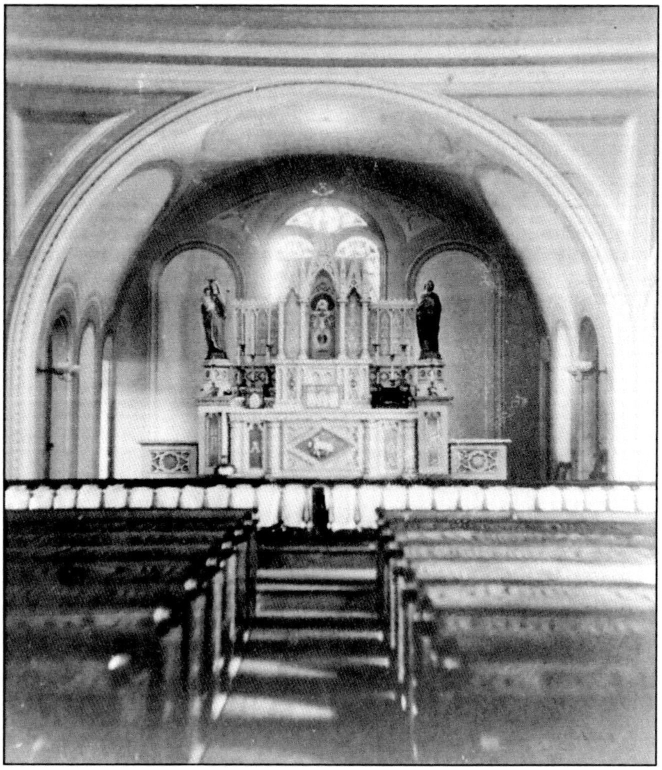

Under the direction of local architect George G. Stevens, the first St. Mary's church received a Victorian appearance in 1868 through the addition of a square tower and Italianate trim on the exterior as well as stained-glass windows and decorative painting on the interior. This photograph focuses on the ornate altar in the arched chancel at the front of the sanctuary.

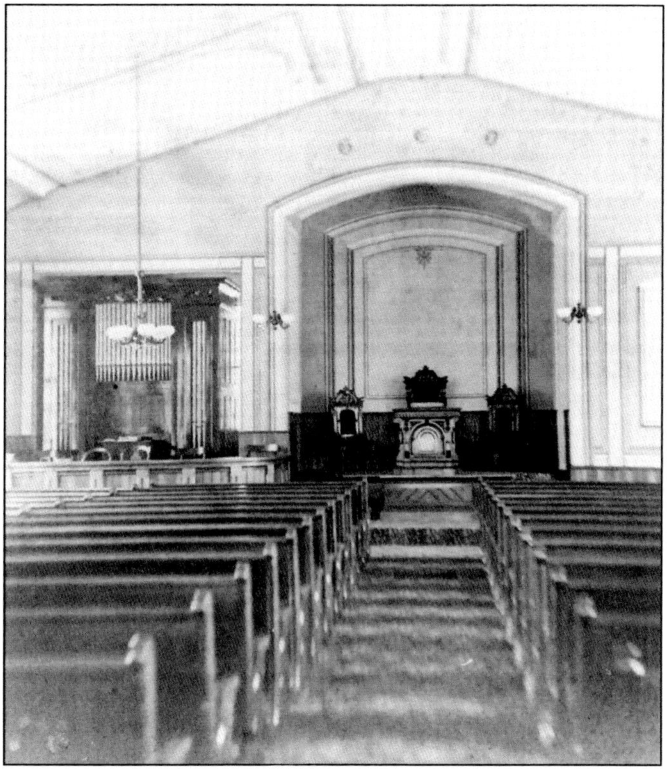

In 1879, the Unitarians replaced their 1833 meetinghouse at State and Oak Streets with a stylish stick-style church designed by the Boston architect Thomas J. Silloway. The 300-seat auditorium was decorated with trompe l'oeil wall and ceiling paintings by George F. Sheppard of Boston. Elim Christian Fellowship now occupies the building.

Three

NORTH END

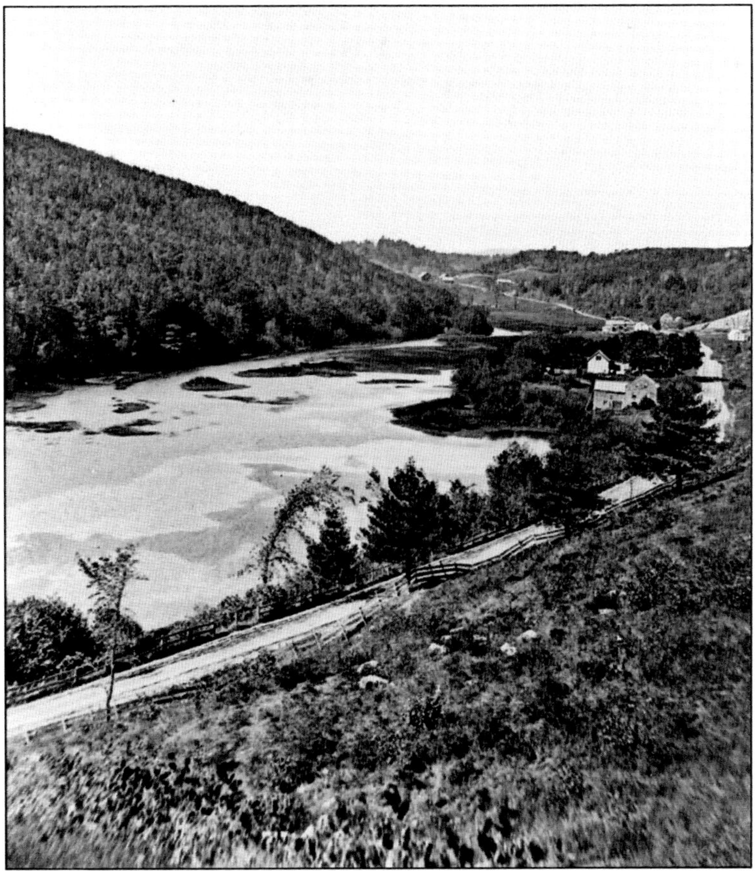

Henry Bailey's camera captured this sweeping view looking north up Bond Brook, paralleled by a rural Mount Vernon Avenue prior to its residential development. The brook takes its name from Thomas Bond, a Massachusetts trader who came to Augusta in 1796 and erected the community's first brick building at Mount Vernon Avenue and Bond Street about 1805. This two-story house was a north end landmark until its demolition for a convenience store in 1983.

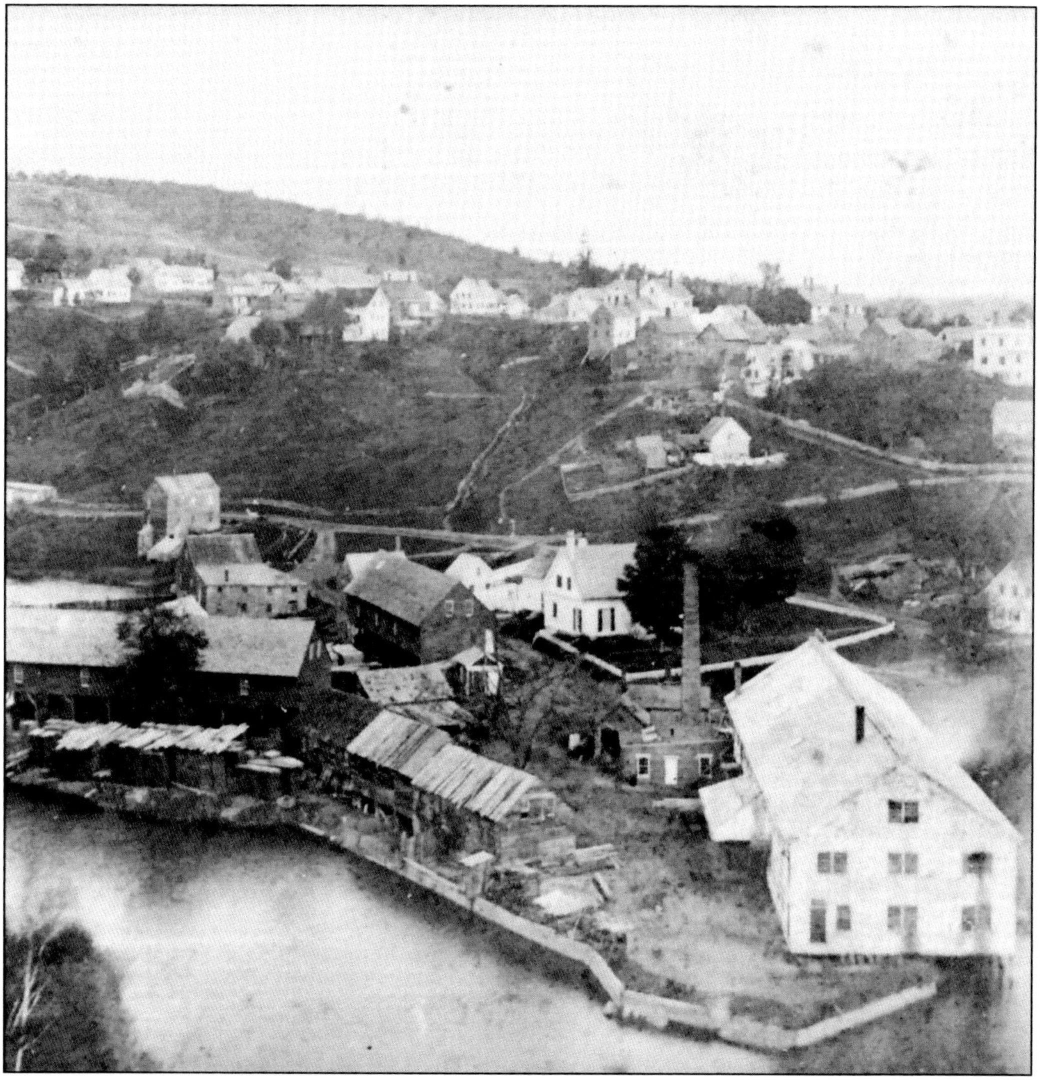

A sawmill was built as early as 1762 on Bond Brook. The sawmill complex shown in the foreground was established in 1856 and was operated from the 1860s to the 1880s by Josiah P. Wyman and Sons, which manufactured doors, sashes, and blinds. The white house adjacent to the mill is Glen Cottage, built in the 1830s by William Bridge and now known as 36 Mount Vernon Avenue. Sand Hill appears in the background.

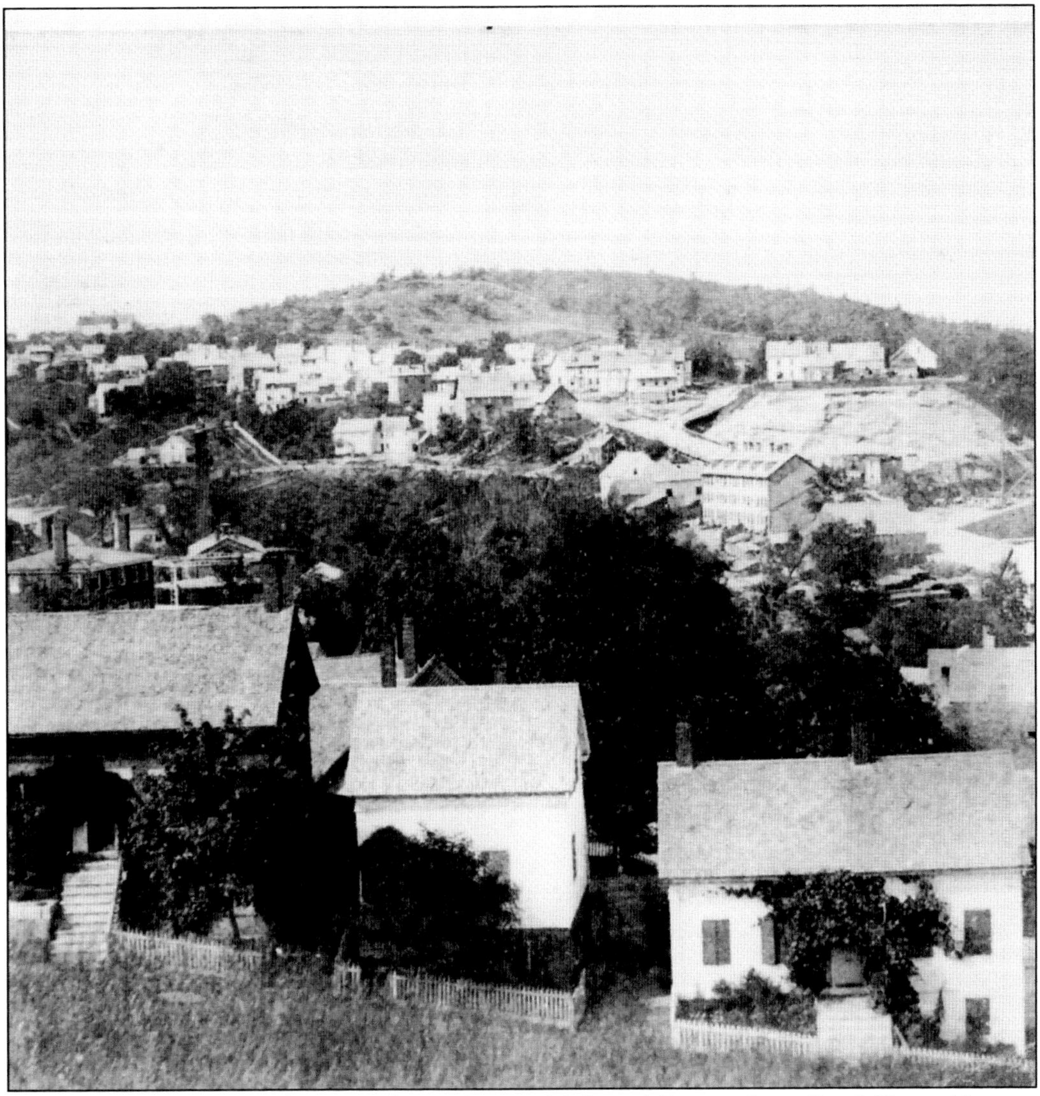

From left to right in the foreground are 13, 9, and 7 Laurel Street, three Greek Revival houses built by Eben Parker between 1847 and 1851. On page 60, 7 Laurel Street can also be seen as the home of Emile Barbier, a later owner. The Thomas Bond house and the gasworks appear at the left above the roofline of 13 Laurel Street. At center right is the Lower Boarding House, built in 1845 as textile mill workers' housing and still standing in modified form at 32–40 Northern Avenue.

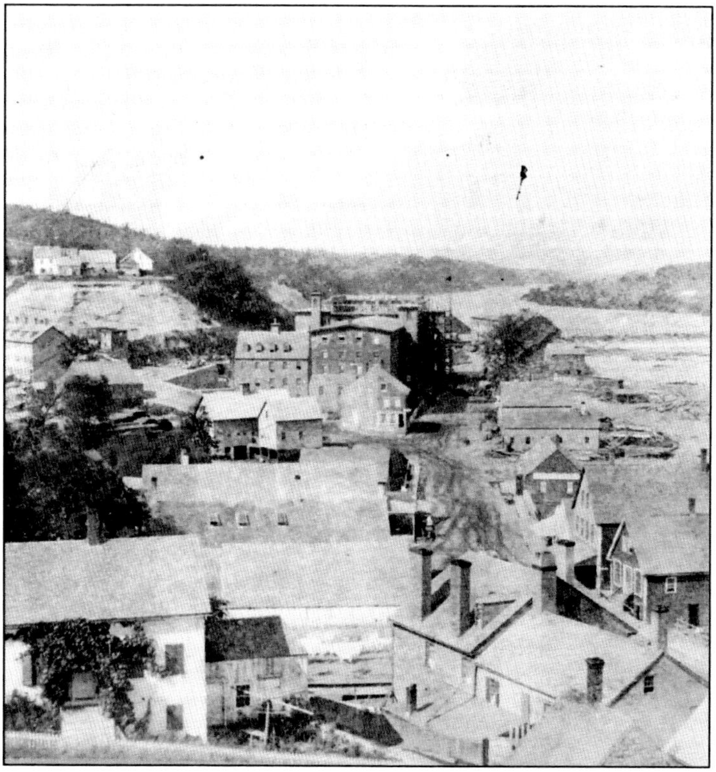

The tall chimneys of Piper's Tavern and 7 Laurel Street appear in the foreground of this view from 1870 looking north to the textile mill complex at Water Street and Northern Avenue. Erected by the Kennebec Company in 1845, mill No. 1 was acquired by the A. and W. Sprague Manufacturing Company of Rhode Island in 1867 and remodeled in 1868. The next year, the Spragues began the construction of mill No. 2, which is shown in progress behind No. 1.

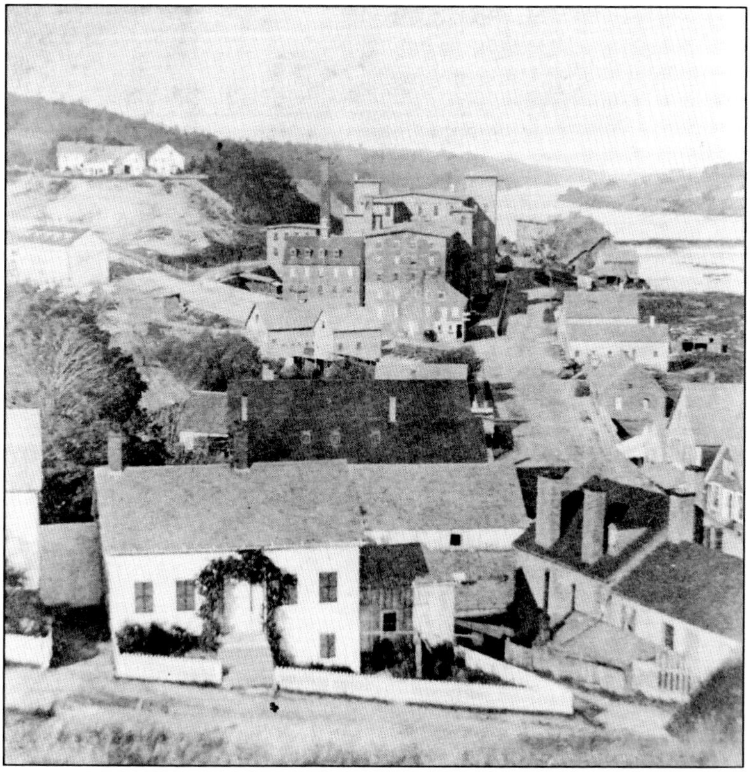

Henry Bailey returned to the same vantage point as the previous photograph to record the completion of the A. and W. Sprague Manufacturing Company's mill No. 2 in 1871. Featuring a square Italianate tower on either side, this massive brick structure rises above mill No. 1. At the left stands the Lower Boarding House on Northern Avenue, and at the right is a glimpse of the mill dam over the Kennebec River.

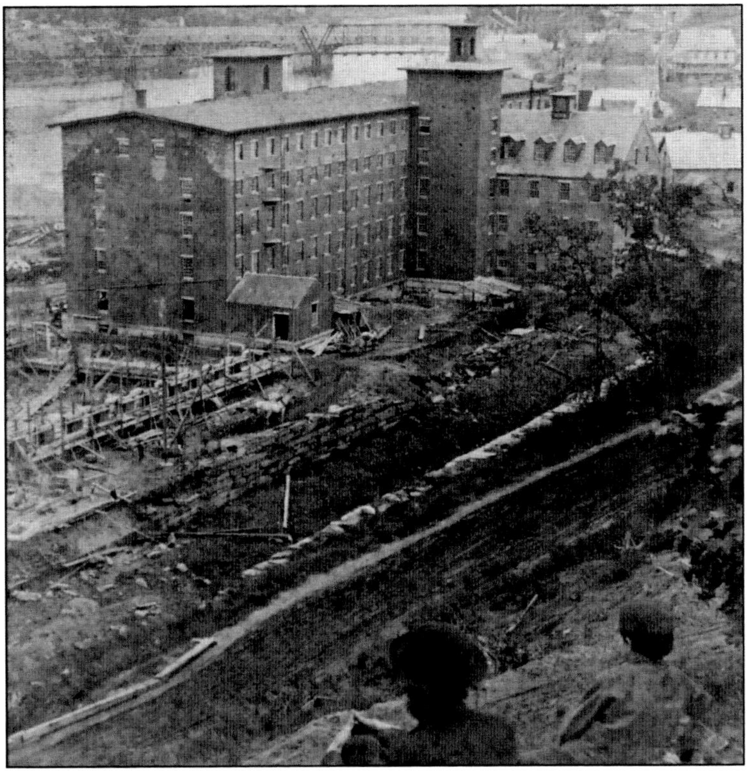

Mill No. 1 looms in the background as the Sprague company begins the two-year construction of mill No. 2 in 1869 at the left. On September 29, 1869, the *Kennebec Journal* reported, "The foundation for the new mill is eleven feet wide at its base and rests on solid ledge. The brick walls of the factory, which are now being laid, are three feet in thickness, of solid masonry. Gangs of men are working day and night."

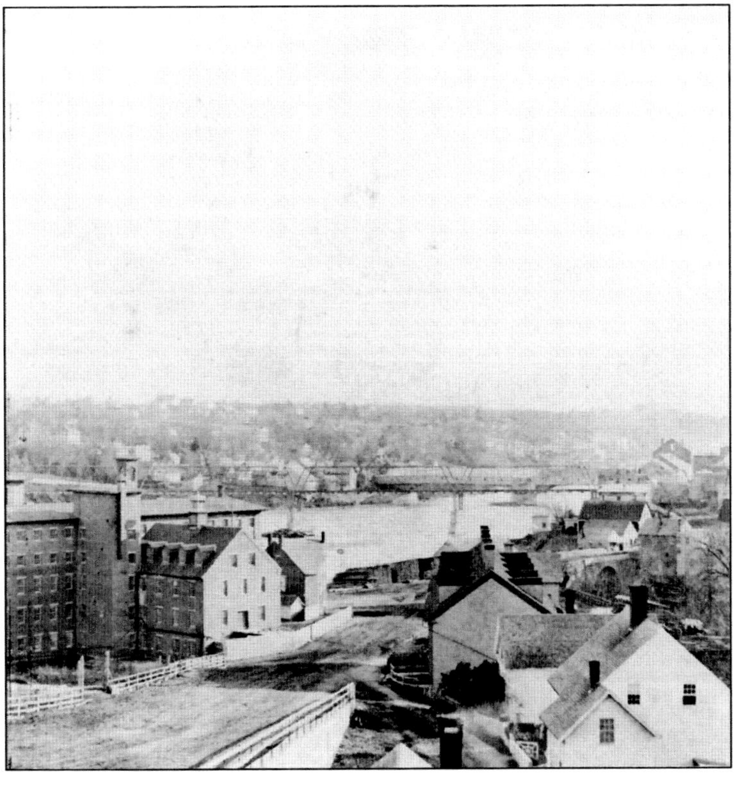

Looking south, this view shows the junction of Northern Avenue and Water Street with mill No. 1 on the left and the Lower Boarding House on the right. The iron Maine Central Railroad bridge and the wooden covered bridge span the Kennebec River to Augusta's east side, which appears in the background.

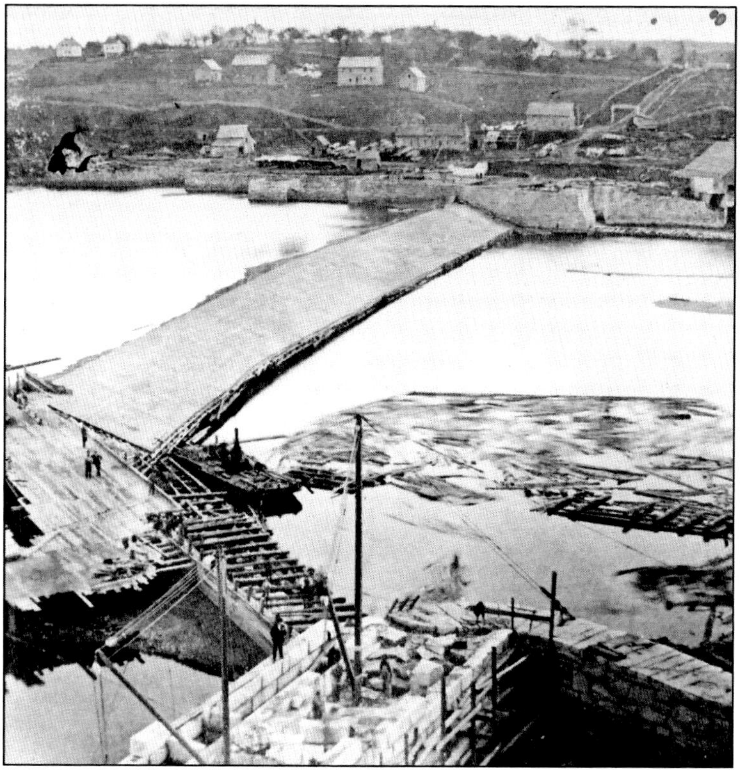

Augusta's efforts to harness the waterpower of the Kennebec River for industrial purposes proved challenging. Completed in 1837, the dam was rebuilt in 1840, 1846, 1855, and here in 1870 after the February flood that year. Consisting of extra stone ballast and heavy timber reinforcement, the 1870 reconstruction withstood the 1896 and 1936 floods.

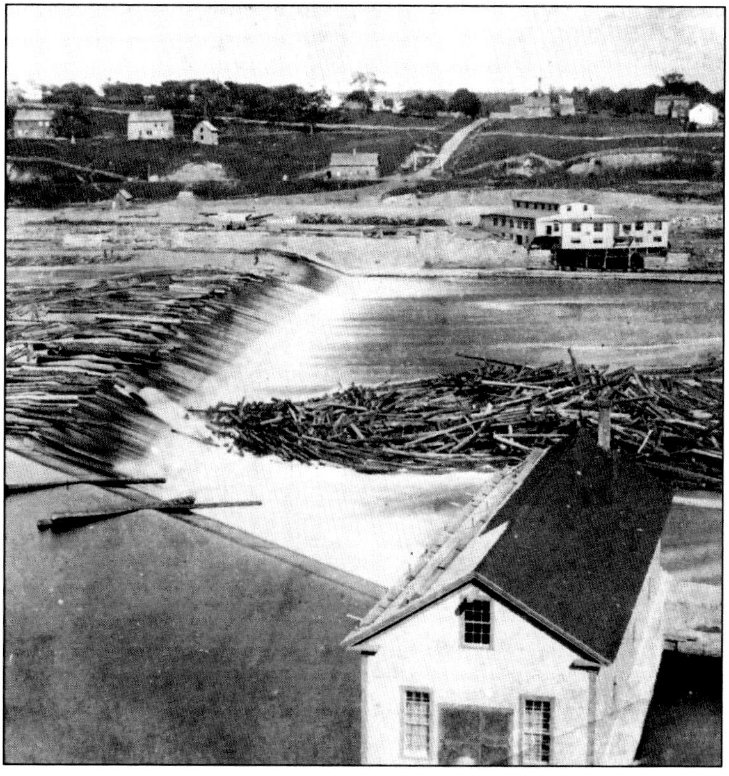

Logs cut in the northern forests adjacent to the Kennebec River flow over the dam reconstructed in 1870 and collect in the current below, awaiting conversion into lumber by local sawmills. In the foreground is the dam's gatehouse, while directly across the river stands the stone lock for the dam and the sawmill that A. and W. Sprague Manufacturing Company built in 1871 and leased to the Kennebec Land and Lumber Company.

The graceful arch of Bond Brook Bridge and its reflection encircle a view of the Kennebec River and the Maine Central Railroad bridge. In 1849, Augusta voted at the town meeting to replace a wooden span over Bond Brook on Water Street with this stone-arch bridge, which was constructed by Ephraim Ballard and remains in use today.

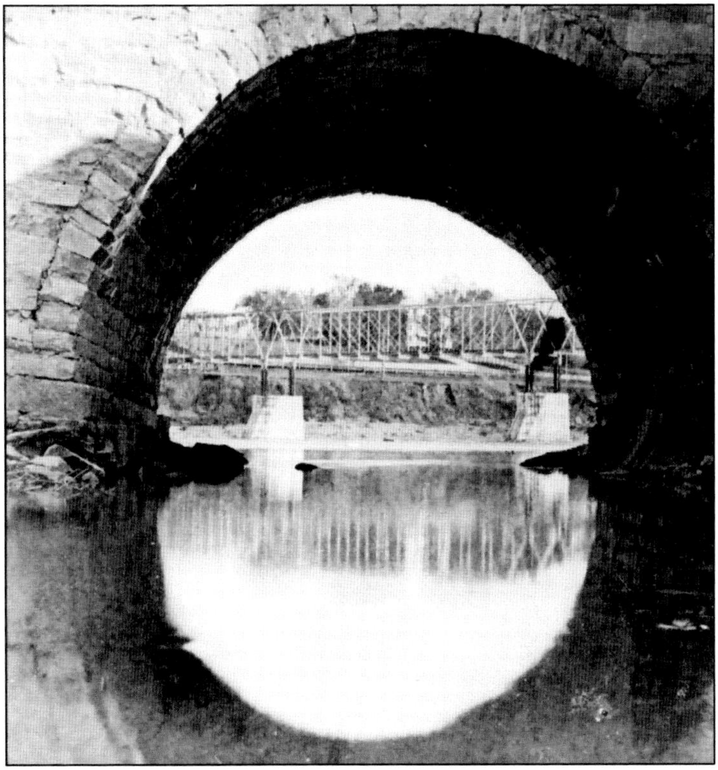

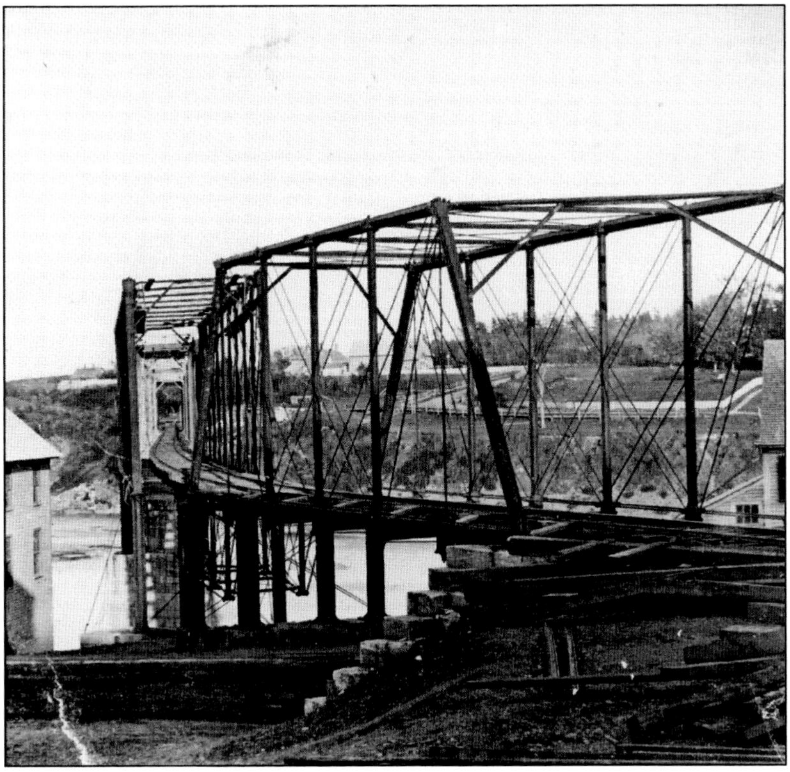

A severe flood destroyed Augusta's railroad bridge over the Kennebec River in February 1870. That summer, the Maine Central Railroad replaced its lost wooden bridge with this 852-foot-long Pratt truss iron bridge made by Kellogg, Clark and Company of Phoenixville, Pennsylvania. The new iron structure rested on four stone piers and two stone abutments.

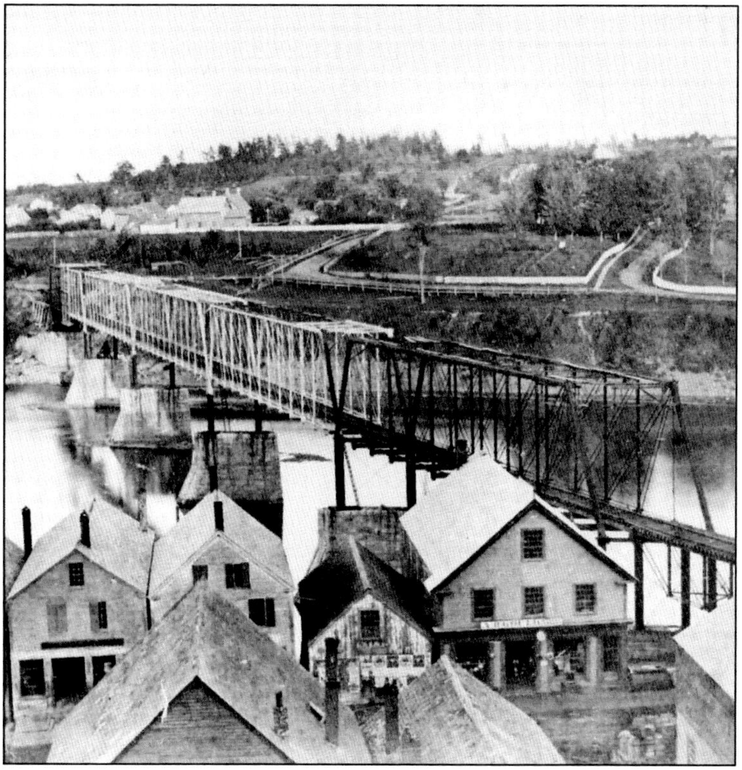

Standing on Cony Street, Henry Bailey took this picture of the new iron railroad bridge. In the foreground is a row of wooden commercial buildings on Water Street, including Albert P. Gould's stove, furnace, and tinware store at the right, adjacent to the bridge. Across the Kennebec River on the east side is Willow Street at center, which turns parallel to the river to join Myrtle Street at the right.

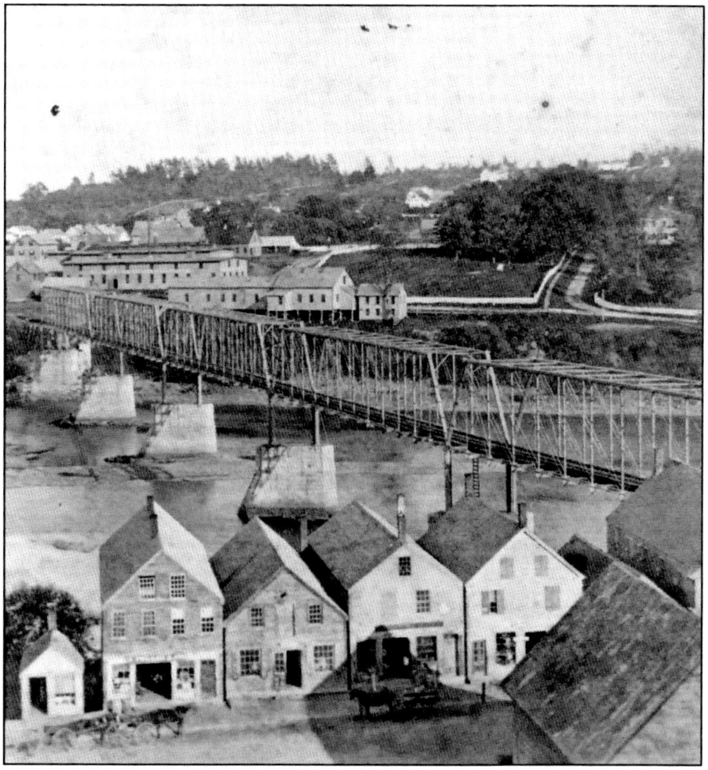

Bailey updated the previous view of the Maine Central Railroad bridge to show the newly constructed manufacturing complex that appears on the east side of the river. Within these sprawling, wooden buildings at the left, Thomas Lambard made freight cars for the railroads from 1871 to 1881.

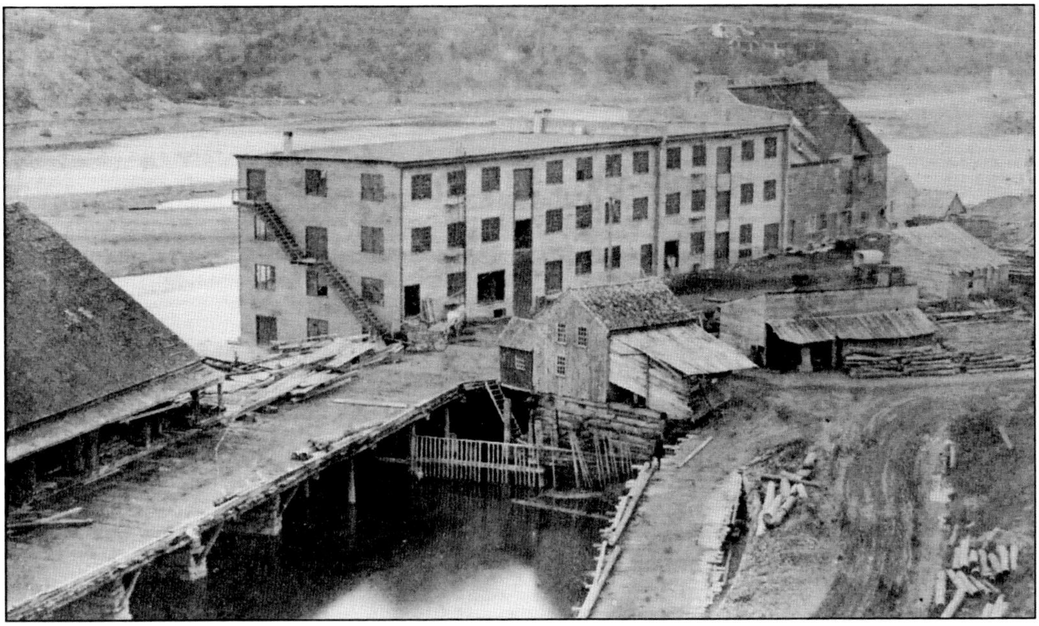

Located below the mill dam, this large wooden building was constructed as a machine shop for the Augusta Water Power Company in 1853. By the time this photograph was taken in the 1870s, the structure housed a machine shop for the A. and W. Sprague Manufacturing Company mills as well as a gristmill, a planing mill, a furniture factory, and a sash factory. The building was removed by the Edwards Manufacturing Company in the 1880s to make way for mills No. 3, No. 4, and No. 5.

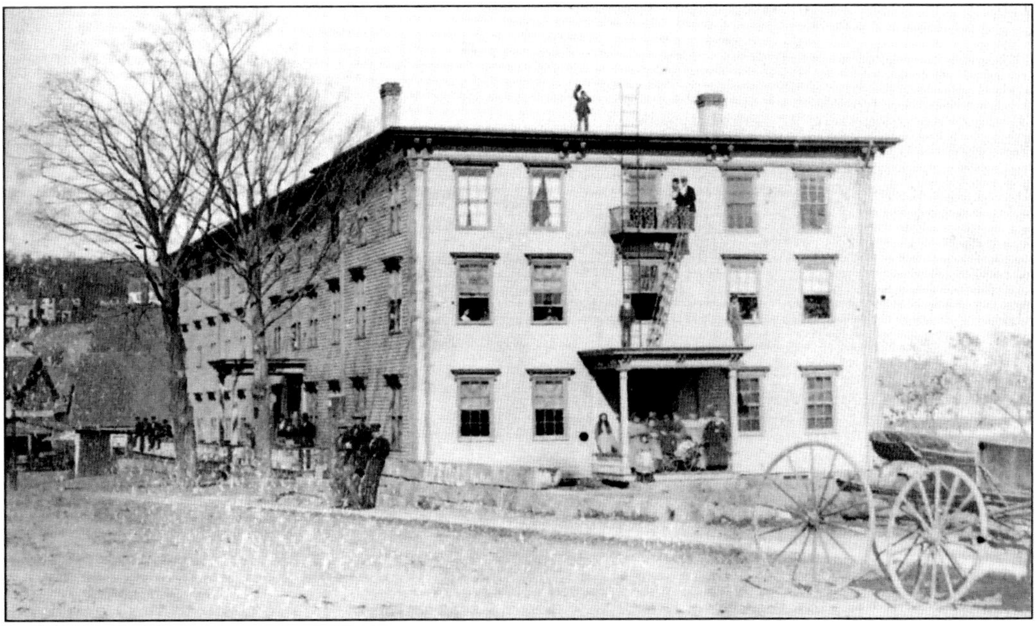

The completion of mill No. 2 in 1871 created the need for a new boardinghouse to accommodate an expanded workforce. By 1875, the Sprague company had built this large frame Italianate block between Water Street and the Kennebec River to house 100 employees. The Sprague boardinghouse now contains apartments.

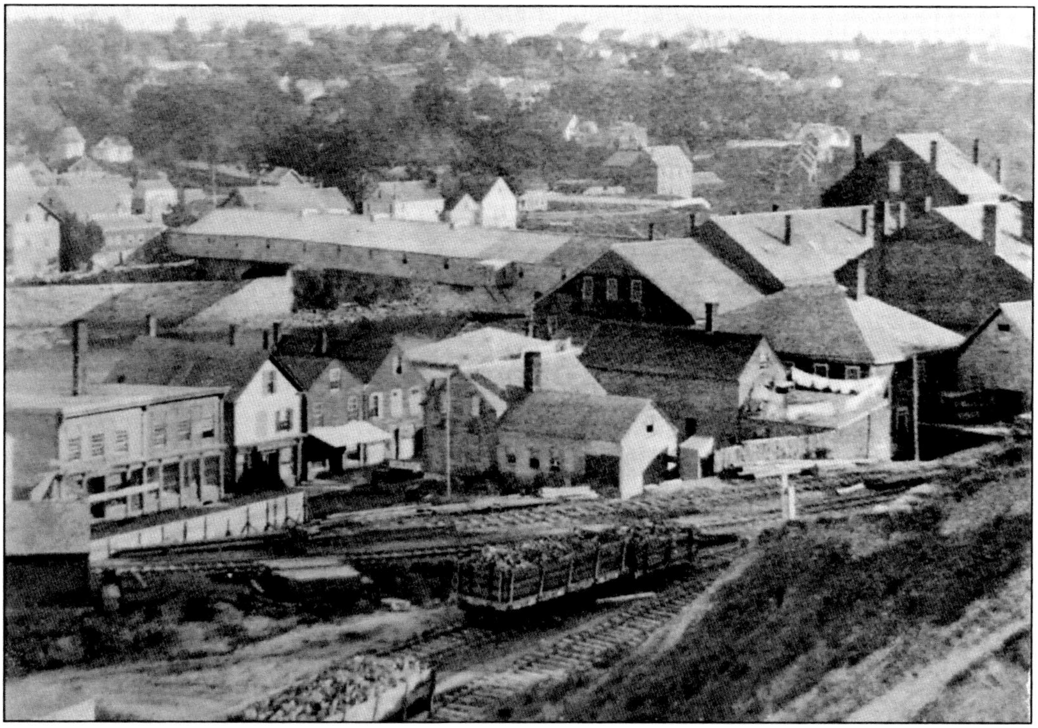

Standing at the north end of Crosby Street, Henry Bailey aimed his camera southeast across the Kennebec River to take in Water Street commercial buildings, the 1827 covered bridge, and Augusta's east side. A spur track in the foreground went to a gravel pit from which the Maine Central Railroad obtained material to build its roadbeds.

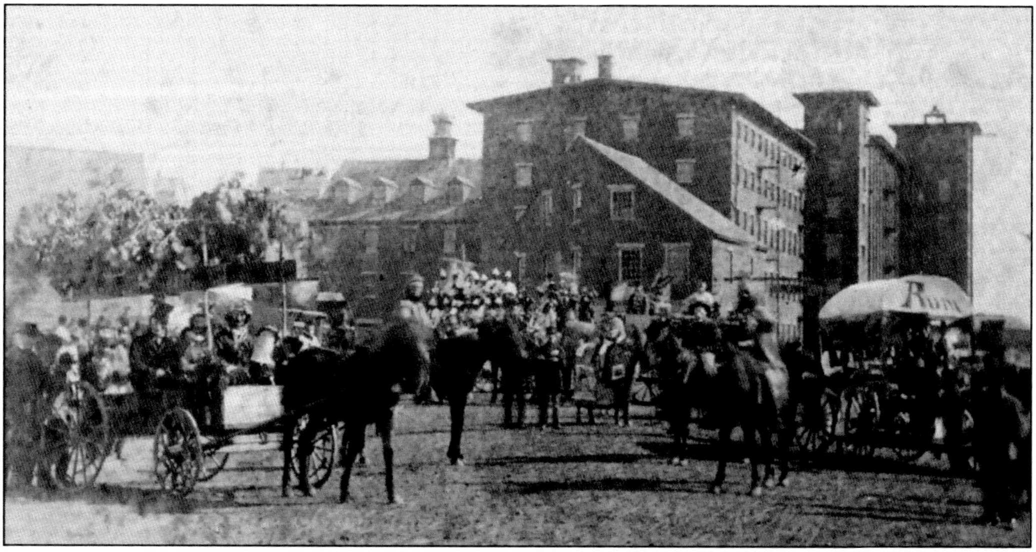

Fourth of July parades in 19th-century Maine featured "antiques" or "horribles," who were individuals dressed in outrageous costumes and masks for the public's entertainment. Here wagons of antiques and horribles on horseback gather on Water Street in front of the A. and W. Sprague Company mill to join the holiday procession through Augusta. Prizes were awarded for the strangest outfits. (Kennebec Historical Society.)

Four

WATER STREET

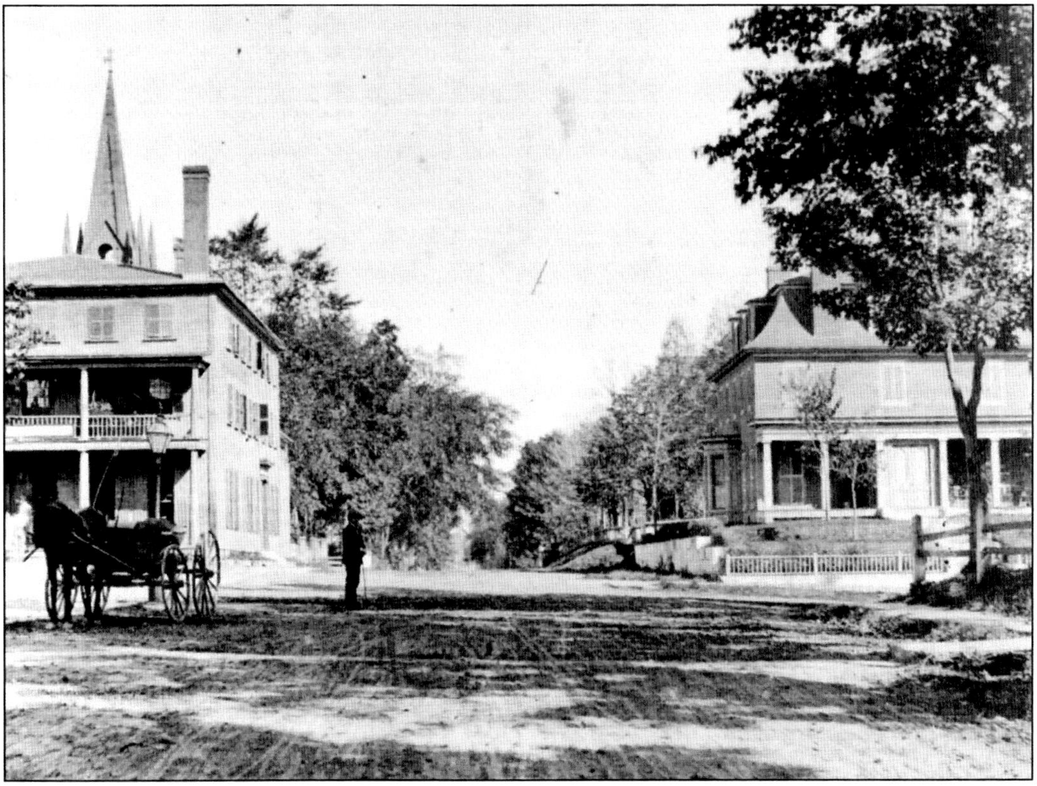

Two lost landmarks appear in this view of State and Winthrop Streets looking north. At the left, the Cushnoc House was built as a residence and store by Amos Partridge in 1803 and was later enlarged to become a three-story tavern. Fire destroyed it in 1892, and Lithgow Library now occupies the site. To the right is the Kennebec County jailor's house, which Ai Staples transformed into his residence in 1863. Staples's home was replaced by the former YMCA in 1914.

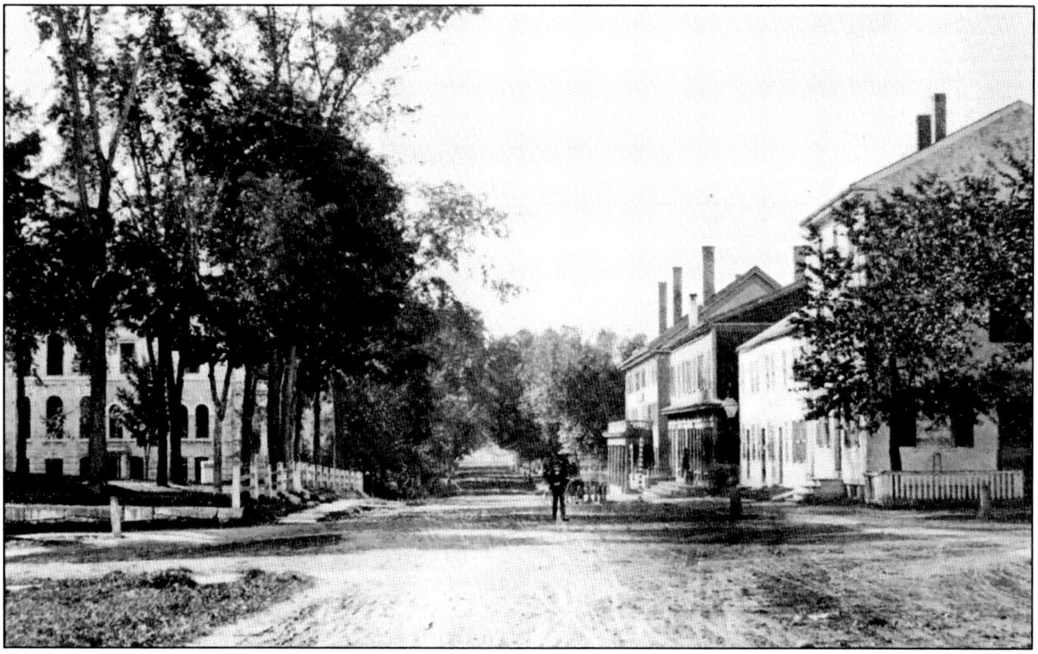

This view looks south on State Street from the intersection of Winthrop Street. Through the trees at the left, the Kennebec County Jail can be seen, while directly across State Street is the Mansion House, marked by its row of three tall, narrow chimneys. A popular 19th-century hotel, the Mansion House stood between Court and Weston Streets until it burned in 1877.

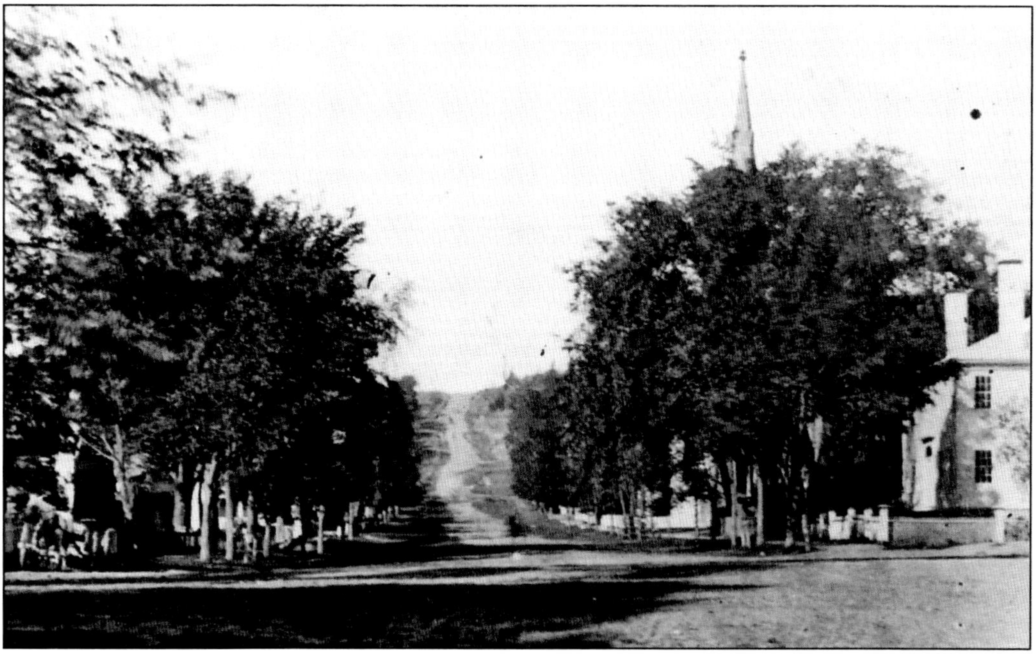

A broad, tree-lined Winthrop Street features prominently in this view looking west from State Street. At the right is the Dr. Issachar Snell house on the corner of Pleasant Street prior to its remodeling into St. Mark's Home for Women. The Universalist church spire projects above the trees.

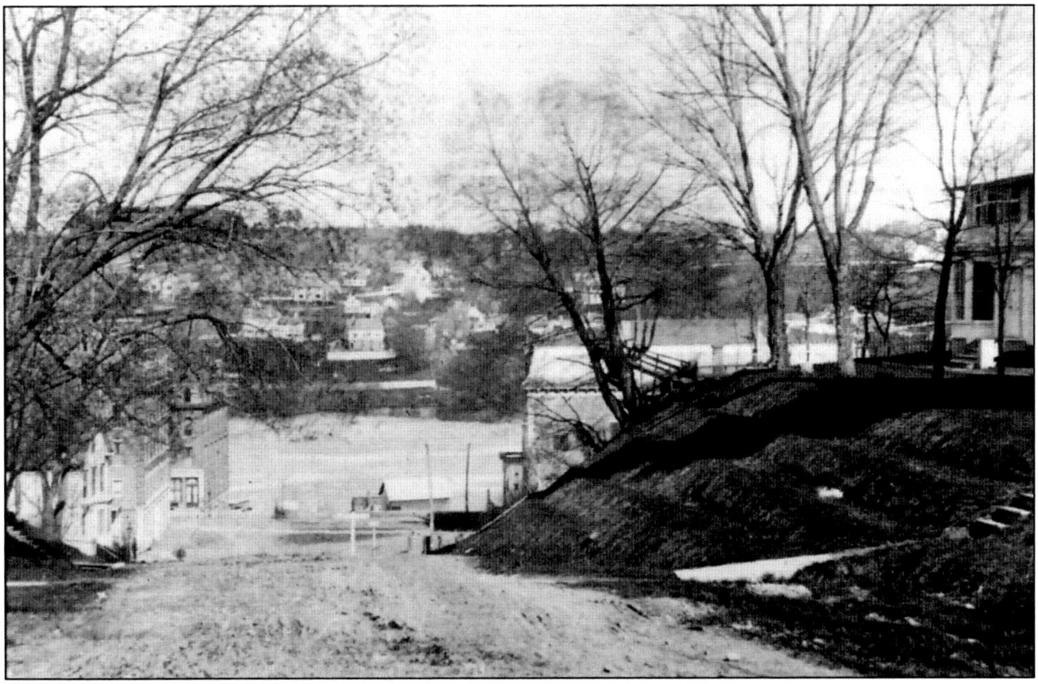

A steep descent characterizes the section of Winthrop Street from State Street to Water Street. The Kennebec River is seen in the background. Above the terraced lawn at the right was a house shared by the Sawyer and Titcomb families.

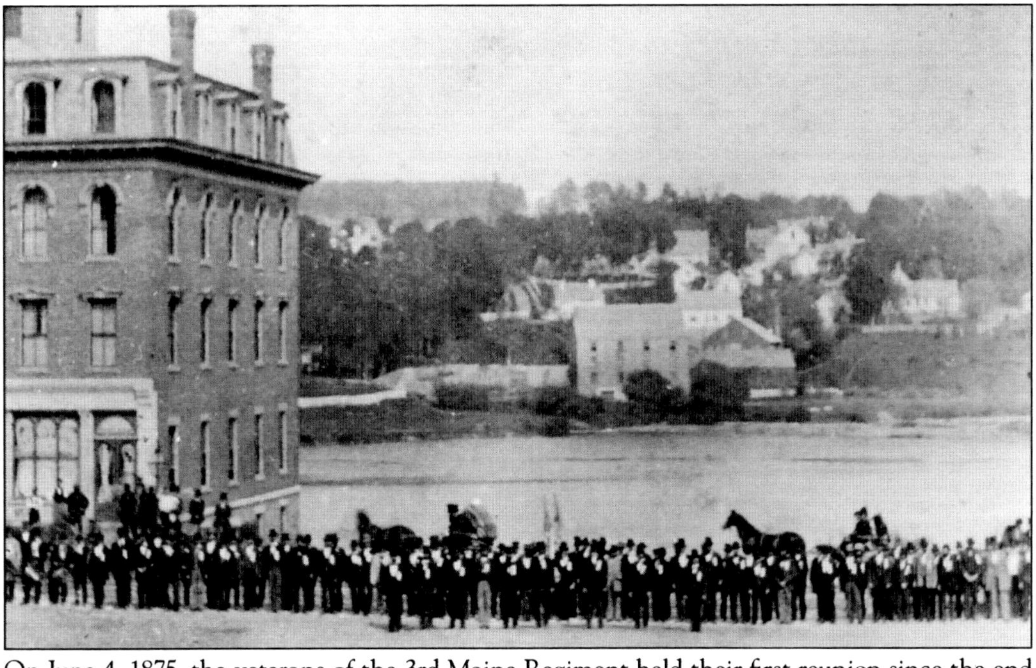

On June 4, 1875, the veterans of the 3rd Maine Regiment held their first reunion since the end of the Civil War. At 3:00 p.m., the regiment formed on Water Street adjacent to the E. C. Allen block, and Henry Bailey took this picture of the former soldiers with the Kennebec River in the background.

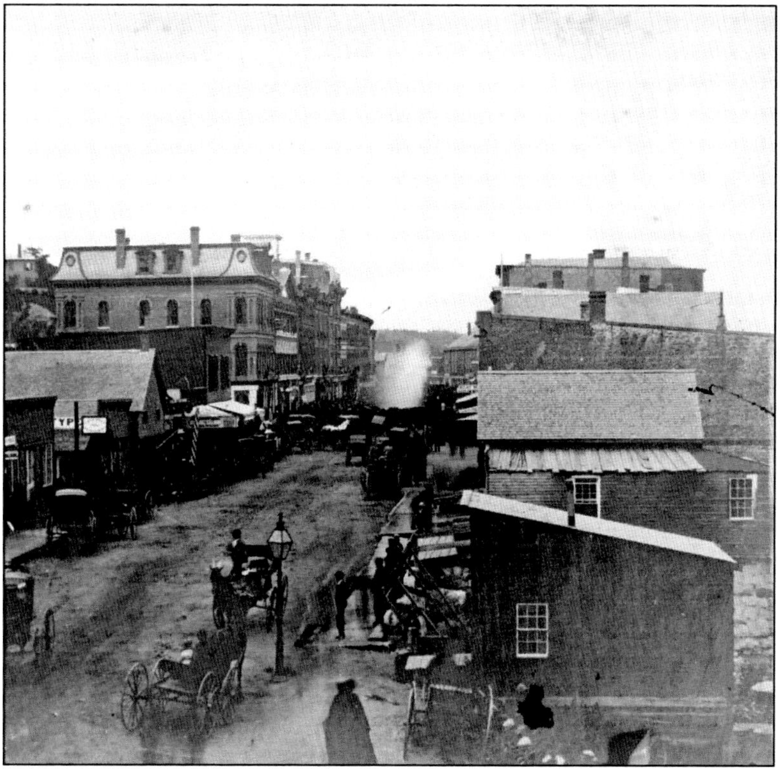

The recovery of the commercial district from the 1865 fire is symbolized in this view looking north on Water Street. In the foreground, the street is lined with one- and two-story wooden shops that were hastily constructed after the fire, while looming in the background are rows of substantial new business blocks. The small frame structure at the right was replaced by the E. C. Allen block in 1871.

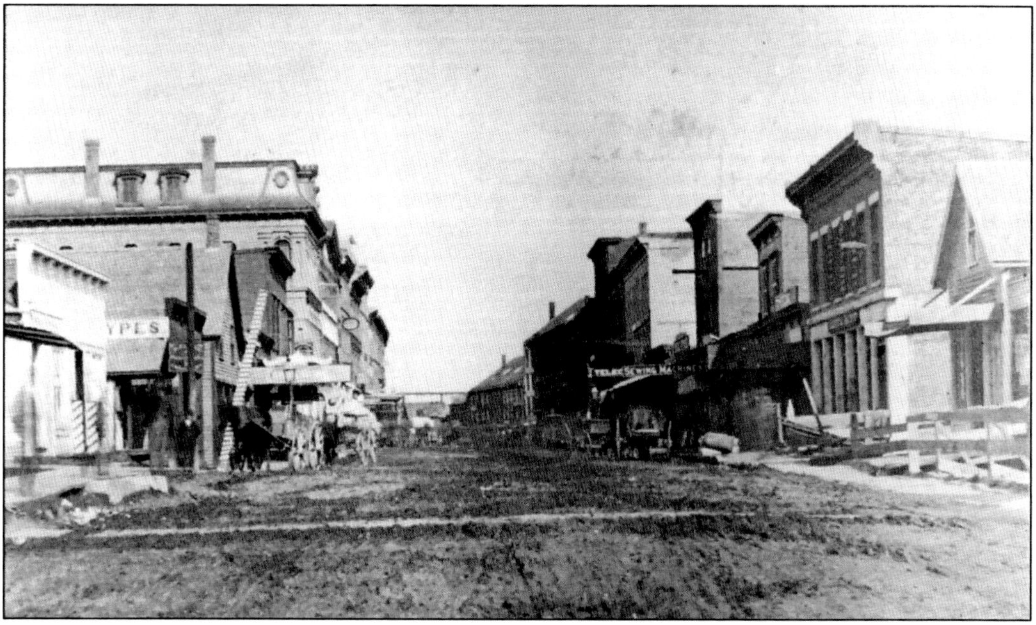

Standing in the middle of Water Street near Market Square, Henry Bailey aimed his camera north to capture this view of the commercial district in transition. Bailey's studio, second from the left with the tintypes sign on the roof, is among the modest structures dwarfed by the Granite National Bank and its adjacent blocks. Second from the right is the two-story brick building constructed in 1866 by Benjamin F. Parrott and H. W. Bradbury to house their grain business.

Featuring a stylish mansard roof and Italianate cupola, the E. C. Allen block dominated the south end of the row of commercial buildings that extended from Market Square to Bridge Street on the river side of Water Street. Constructed in 1871 from designs by George G. Stevens, the Allen block housed a highly successful publishing business that produced large runs of family magazines for national distribution.

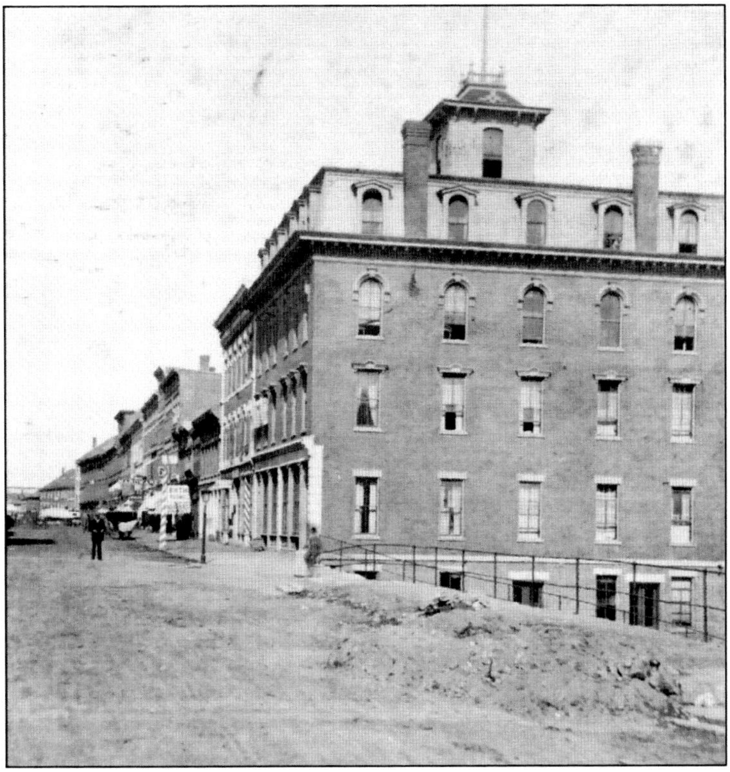

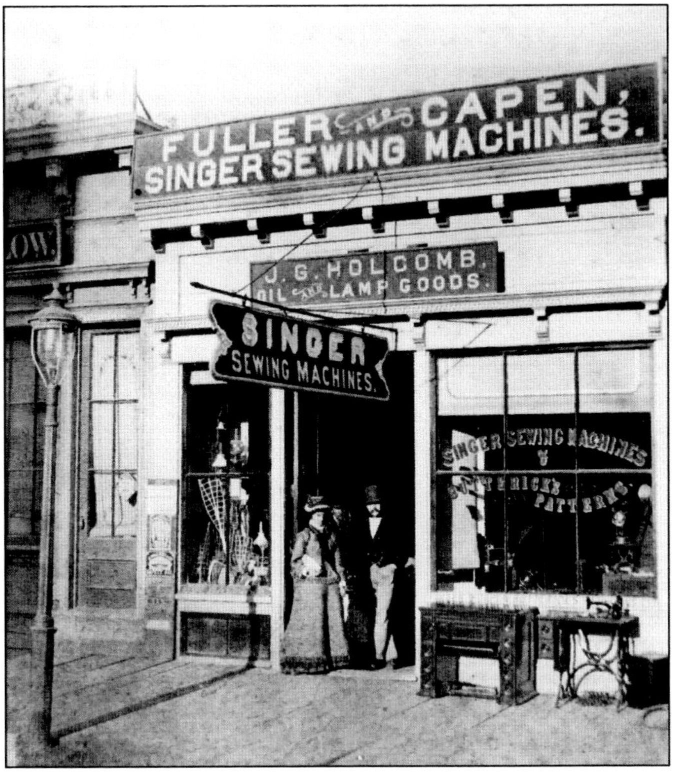

This small one-story shop is typical of the temporary wooden commercial buildings constructed on Water Street after the 1865 fire. Located on the east side opposite Oak Street, this store was occupied by Hosea Y. Fuller and Rodney B. Capen, who sold Singer sewing machines and Butterick clothing patterns from about 1872 to 1877, when the building was replaced by Benjamin F. Parrott's brick block. Jonas G. Holcomb's oil and lamp business shared the space.

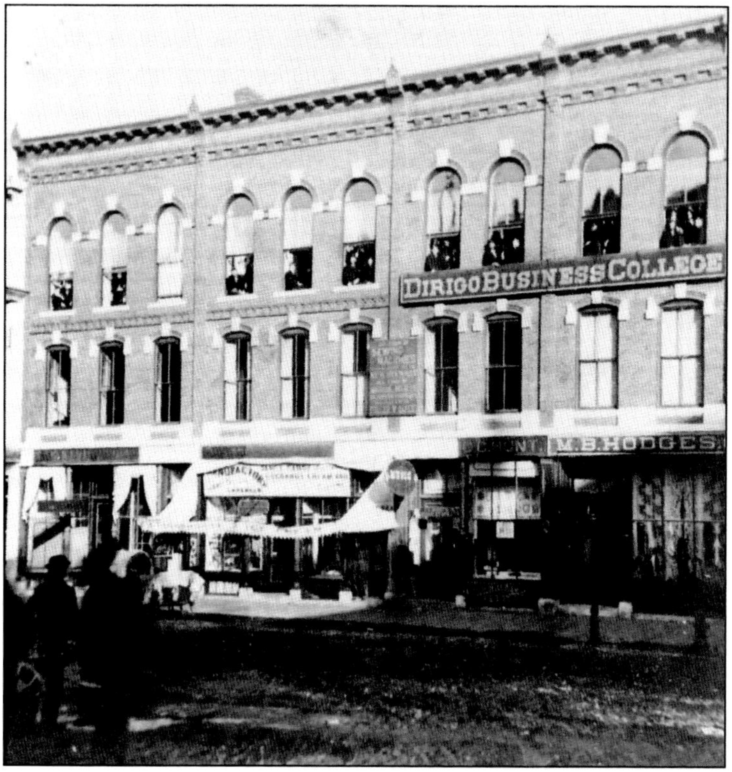

Dirigo Business College, founded in 1865, moved to the third floor of Benjamin F. Parrott's new block on Water Street in 1877, as witnessed by students posing for the photographer from the open windows. First known as the Augusta Commercial College, the school became incorporated as Dirigo in 1867 when Daniel M. Waitt assumed its leadership.

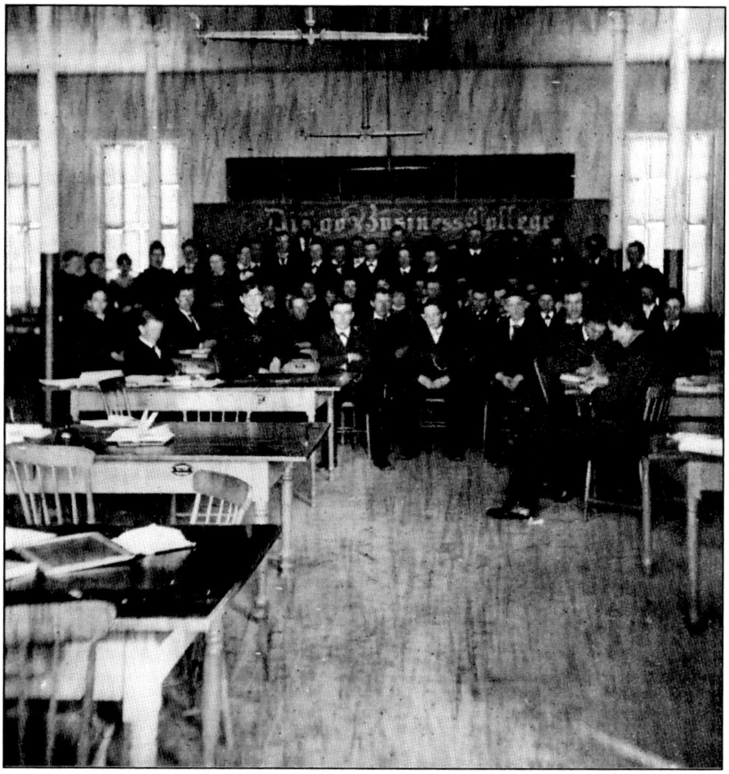

Well-dressed students fill a classroom at the Dirigo Business College. At the left is a small cluster of women in an otherwise male group. An 1880 prospectus for the school offered a "thorough and practical everyday business training for boys who wish to become good bookkeepers, salesmen, practical men to fill official stations, for young ladies who desire to become accountants, telegraph operators, etc."

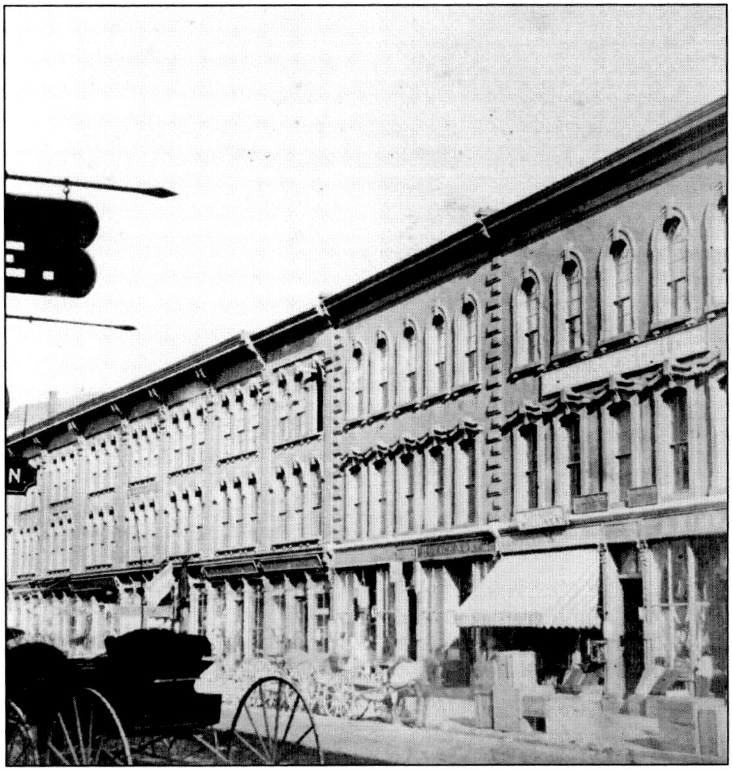

The rebuilding of Water Street after the 1865 fire resulted in rows of brick commercial blocks such as these on the east side near Bridge Street. The two buildings at the right comprised James W. North's block of 1866 with its elaborate Italianate brickwork sheathed in mastic to simulate brownstone. The seven-unit Italianate row to the left was constructed in two parts from designs by Francis H. Fassett and the northern three units by Reuel Williams in 1862, with the balance by his son Joseph Williams in 1866.

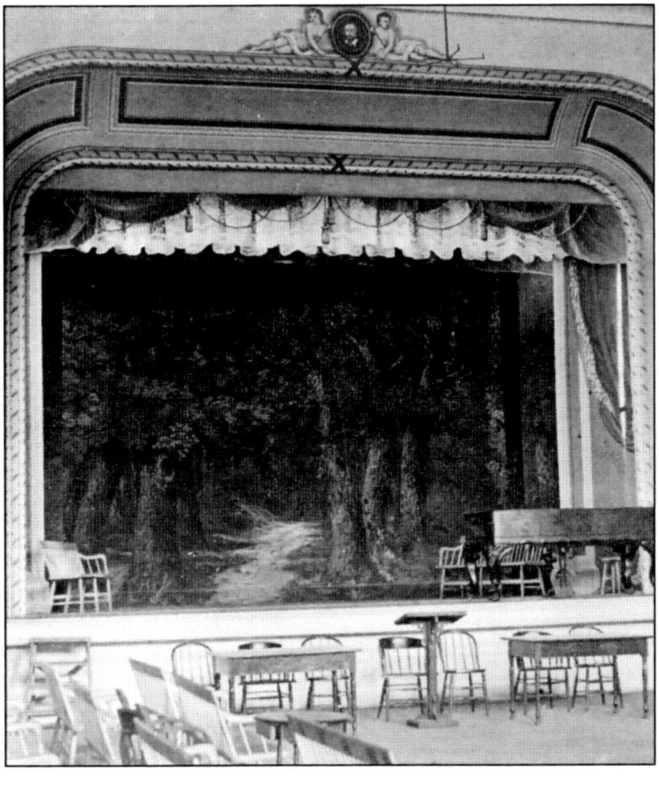

In an age before movies, television, and DVD players, assembly halls on the upper floors of Water Street blocks played an important role in the social and cultural life of Augusta, hosting dances, lectures, political rallies, and fraternal meetings. One of the city's favorite gathering places was Meonian Hall, originally constructed by James W. North on the east side of Water Street in 1856 and rebuilt by him after the 1865 fire. This view shows the stage of the second Meonian Hall, in use from 1866 to 1904. The decorative painting was the work of Charles J. Schumacher, a German-born artist from Portland.

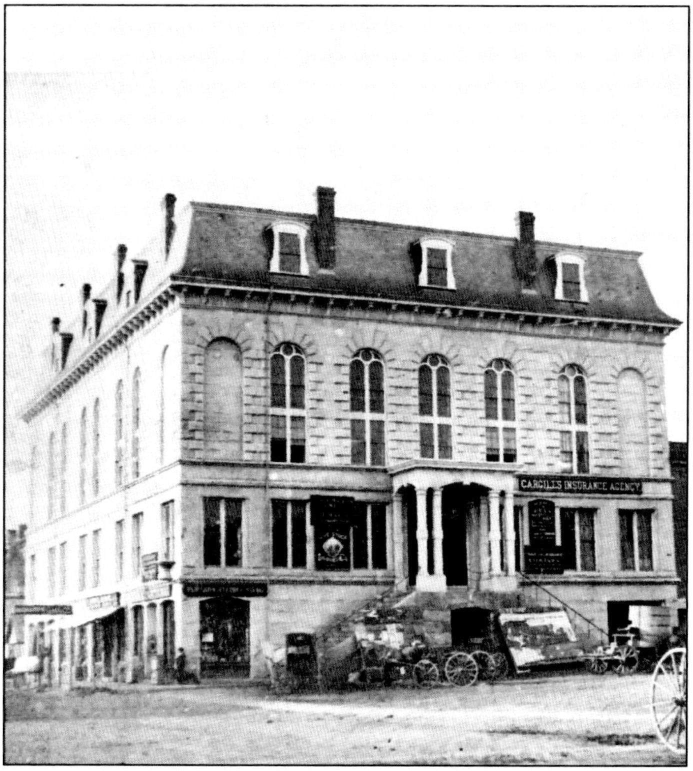

Built at Market Square and Water Street in 1865 and 1866, Granite Hall was designed by Francis H. Fassett for George W. Ricker to accommodate stores, offices, and a grand assembly hall measuring 104 feet long and 62 feet wide. The block was rebuilt after fires in 1890 and 1896 and was remodeled for the Capitol Theater in 1930. A third fire in 1976 led to its demolition in 1983.

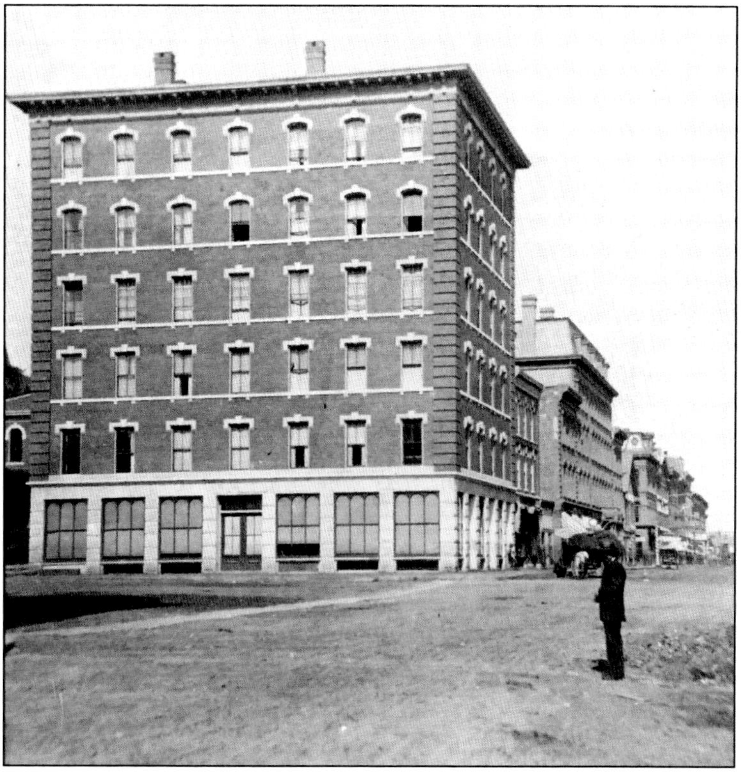

So successful was E. C. Allen's magazine publishing that he added a second Water Street building in 1877 next to his first one of 1871. Further increases in business resulted in Allen constructing this six-story block across the street in 1880. The architect was George G. Stevens. Both the third Allen block and North's Hotel, at the right, were demolished in 1987 for the Key Bank plaza.

The burning of the Mansion House on State Street in 1877 left a gap in accommodations that was filled by the construction of North's Hotel on the west side of Water Street between Winthrop and Oak Streets. Built between 1877 and 1879 by James W. North and Benjamin F. Davis, this five-story, 80-room hotel featured the latest innovations of steam heat and indoor plumbing. The main building and its three-story flanking wings were replaced by the Key Bank plaza in 1987.

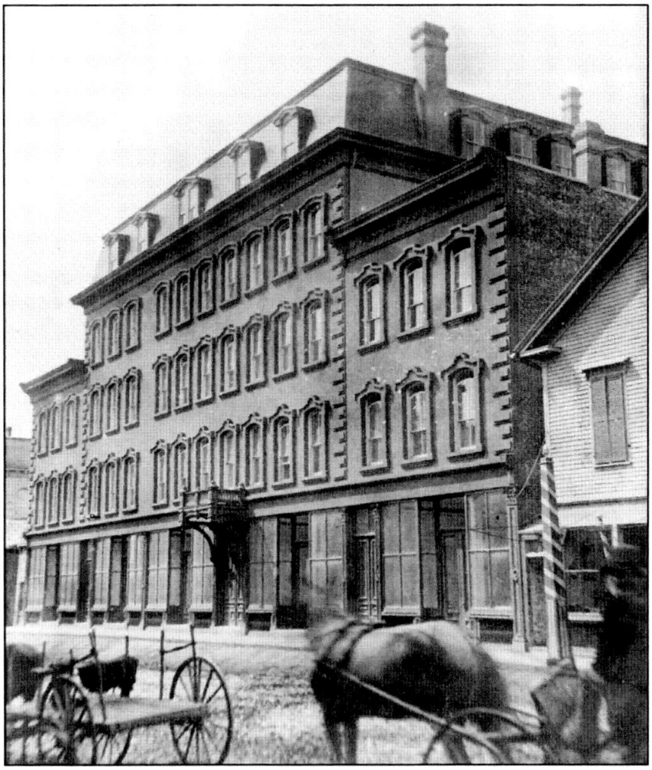

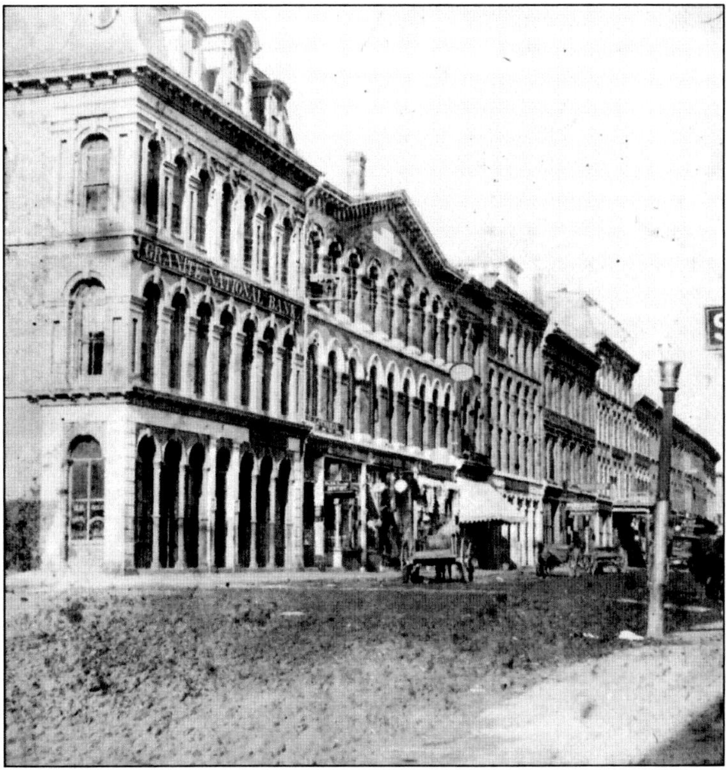

After the 1865 fire, the west side of Water Street from Oak Street to Bridge Street was rebuilt with handsome brick and stone commercial buildings. Prominent among them was the Granite National Bank at the left, an elegant mansard-roofed block constructed in 1866 from designs by Fassett with Rodney L. Fogg as contractor. The bank originally shared the first floor with the post office but in 1870 moved to the second story to allow for expanded postal facilities at the street level.

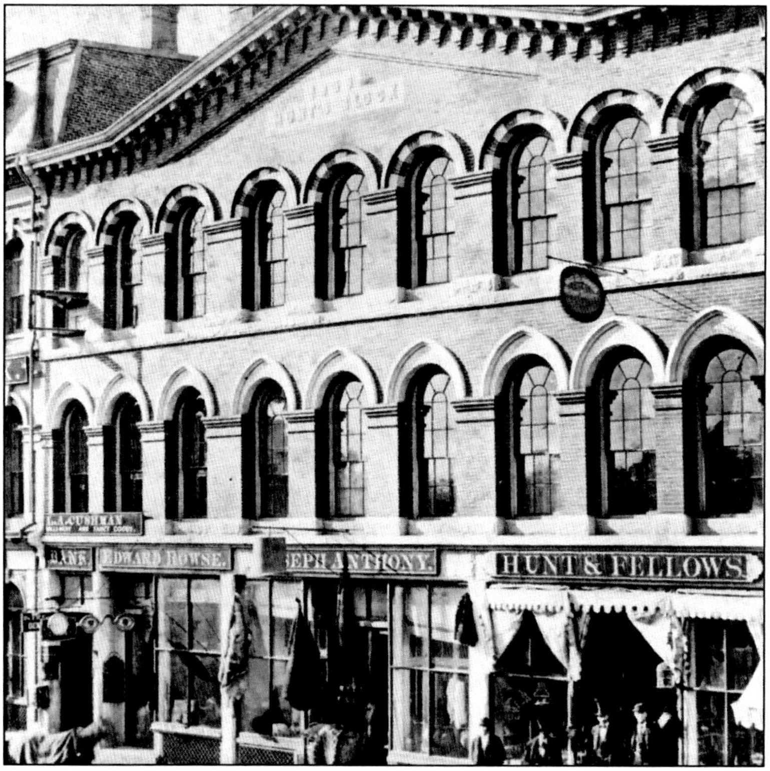

Built next to the Granite National Bank in 1866 for George Hunt, this brick and stone commercial building featured a distinctive Italianate facade designed by Francis H. Fassett and constructed by George G. Stevens and James Savage. Occupants of the Hunt block included jeweler Edward Rowse, clothier Joseph Anthony, and grocers Hunt and Fellows.

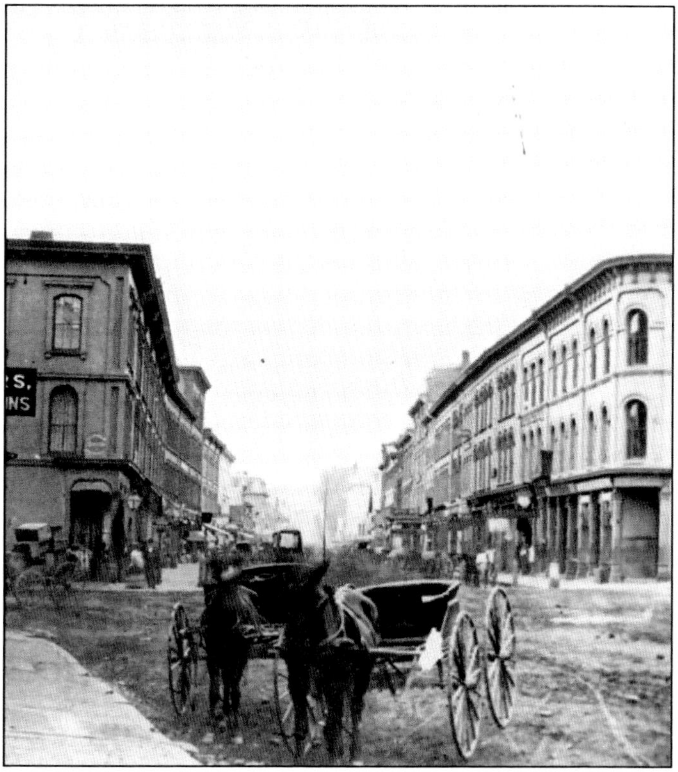

The rows of new commercial buildings on Water Street ended at the intersection of Bridge Street, as seen in this view looking south. On the left, the corner block was built by Joseph H. Williams and Stephen Deering in 1863 from plans by Fassett. Across the street, the three-unit block with the distinctive curved corner was designed in 1867 by John C. Tibbetts for Joseph Anthony, Ira Sturgis, and Erastus Haskell.

Among the many losses in the 1865 fire was the Portland and Kennebec Railroad station, which stood on Commercial Street. In 1866, the Portland and Kennebec Railroad constructed this station near the site of the previous one. Designed by Fassett in the Italiantate style, Augusta's new depot consisted of an attractive two-story brick building that featured an elaborate platform extending from Winthrop Street to Oak Street.

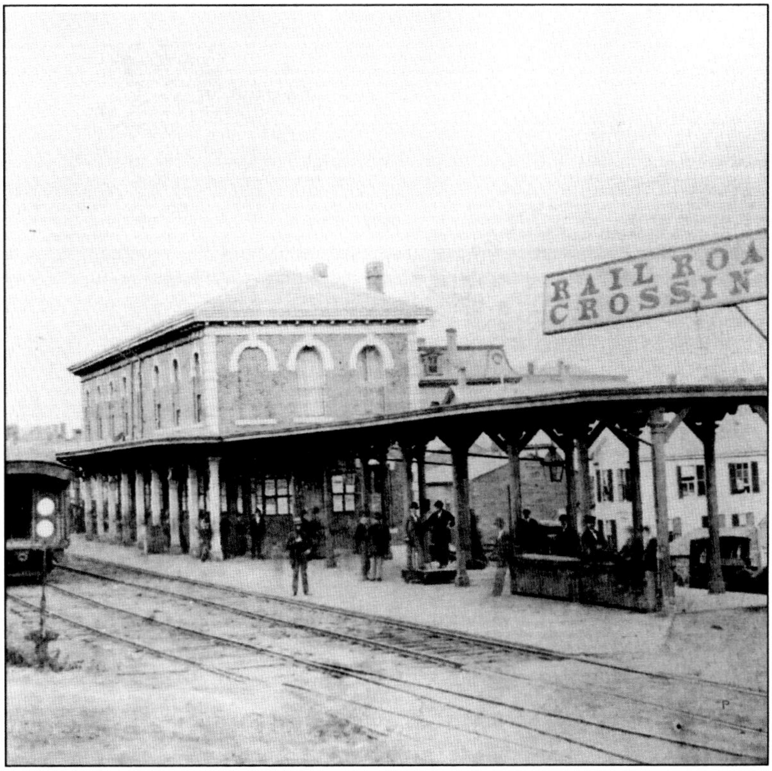

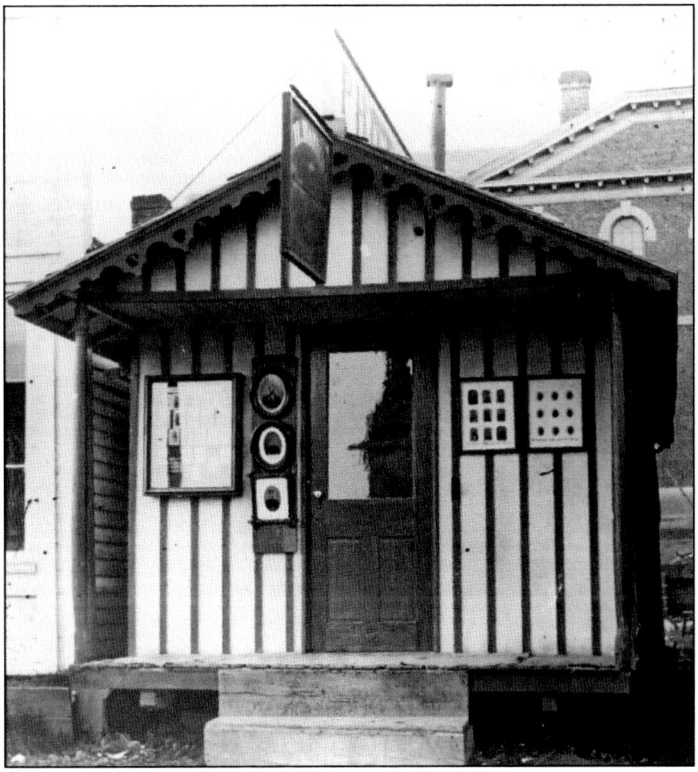

In May 1867, Henry Bailey purchased this small photographic building on the west side of Water Street adjacent to the railroad station. This shop contained a display space at the front and a studio with a skylight and a darkroom at the rear. Glass cases of tintypes and framed tintype portraits hung on the exterior. Bailey conducted business at this location until May 1877, when he was displaced by the construction of North's Hotel.

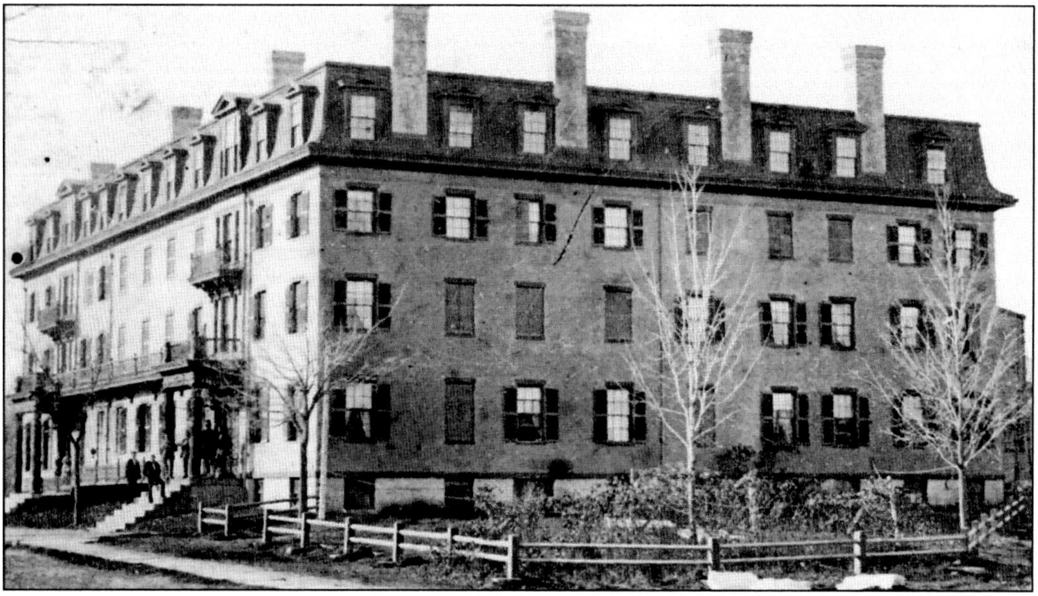

In anticipation of visitors to the first legislative session in Augusta in 1832, the Augusta House was built near the statehouse on State Street and Western Avenue. Erected in 1831, this popular hotel was enlarged in 1864 due to increased business in the capital city during the Civil War. Architect Francis H. Fassett's expansion included a five-bay addition at the south end and a mansard roof. The Augusta House was expanded again in 1910 and then demolished in the 1970s for the Casco Bank building.

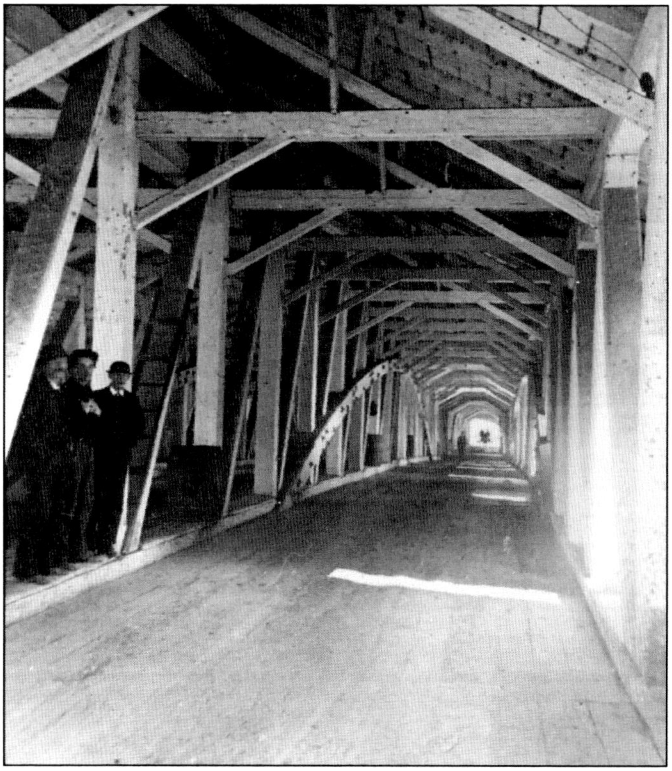

This two-lane, wooded covered bridge linked the east and west sides of Augusta from 1827 to 1890. The third bridge since 1797 to span the Kennebec River at this site, the structure was built under the supervision of Ephraim Ballard. From 1827 to 1867, tolls were charged, after which the bridge was maintained by the city as a free public way.

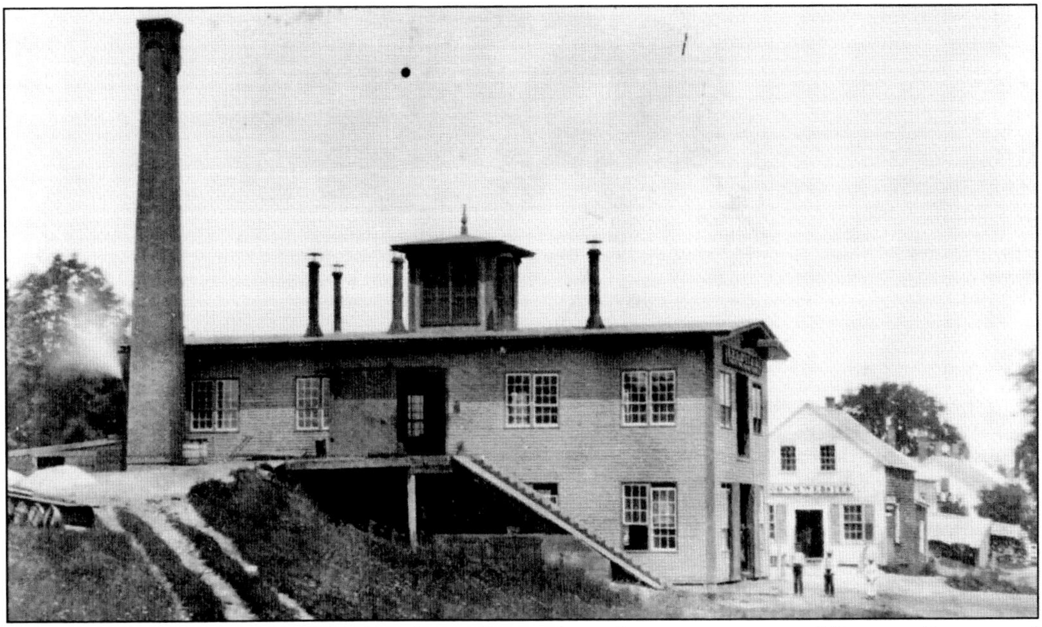

The Pettingill Corner neighborhood was located at the intersection of Bangor Street and Belfast Road (Route 3). After the Civil War, blacksmith Henry H. Harvey erected this two-story wooden foundry at Bangor and Lock Streets across from Belfast Road. In this stylish Italianate building, Harvey manufactured tools for the then-thriving granite industry. John M. Webster's store appears in the background.

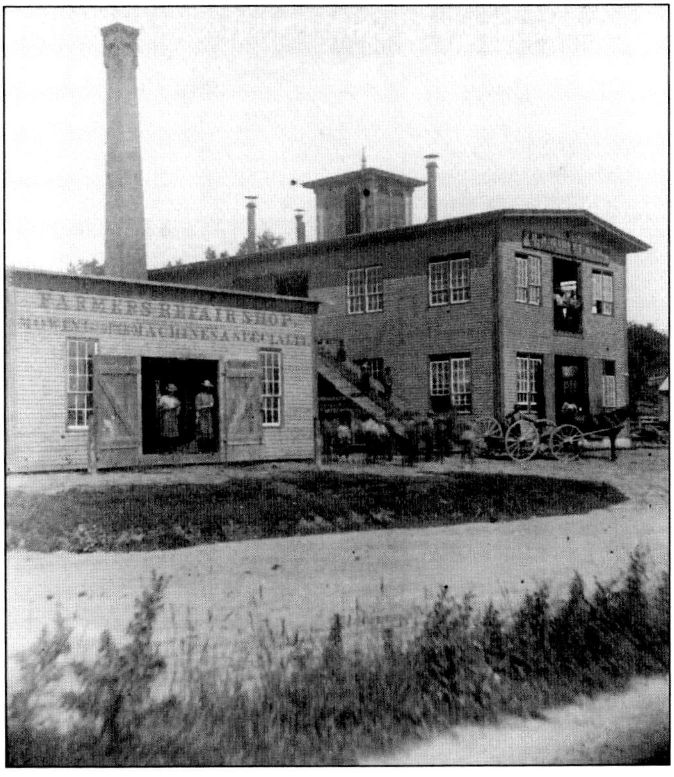

In the 1880s, Harvey added this one-story frame structure adjacent to his foundry to repair farm equipment. The sign reads, "Farmers Repair Shop. Mowing & Other Machines a Speciality." The Harvey foundry ceased making tools in 1918, probably due to the demise of the granite industry.

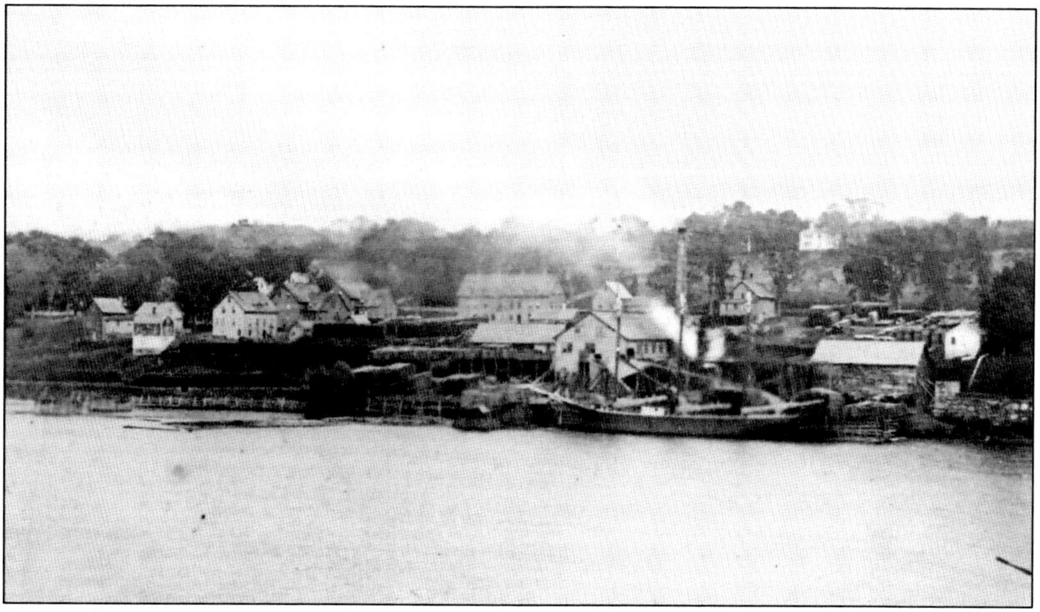

During the 19th century, the Kennebec River provided the highway for transporting timber from the forests to Augusta, where it was sawed into lumber. On the east side of the river, just north of the arsenal, stood the sawmill that Ira D. Sturgis established in 1863 as the Kennebec Land and Lumber Company. After the yard burned in 1875, the business became Sturgis, Lambard and Company in 1876 (shown here), followed by the Augusta Lumber Company in 1889.

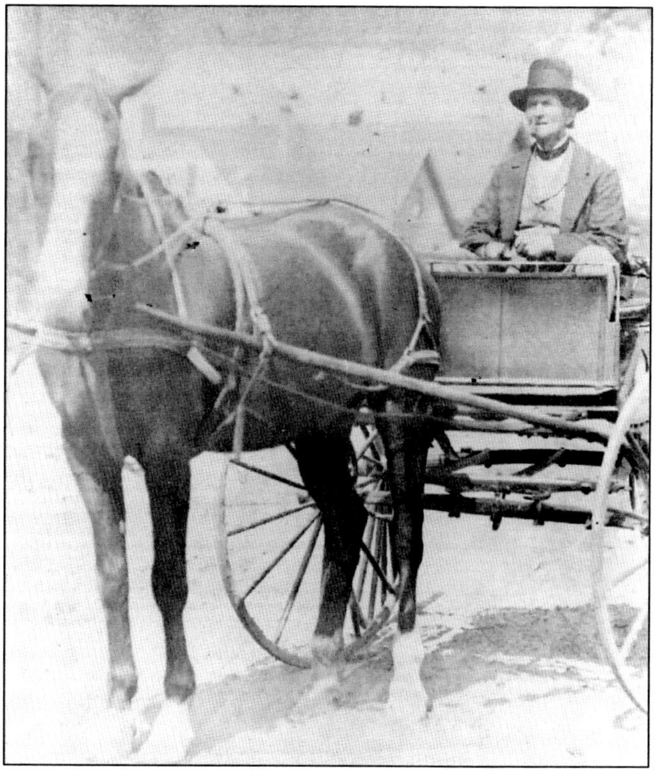

Russell Eaton was a familiar figure on the streets of Augusta for 65 years. In 1825, Eaton and his partner, Luther Severance, started publishing weekly issues of the *Kennebec Journal*. Eaton left the newspaper in 1833, and from 1844 to 1858, he published the *Maine Farmer*, another widely read weekly newspaper. Born in Montague, Massachusetts, in 1797, he died in Augusta in 1890.

Five

Residences

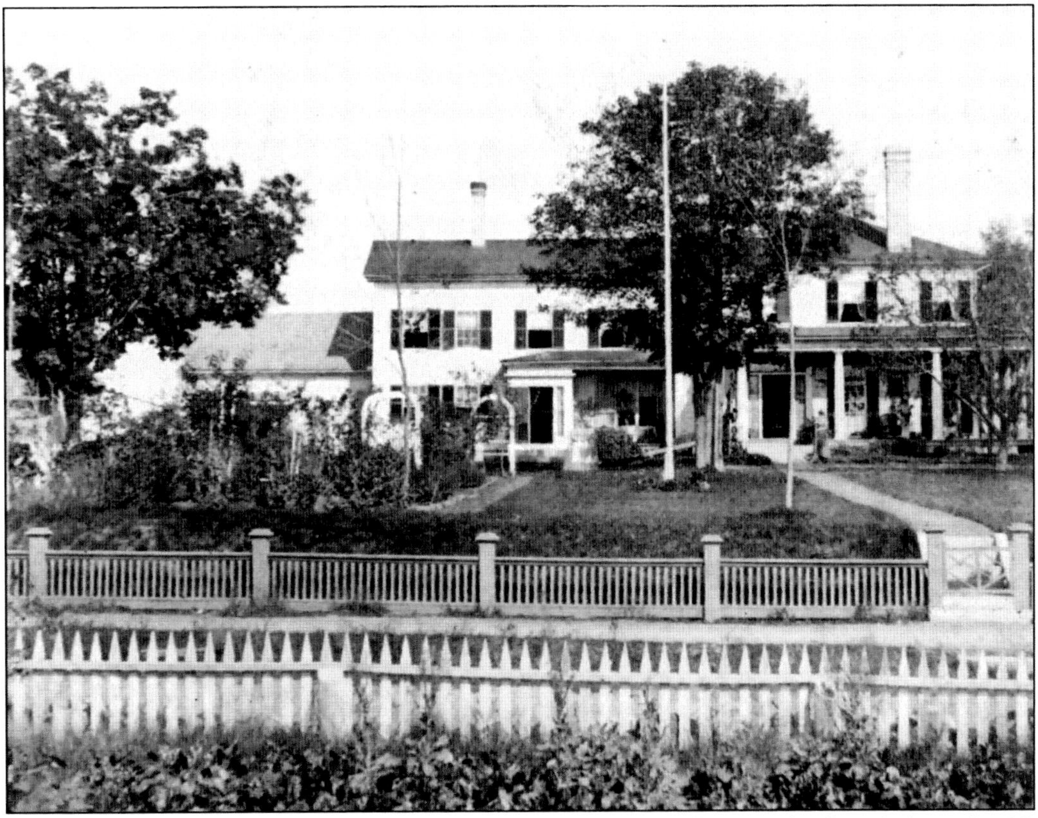

Born in 1802, James W. Bradbury graduated from Bowdoin College in the famed class of 1825, became an attorney, and served a term as a U.S. senator before the Civil War. About the time of his marriage in 1834, Bradbury built this elegant transitional Federal–Greek Revival residence on Green Street, where he lived until his death in 1901. The house was demolished in 1927 for the Central Maine Power Company office building.

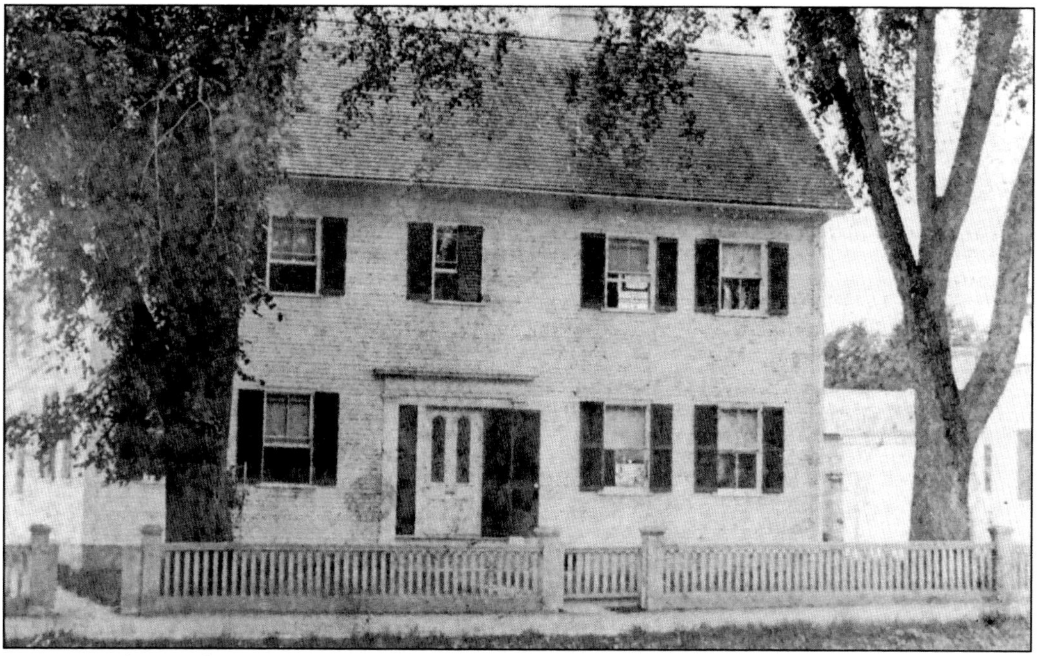

A pre–Civil War photograph of 58 Winthrop Street shows a two-story, Federal-style house with a hipped roof, which was built by Elisha Child in the 1830s. By the time Henry Bailey made this view about 1880, the roof had been changed to a gable, and the house was owned by the Johnson family.

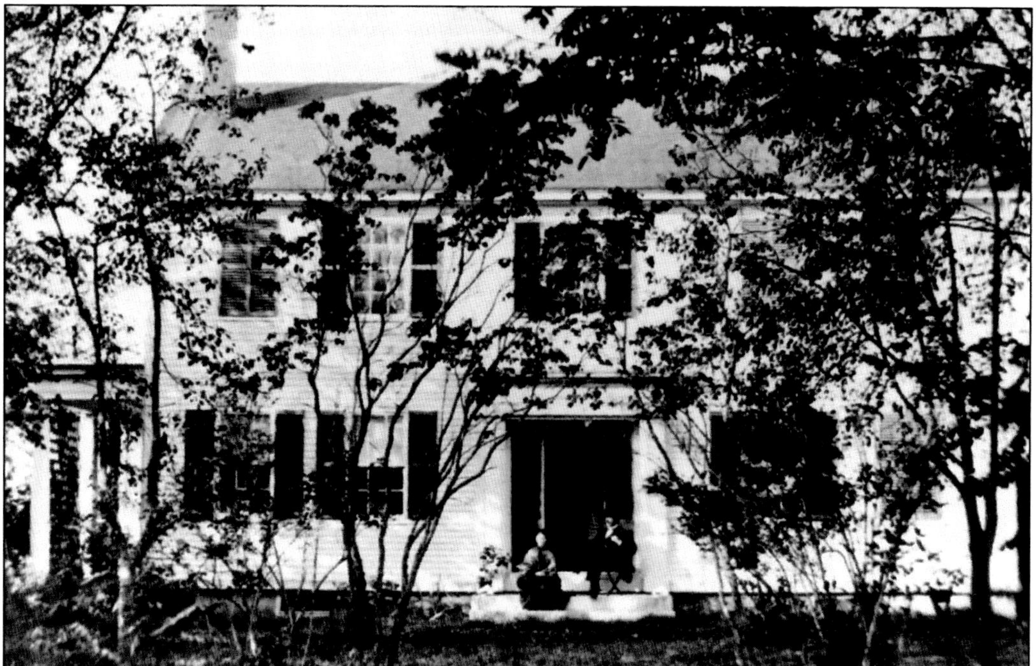

Bailey's camera captured the transitional Federal–Greek Revival appearance of the house at 25 South Chestnut Street before its Victorian remodeling by Sewall Lancaster, an attorney who lived there from the 1850s to the 1880s.

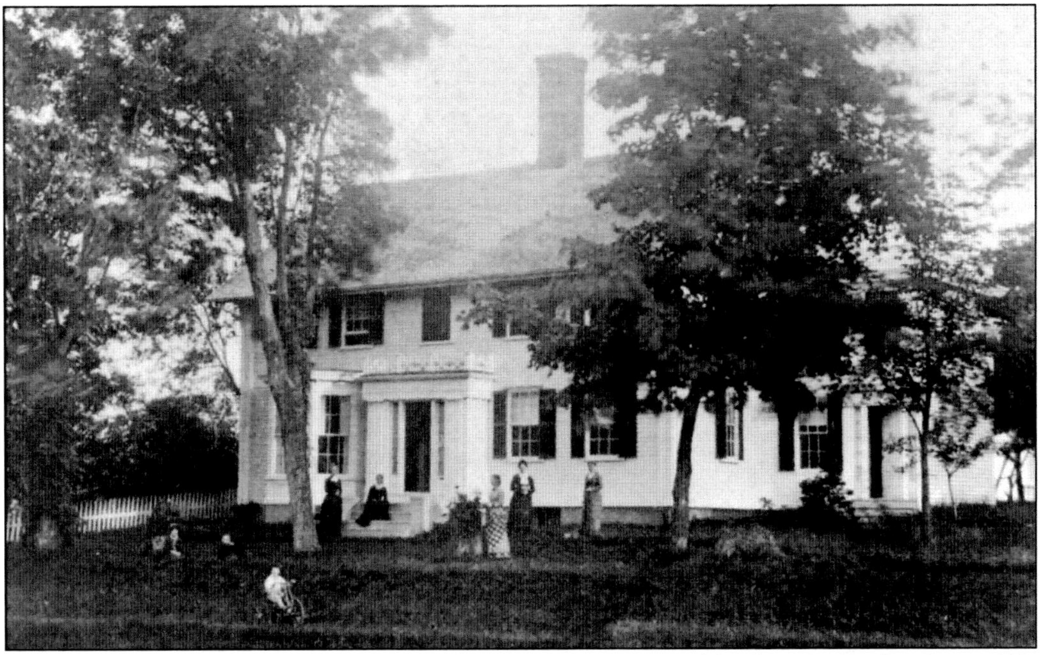

This early house, which stood at 26 Winthrop Street, was owned by the Weston family in 1838. After the Civil War, Eben H. Sawyer, a shipbuilder, lived there with his wife, Lucy. When Eben died in the 1870s, Lucy converted the house into a duplex that she shared with druggist Lewis H. Titcomb.

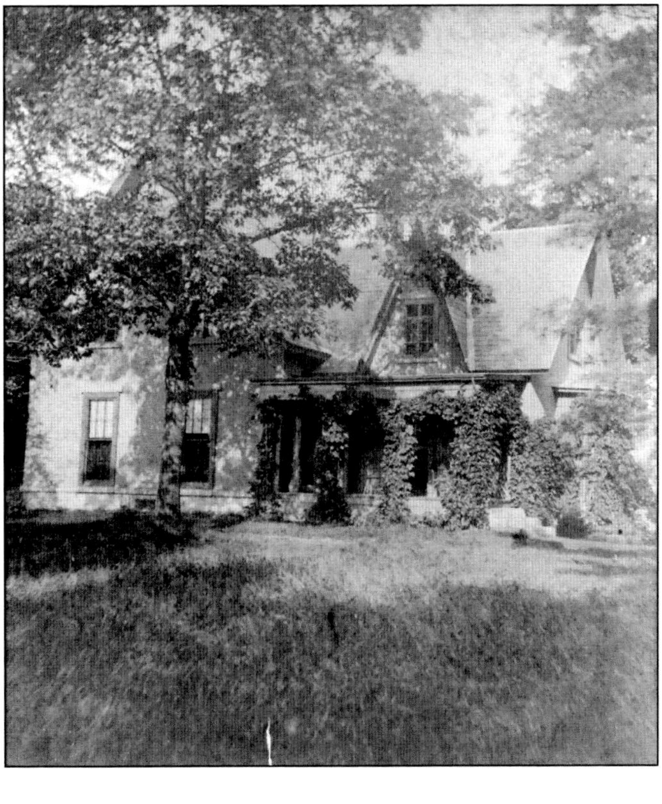

In 1846, the noted Unitarian clergyman and novelist Rev. Sylvester Judd, built Riverside, a picturesque Gothic Revival, brick cottage at Arsenal and Williams Streets, basing its design on plans in Andrew Jackson Downing's *Cottage Residences* from 1842. Judd served as minister for Augusta's Unitarians from 1840 until his death in 1853. His wife, Elizabeth, a daughter of Reuel Williams, continued to reside in the house, which is now part of an office complex.

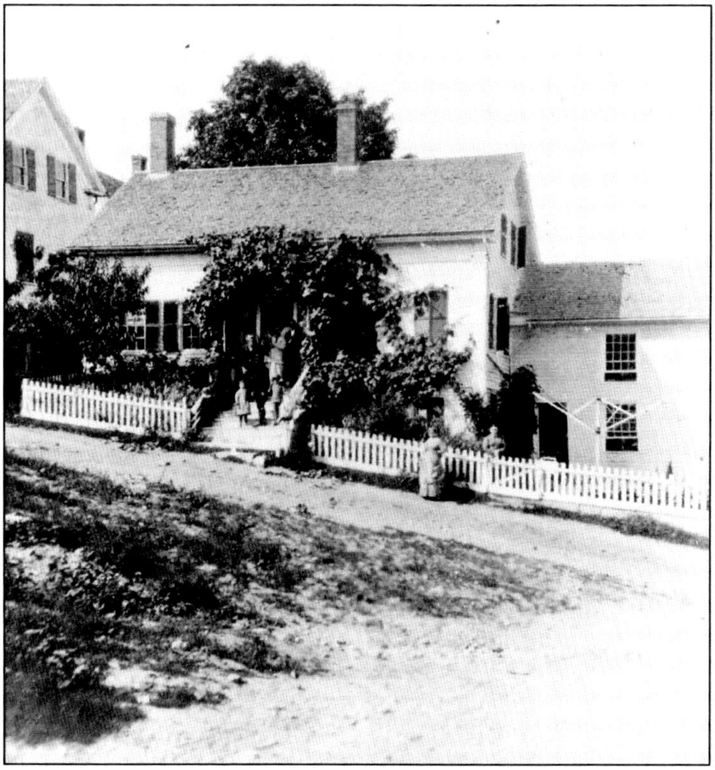

This modest Greek Revival cape, now gone, was built at the foot of Laurel Street by 1851. When Henry Bailey photographed the house in the post–Civil War period, it was the home of Emile Barbier, who operated a steam dyeing plant nearby on Water Street.

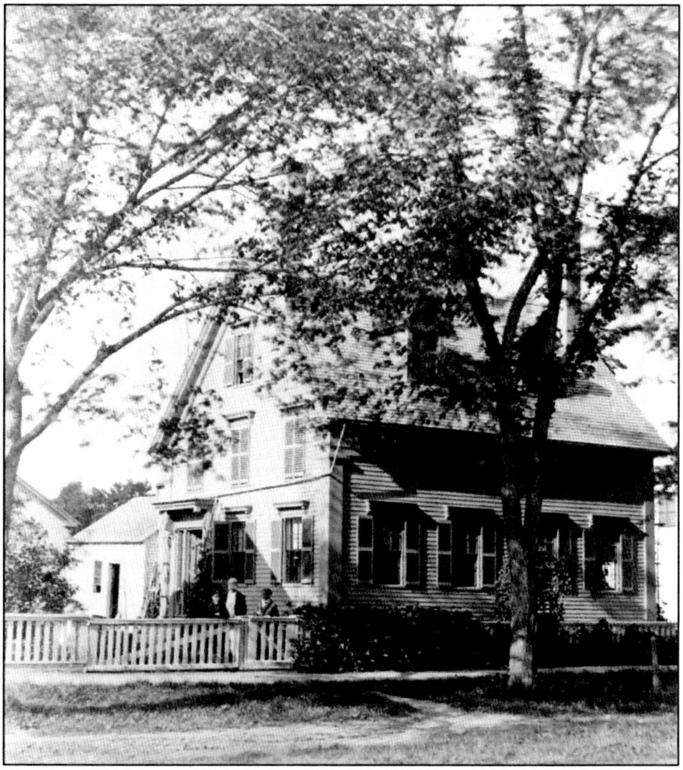

John S. Cushing's stylish one-and-a-half-story Greek Revival house still stands at 56 Winthrop Street. The treasurer of the Portland and Kennebec Railroad, Cushing built this home between 1851 and 1856, using such distinctive features as a gable end main entry and small oval windows in the cornice facing Winthrop Street.

This home, which once stood at 17 Winthrop Street, appears on the 1851 Augusta map as being owned by the Whitehouse family. When Henry Bailey photographed the house on August 15, 1881, he noted that John P. Whitehouse, a bookkeeper, lived there. Family members pose for the photographer on the front lawn.

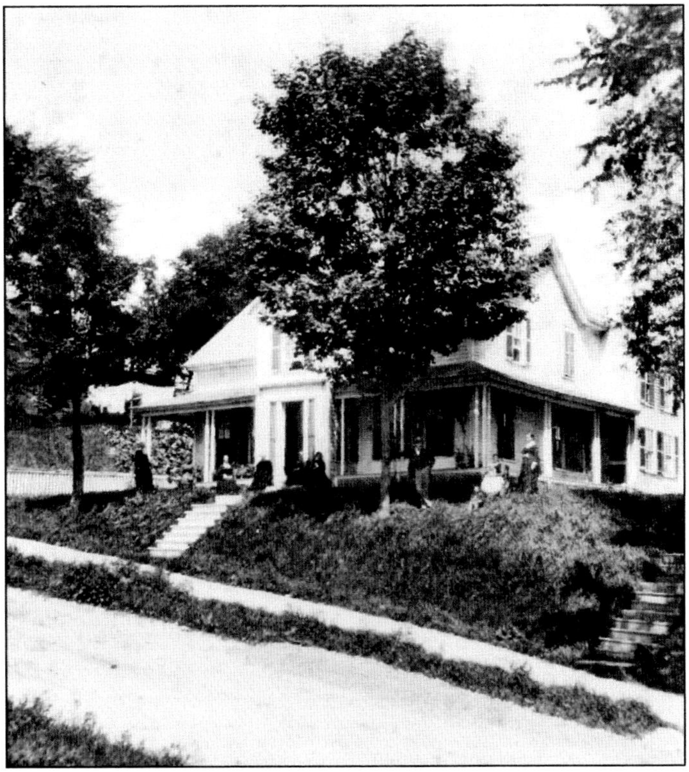

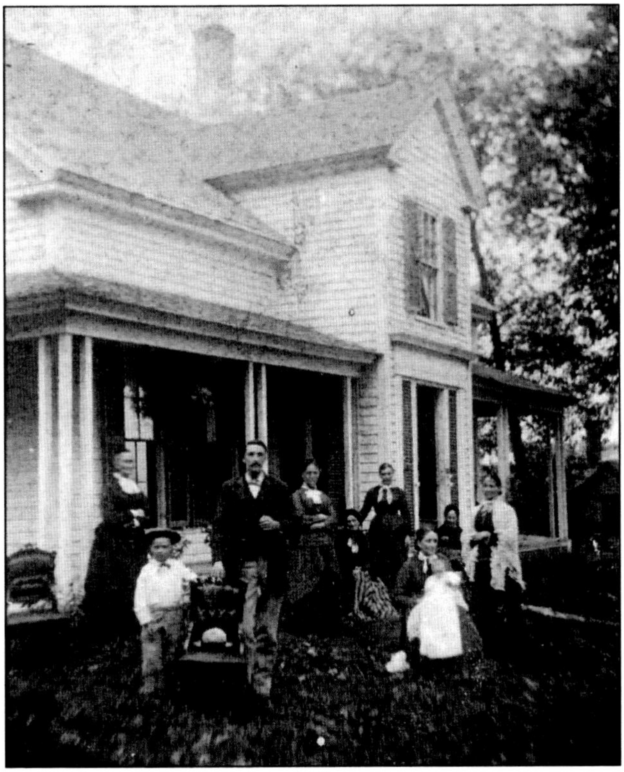

This close-up of John P. Whitehouse and his family standing in front of their 17 Winthrop Street home in 1881 is a classic Victorian photographic portrait, the kind that Bailey and his contemporaries often were called upon to make. A study of faces indicates that as many as four generations may be present.

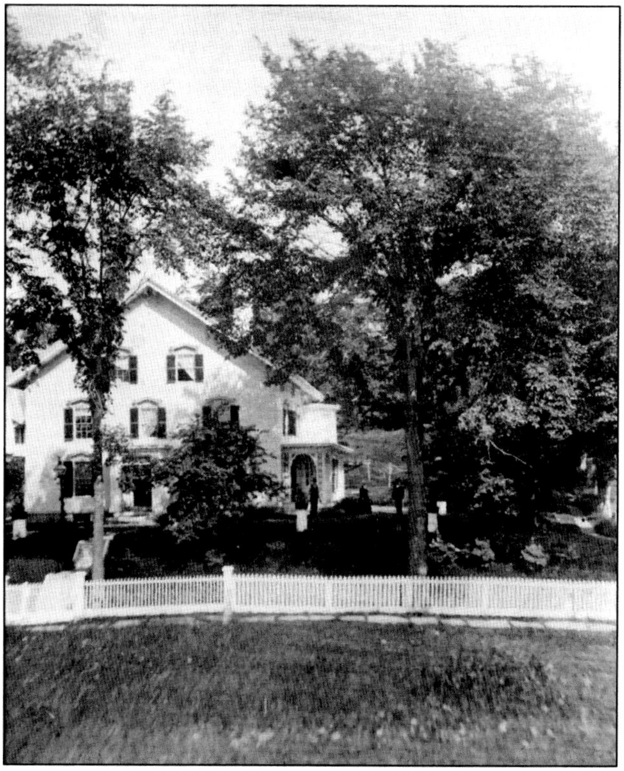

Built by Thomas Sewall in the late 18th century, this house, which stood at 25 Howard Street, was acquired in 1826 by Allan Lambard, who gave it its Victorian appearance in 1865. Lambard was one of Augusta's leading businessmen, first operating a distillery, then an iron foundry. During the California gold rush, he established a foundry and a flour mill in Sacramento. In retirement, he operated a large east side farm near his home.

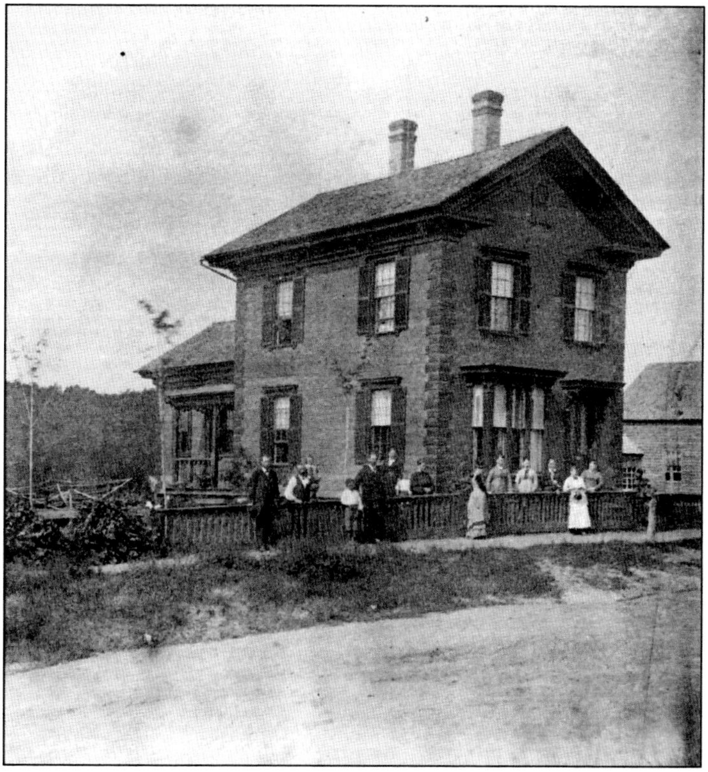

In 1867, the A. and W. Sprague Manufacturing Company of Rhode Island purchased the Kennebec Company's textile mill, dam, waterpower, and land at the north end. That year, the company's overseer, Jefferson Higgins, built this stylish Italianate house at 124 Northern Avenue to live in close proximity to his firm's holdings. Higgins resided there until 1880. The house stands today in an altered condition.

Less elaborate in its Italianate features than the Jefferson Higgins house is the home that carpenter Ira L. Mackie built for himself at 5 York Street in 1872. Mackie lived in this north end residence until 1912, after which it was converted into three apartments that are still in use.

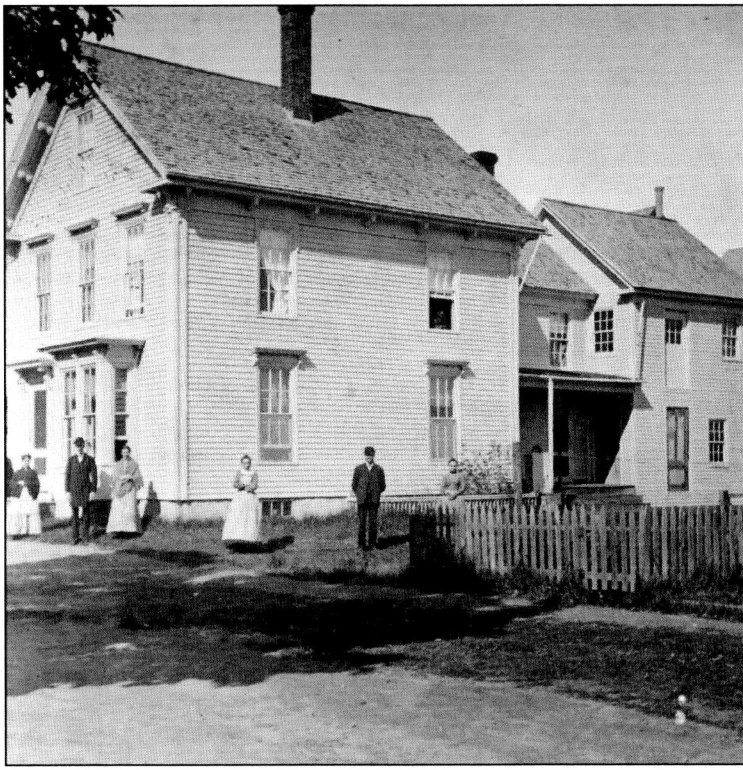

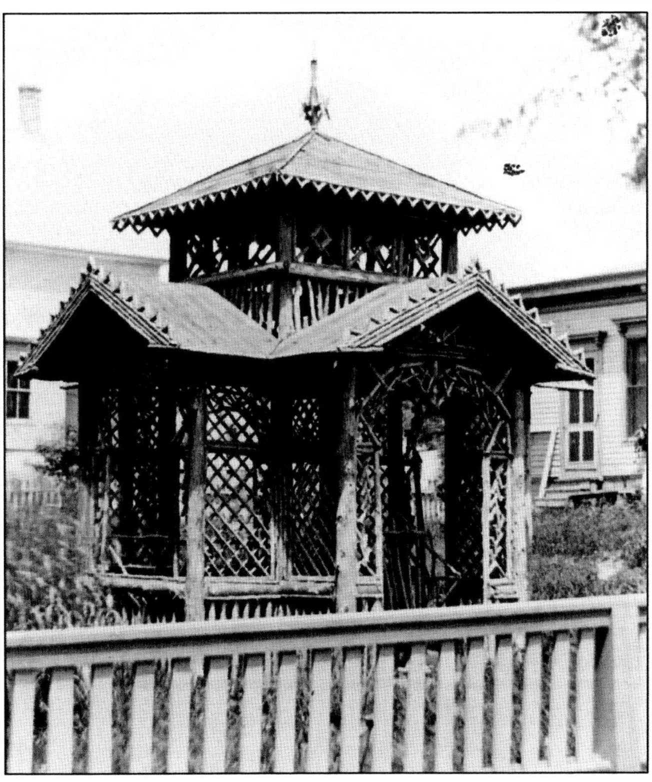

On July 14, 1873, the *Kennebec Journal* reported that "George F. North has built this past season on his lot, corner of Green and Melville streets a rustic summer house after his own design and mostly of his own workmanship." This picturesque ornament to North's grounds vanished long ago, but his Italianate residence still stands.

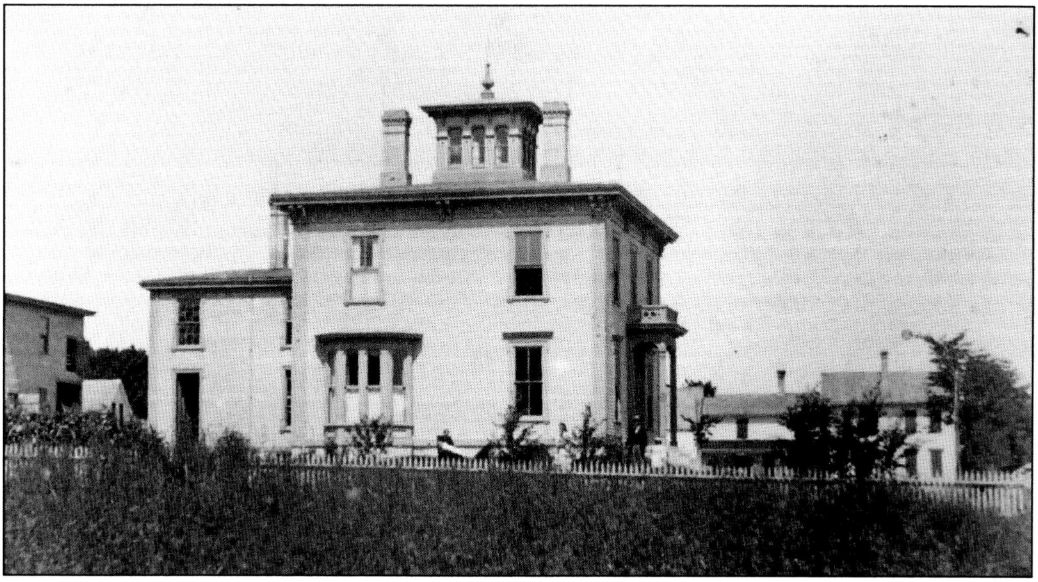

Levi L. Lincoln's stately two-story Italianate house, with its ornamental cupola, stood at Sewall and Lincoln Streets from 1869 until its demolition for St. Mary's School. Lincoln was the superintendent of the Portland and Kennebec Railroad. The undeveloped land in the foreground is now a parking lot at Western Avenue and Sewall Street.

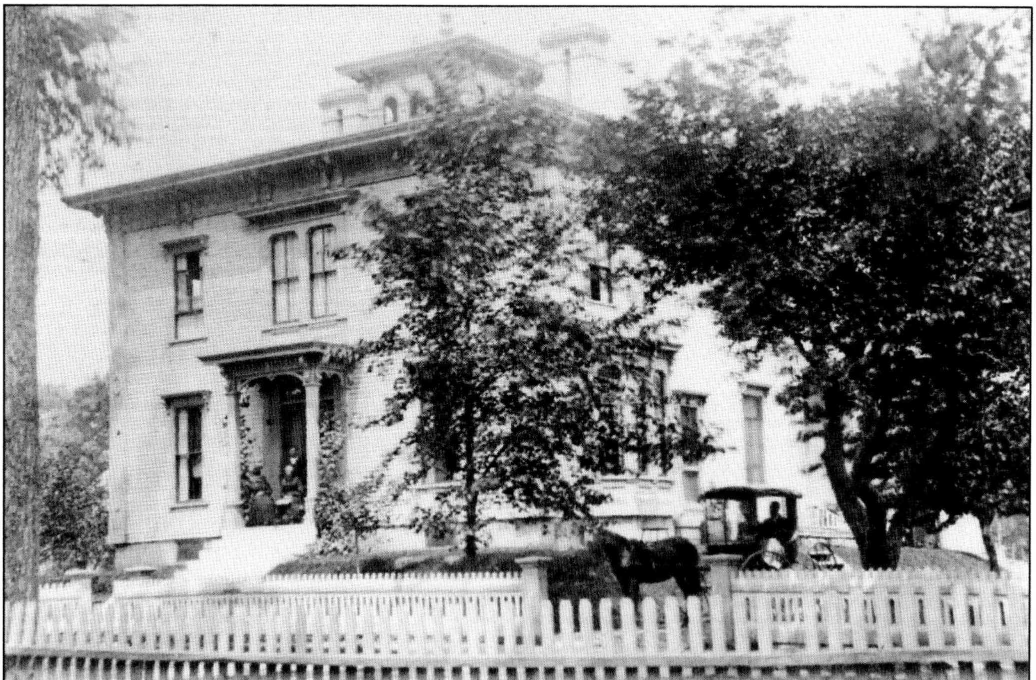

This handsome Italianate house at 51 Green Street, with its bracketed cornice and cupola, was built in 1869 for James M. Sanborn, a grocer on Water Street. The architect was George G. Stevens of Augusta, who designed many local Victorian commercial buildings and homes. After Sanborn's death in 1881, the house was owned by Charles and Emma Huntington Nason. Emma wrote *Old Hallowell on the Kennebec*.

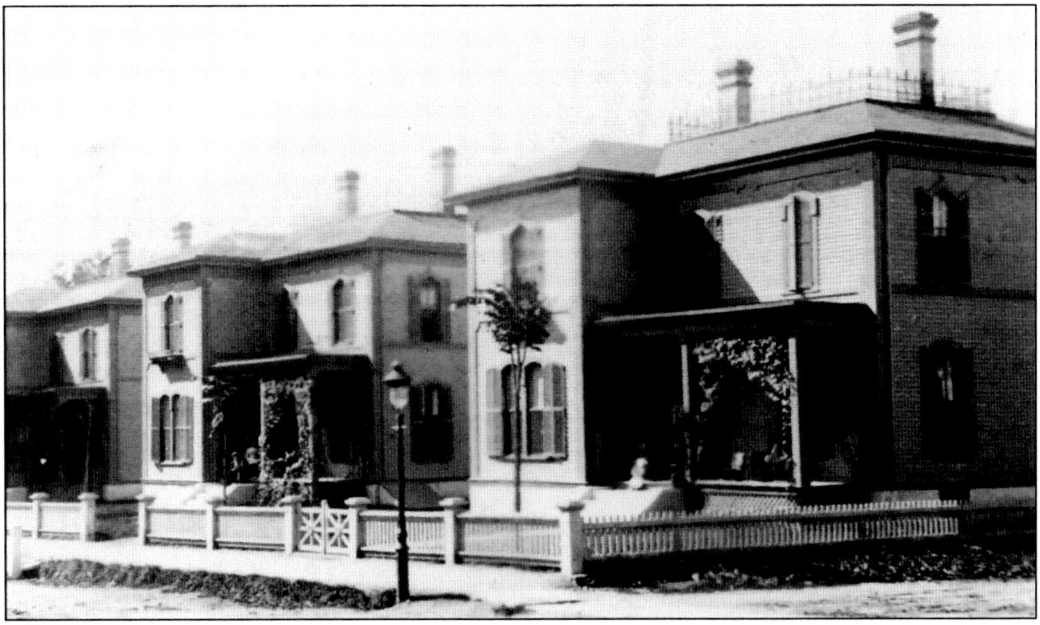

In 1880, publisher Peleg O. Vickery built these three identical Italianate houses at State and Court Streets on the site of the Mansion House, a hotel that burned in 1877. Known as the Vickery triplets, these homes were based on a design in Elisha Charles Hussey's *National Cottage Architecture*, an 1874 architectural plan book. The October 22, 1880, *Kennebec Journal* described them as "three tasty modern dwellings."

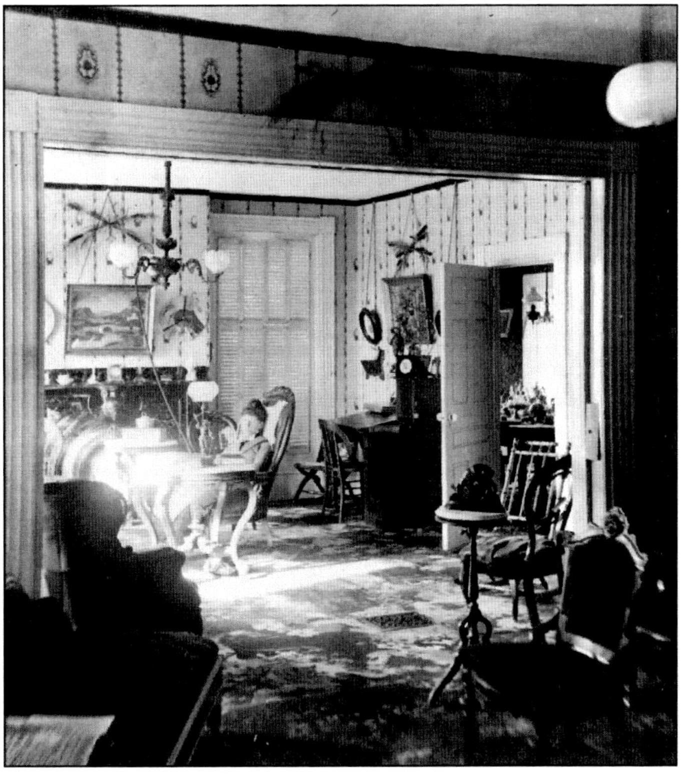

In Victorian times, fashionable middle-class homes featured adjoining family and formal parlors, one for the social activities of daily life and the other for such special occasions as holiday celebrations, weddings, and funerals. Here Martha M. Pray relaxes in an armchair in the family parlor of her State Street home, which stood opposite the Augusta House hotel.

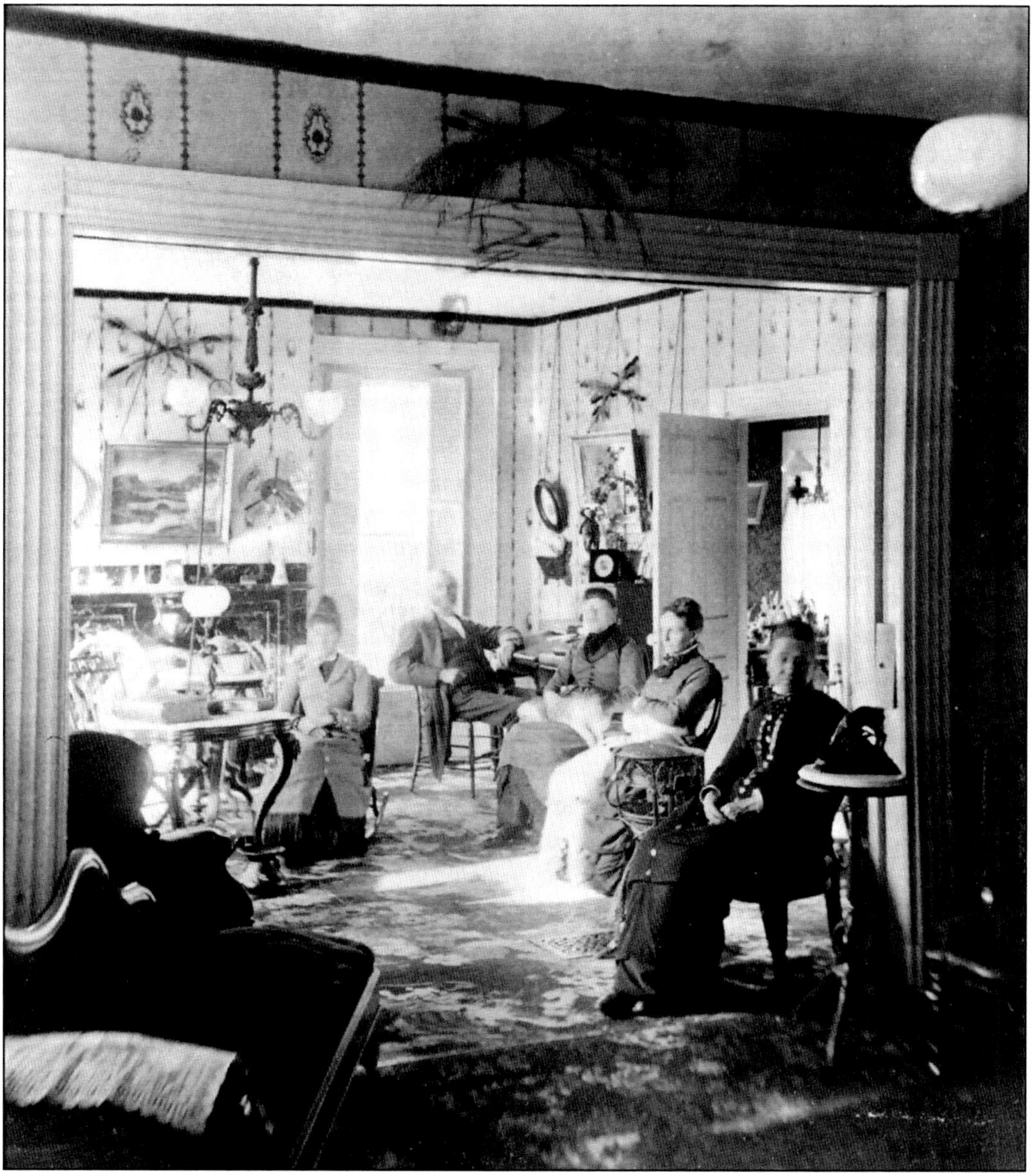

Those pictured in this May 1880 photograph of the Pray family parlor, from left to right, are Martha M. Pray at the center table, Deane Pray at his desk, and three unidentified women. A large family Bible rests on the marble-top table, while a spittoon for chewing tobacco stands next to the table leg.

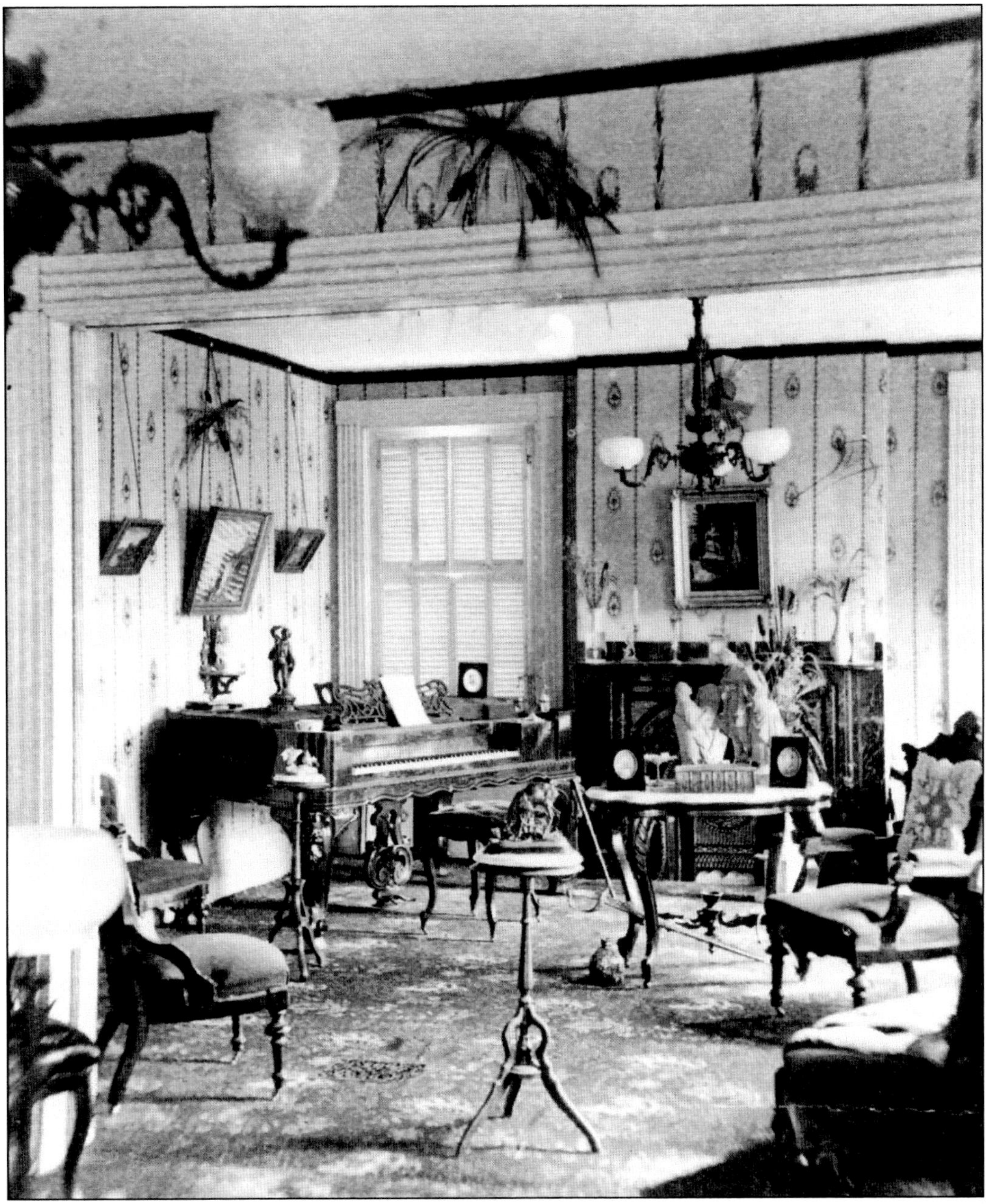

Pray's success as a clothing merchant on Water Street allowed his wife to furnish their formal parlor with a costly piano and display a copy of the famous John Rogers statue *Going to the Parson* on a marble-top center table. The Victorian decorative aesthetic of "more is better" made for a challenging navigation of a room so full of chairs and stands.

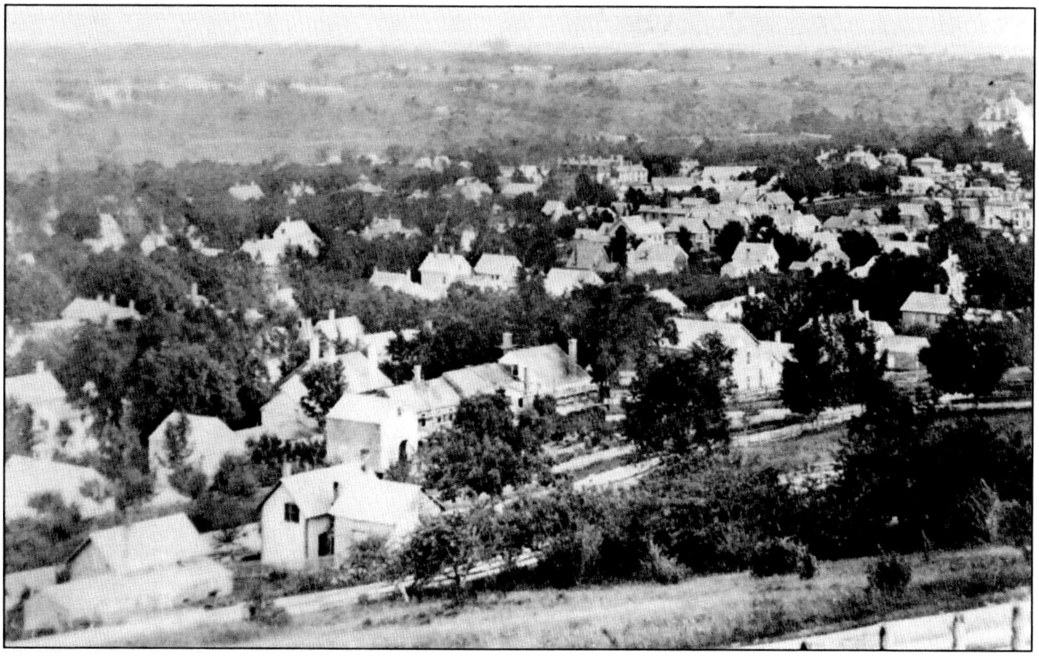

Standing on Granite Street, Henry Bailey directed his camera southeast across the Winthrop Street residential neighborhood to create this panoramic image of its many tree-lined streets. Two remaining Winthrop Street landmarks are the Lot Morrill house in the center foreground and the brick schoolhouse, partially obscured, to its right.

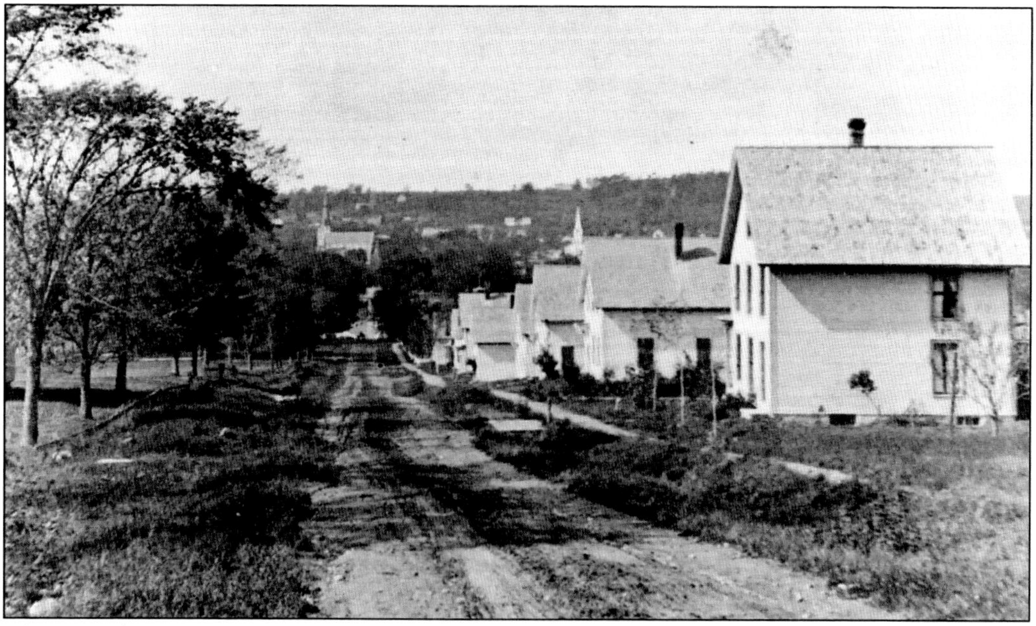

The east side's Cony Street is a rutted dirt road lined on the right by a row of modest workingmen's homes. Looming center left in the background is the South Parish Congregational Church, standing on an elevated site across the Kennebec River. The white steeple appearing center right belonged to the Free Will Baptist Church on State Street, also located on the west side of the river.

Six

Capitol Park

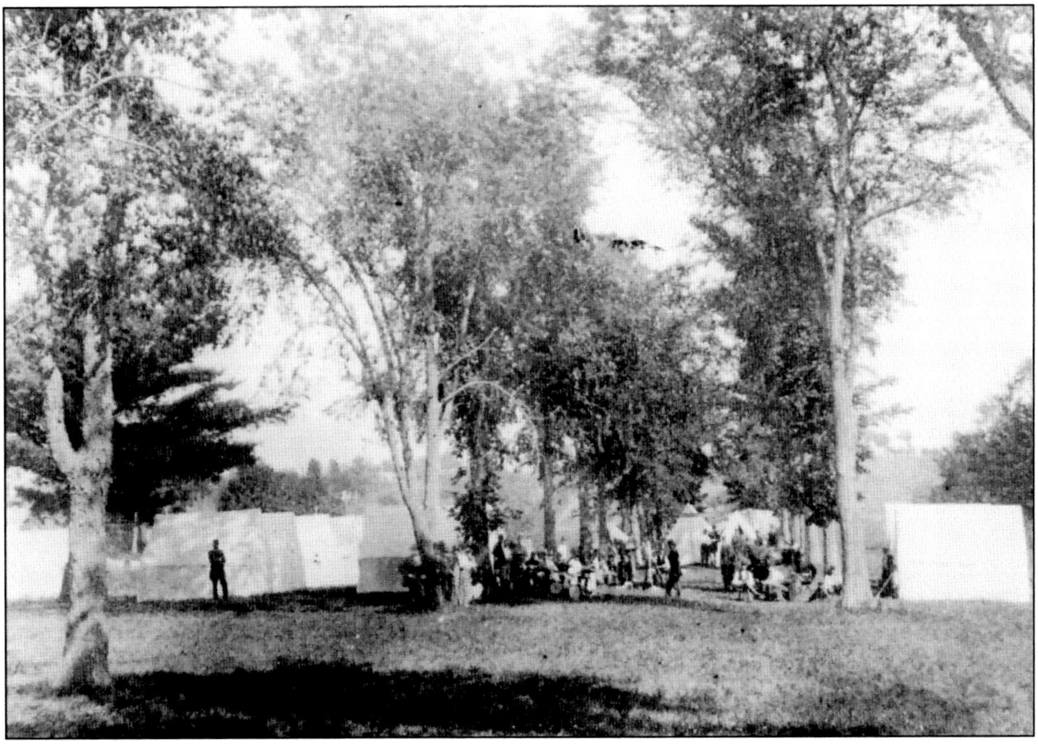

When the decision was made in 1827 to move the state capital from Portland to Augusta, Gov. Enoch Lincoln, the executive council, and a local committee selected Weston's Hill, south of the village, as the site for a new statehouse. That section of the property that extended from the newly laid out State Street to the Kennebec River was designated as Capitol Park, which was planted with two rows of trees down the center in the fall of 1827. These trees were increased to double rows by 1851.

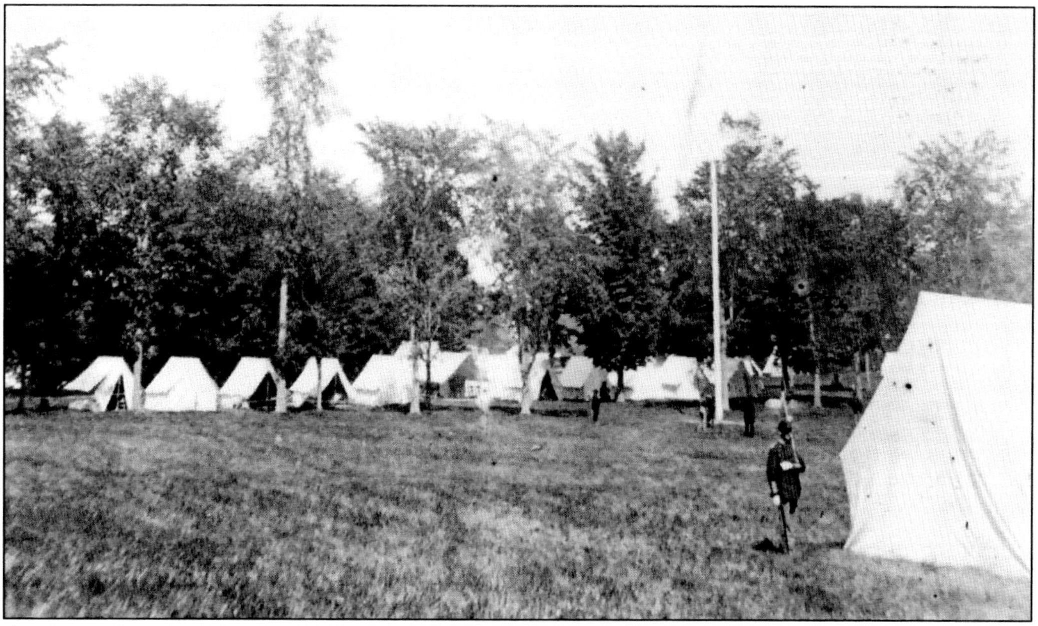

At the outbreak of the Civil War, Capitol Park was used by several Maine regiments as a camp site and training ground. The May 22, 1862, *Maine Farmer* reported that "tents and stables and barracks have been spread over them, infantry, artillery, and cavalry have practiced their drill there." After the troops left for the war, the grounds were ploughed and fertilized in 1862. The following year, the state leased Capitol Park to a farmer to grow grain there.

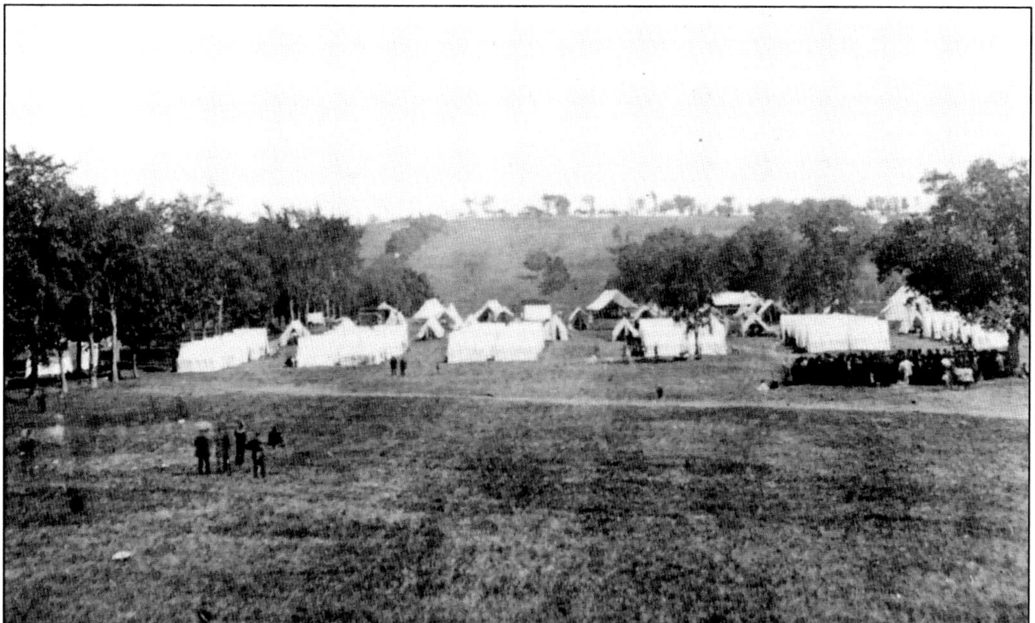

In August 1877, Capitol Park hosted a six-day encampment of the Maine militia under the command of Gen. Joshua L. Chamberlain, Civil War hero and former governor. The troops who pitched their tents and conducted exercises in the park were from the 1st Maine Regiment, the Androscoggin Light Artillery, three unattached companies, and four cadet companies.

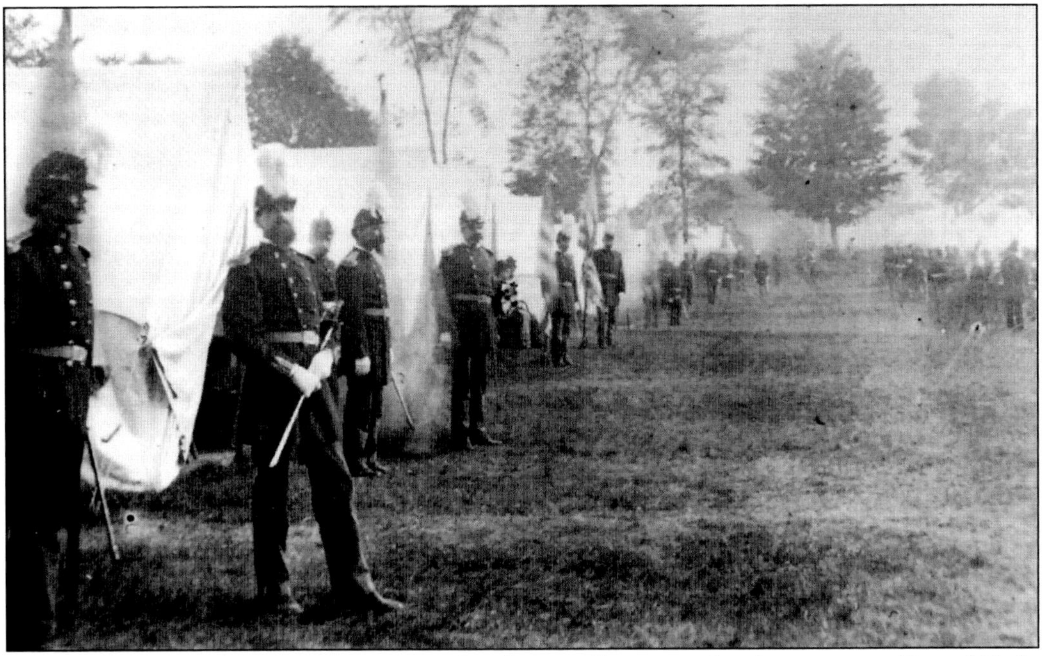

During the 1877 military exercises, several infantry officers pose by their tents in Capitol Park. These officers are wearing blue double-breasted frock coats with brass buttons bearing the state seal and sport visored caps with white plumes. Their swords are a further indication of their commissioned status.

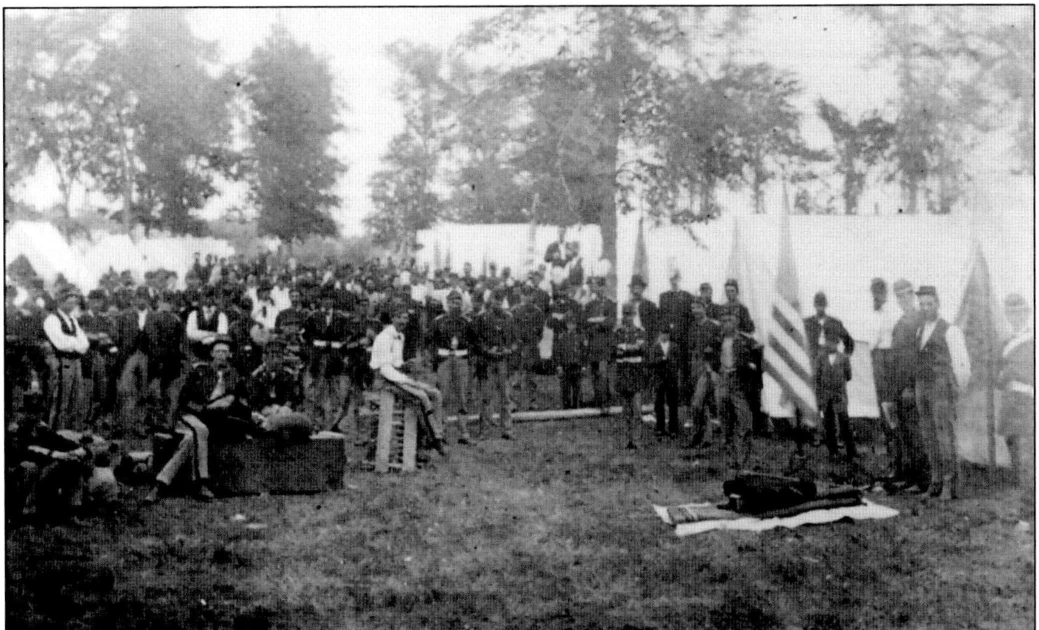

A sea of faces appears in this photograph of enlisted men who gather between rows of tents at the 1877 encampment. These infantrymen are wearing blue uniforms with state of Maine brass buttons and blue forage caps without plumes. The August heat has reduced a few men to shirtsleeves.

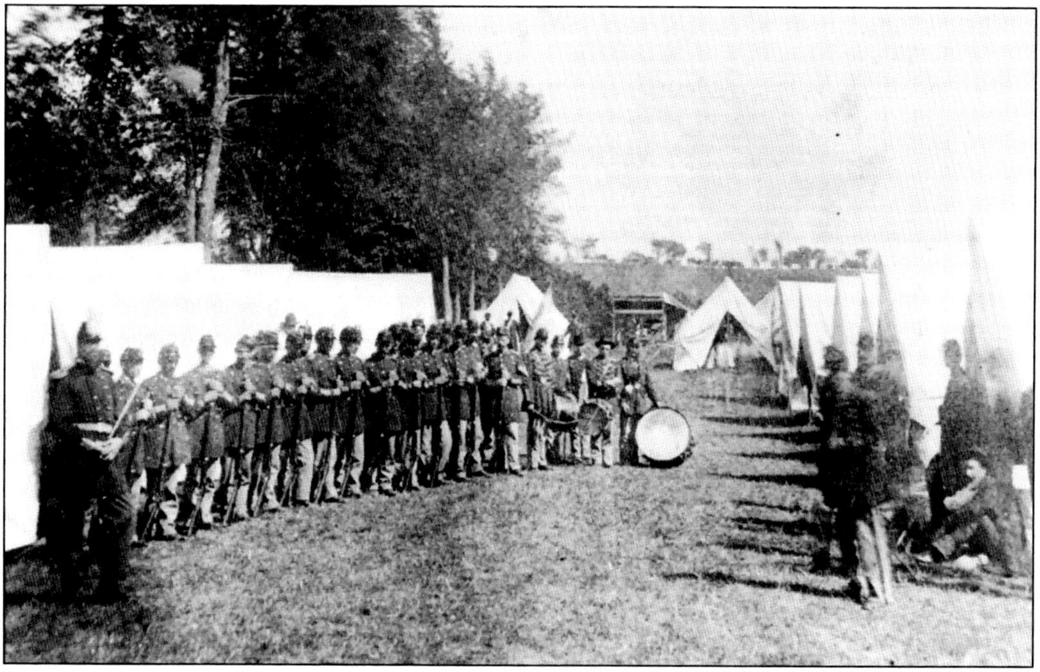

Sword in hand, an officer commands a company of infantrymen standing at parade rest with their rifles in front of them. At the center is a military band complete with drums for marking cadence during marching exercises.

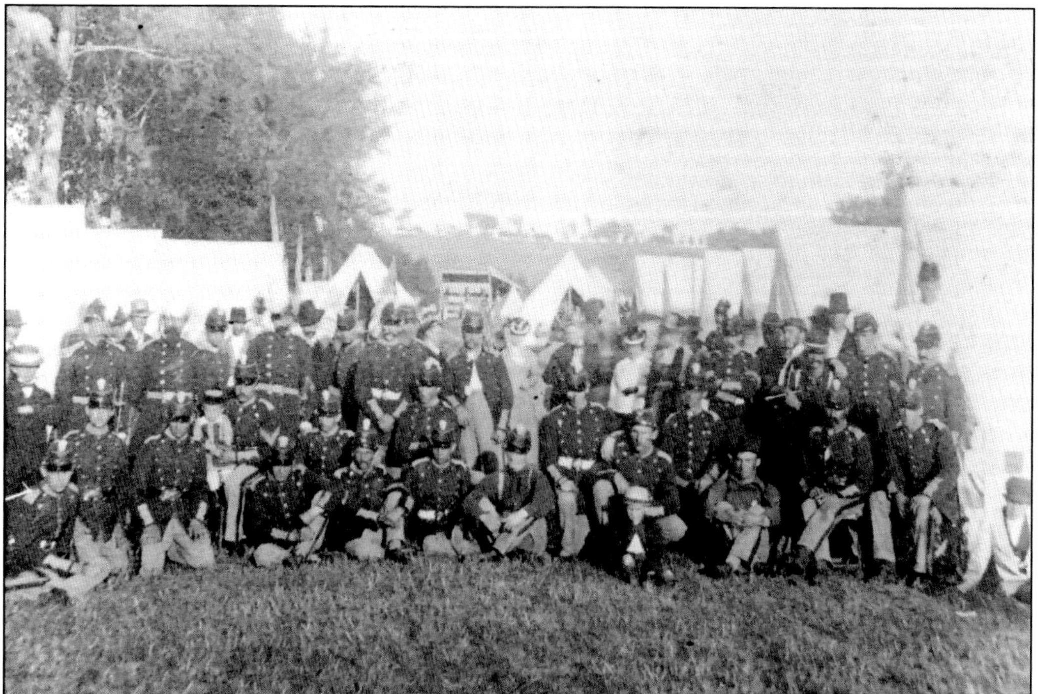

Civilian visitors, including men, women, and children, mix with officers and enlisted men in this view of the 1877 Maine militia encampment in Capitol Park.

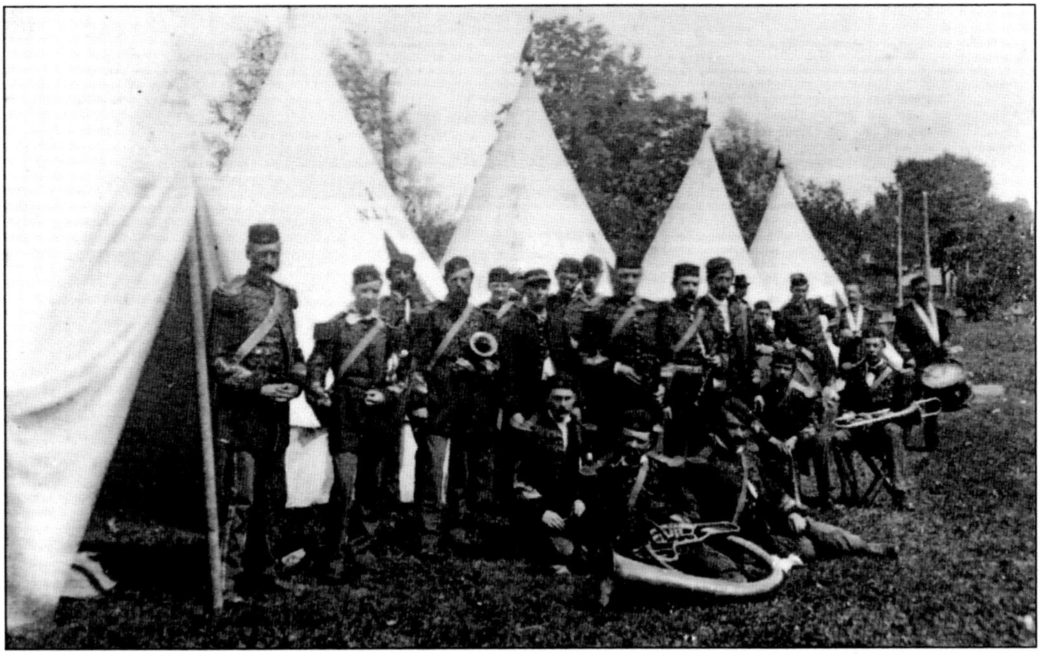

Members of Chandler's Band of Portland are assembled in front of their pointed Sibly tents, which were popular during the Civil War. These bandsmen wear decorative uniforms, and many of them have visorless caps. A bugle, a drum, and two large over-the-shoulder Civil War–era horns are in evidence.

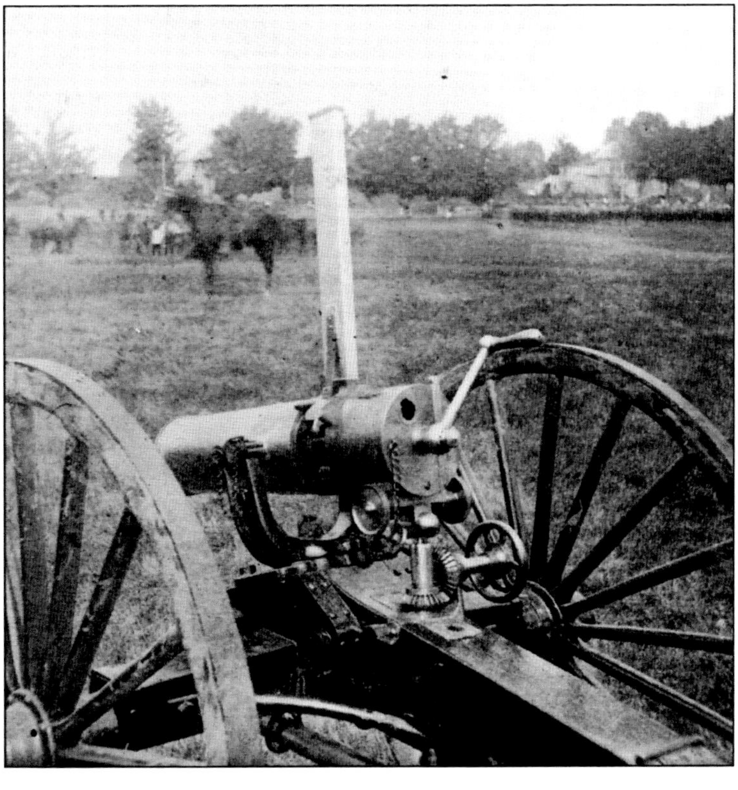

The encampment included a demonstration of the Gatling gun that the state had acquired recently from the federal government. Invented by R. J. Gatling, this machine gun consisted of a cluster of barrels revolved by a crank that could fire up to 600 shots a minute.

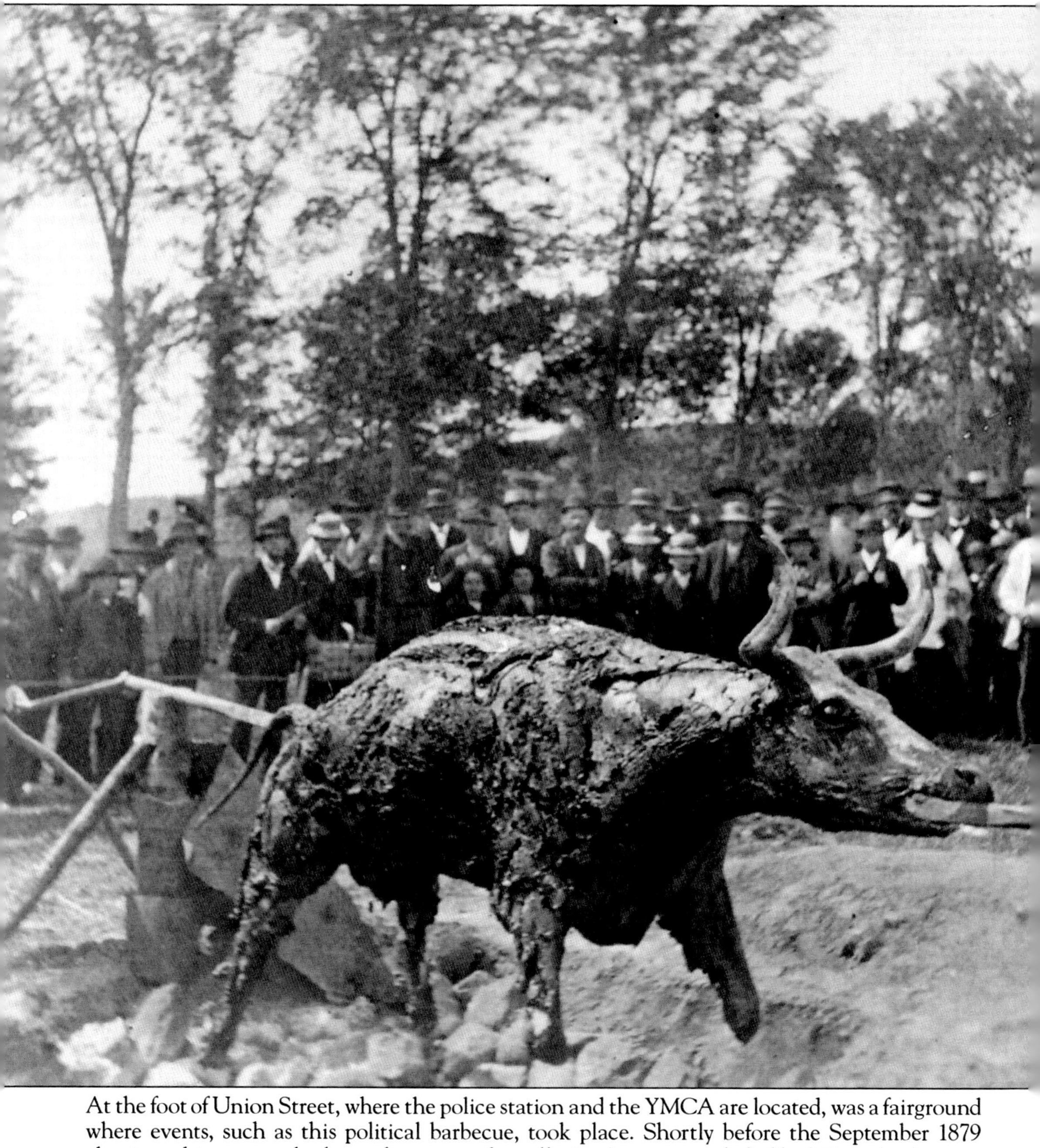

At the foot of Union Street, where the police station and the YMCA are located, was a fairground where events, such as this political barbecue, took place. Shortly before the September 1879 election, this ox was barbecued as part of a rally in Augusta on behalf of Greenback party candidates, who supported an expanded use of paper currency.

Seven

TOGUS

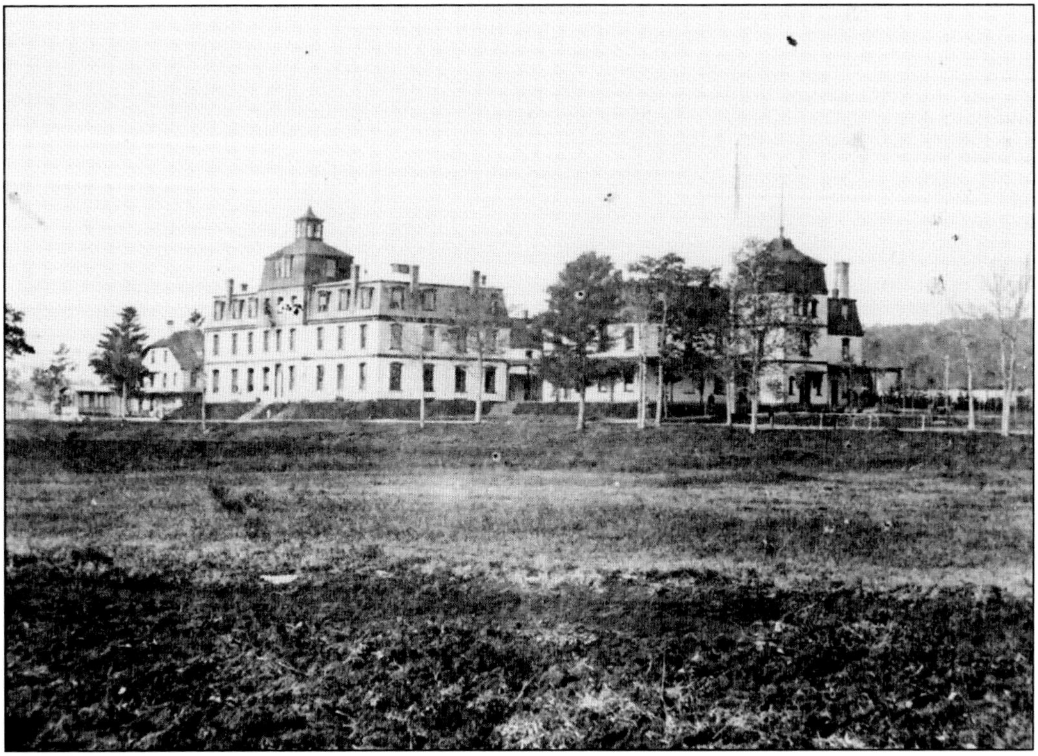

The eastern branch of the National Home for Disabled Volunteer Soldiers was established in 1866 at Togus in Chelsea in a large wooden summer hotel built prior to the Civil War. When the former hotel burned in 1868, it was replaced that year by four 100-by-50-foot brick buildings that formed a square with a courtyard in the center. Two of these structures are shown here along with the hospital built in 1878 at the left.

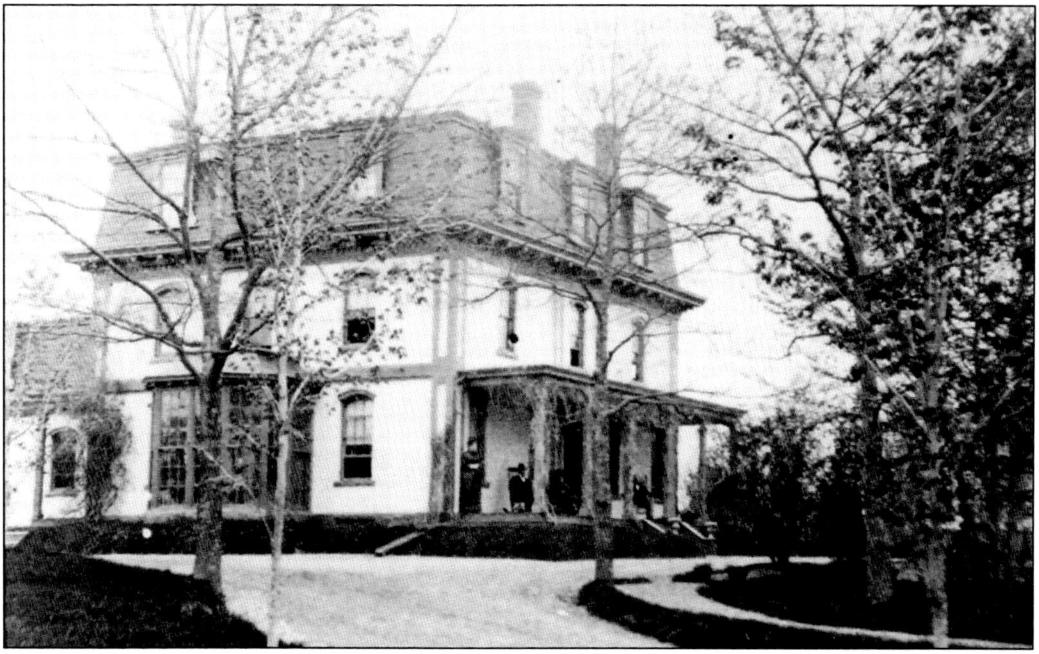

This brick mansard-roofed house was built in 1870 for Togus's commanding officer. Its first resident was Gen. William S. Tilton, who served as governor of the institution from 1869 to 1883. Designated as a national historic landmark in 1973, the governor's house is Togus's oldest building.

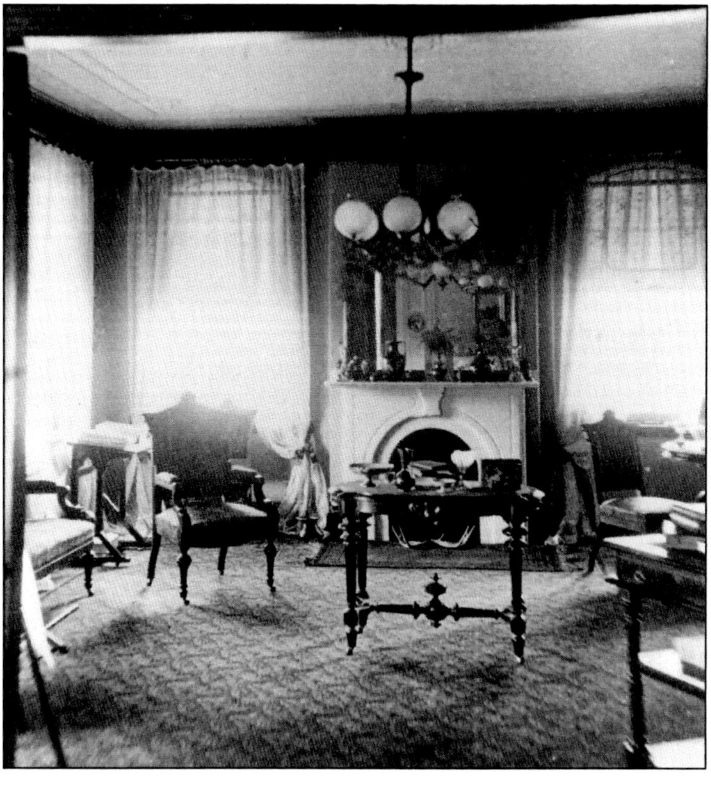

A native of Newburyport, Massachusetts, Tilton enlisted in the 22nd Massachusetts Regiment at the beginning of the Civil War and rose to become its commander. Tilton and his family were the first residents of the governor's home at Togus, living there from 1870 to 1883. The Tilton parlor was decorated in the Victorian elegance of the period, with wall-to-wall carpeting, floor-length drapes, a marble mantelpiece, frescoed walls, and a suite of elaborate furniture.

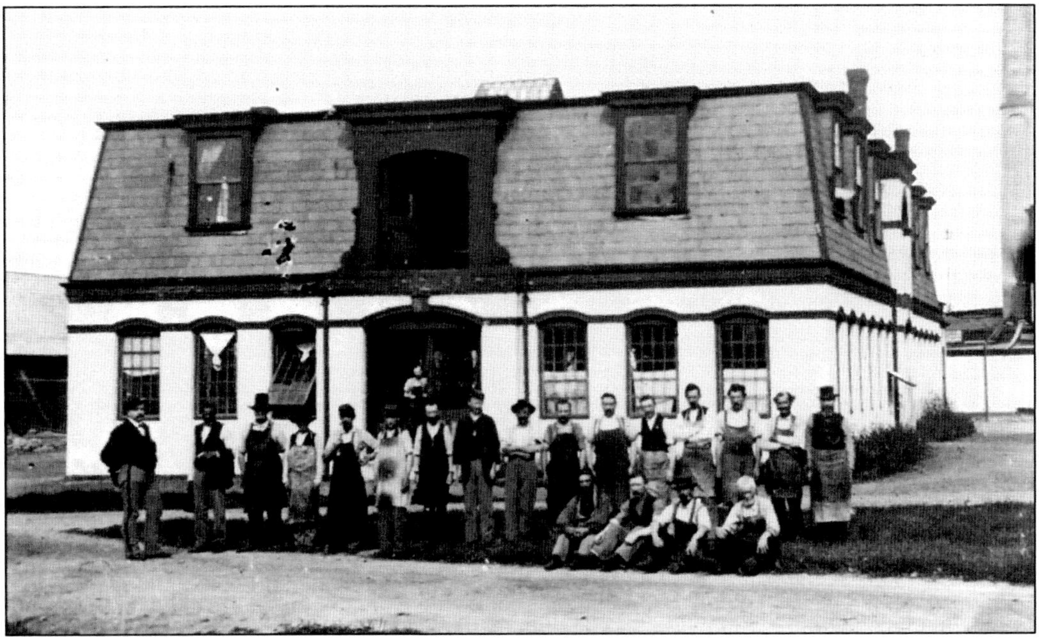

Some Togus residents worked in the brick shop building, which opened in June 1870 to manufacture boots and shoes. With the exception of a brief closure in 1875, this factory operated until 1883, producing 30,000 pairs of footwear a year and making profits that were applied to the purchase of clothing for the residents.

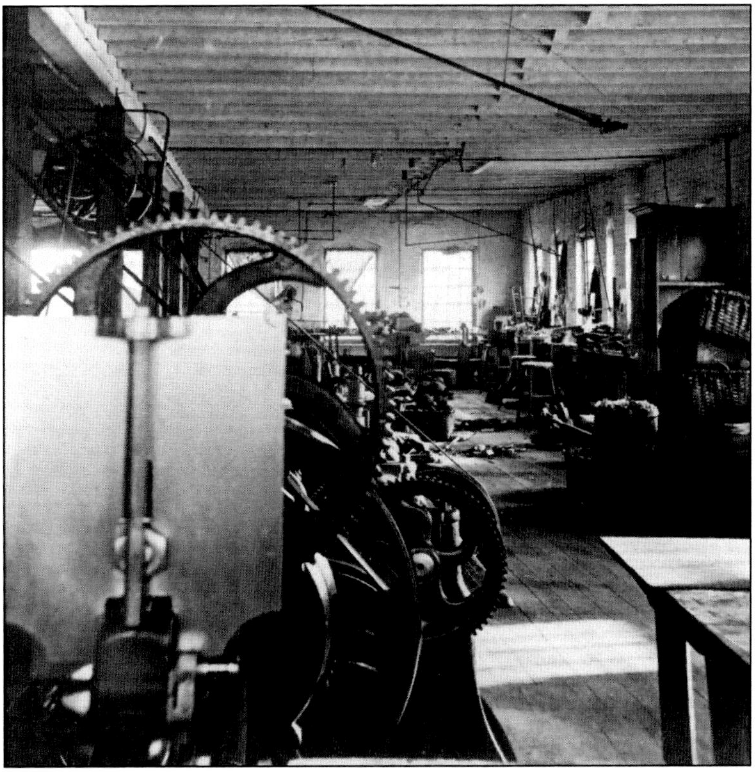

From 1870 to 1883, a workforce of approximately 50 residents was employed here making shoes. The 30,000 pairs produced annually supplied the needs of those at Togus and other veterans' homes, with the balance being sold to the U.S. Army and the New York market.

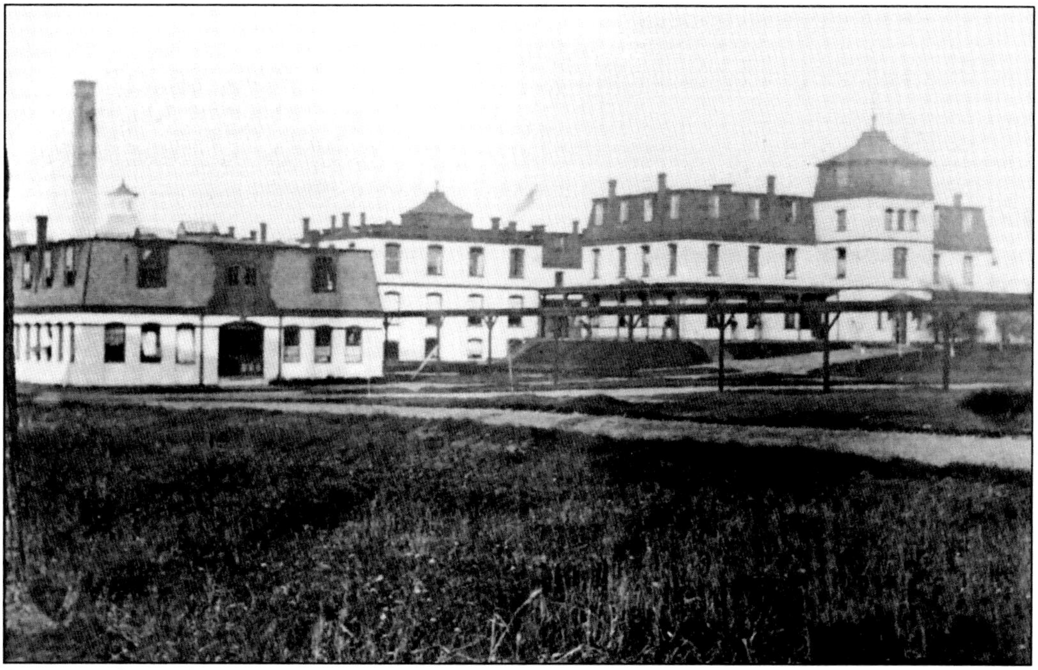

Boston architect Benjamin F. Dwight designed several of the early mansard-roofed buildings at Togus. At the left is the shop of 1870, where boots and shoes were made, while at the right is Company B barracks, one of the three major structures erected in 1868 to house the veterans.

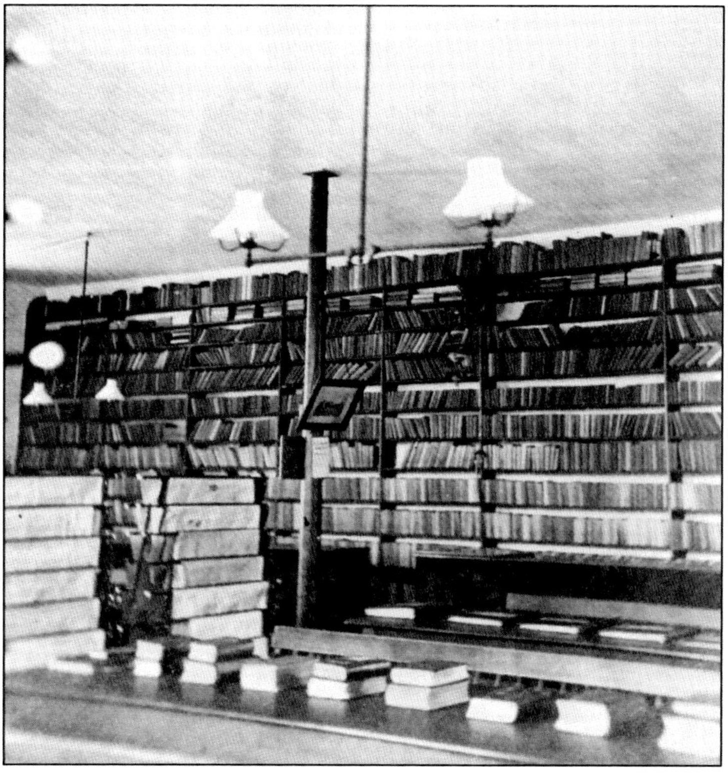

In 1879, the Togus library contained 4,300 books. Newspaper racks at the left held 22 daily newspapers and 115 weeklies, along with magazines in English, French, German, and Italian. Especially during the winter months, this reading room was visited frequently by the veterans.

Dedicated on November 25, 1871, the amusement hall contained a 500-seat auditorium on the first floor, a dormitory on the second floor, and a billiard room, guardhouse, and police headquarters in the basement. The building was later converted into a library and reading room.

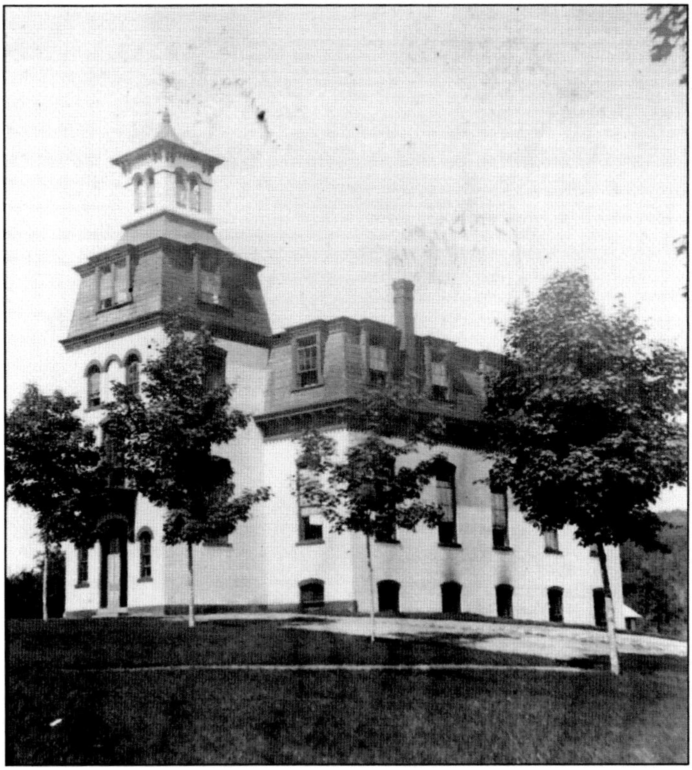

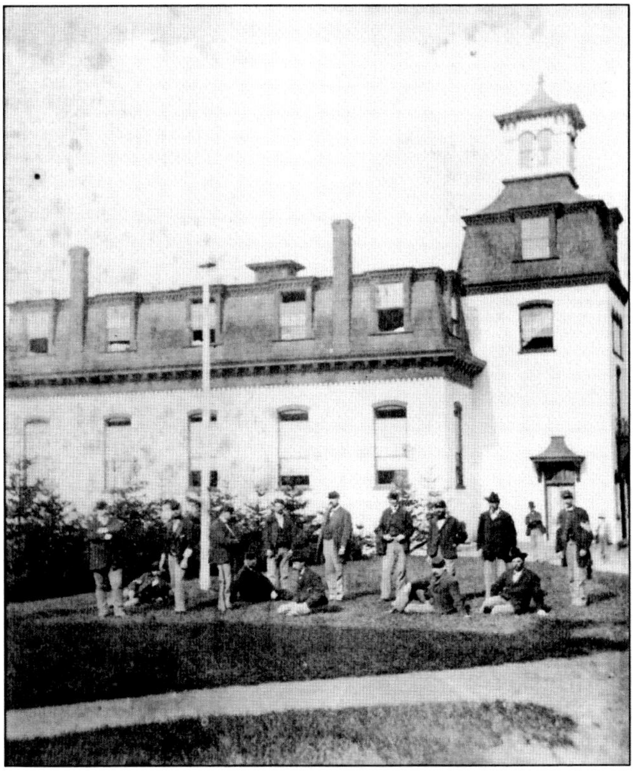

Veterans gather in front of the amusement hall, appearing to have time on their hands. An 1879 guidebook to Togus stated that "the sources of amusement are a theater, lectures, and various other entertainments during the winter months, besides billiard tables, checkers, dominos, and a bowling alley. Gambling is positively prohibited."

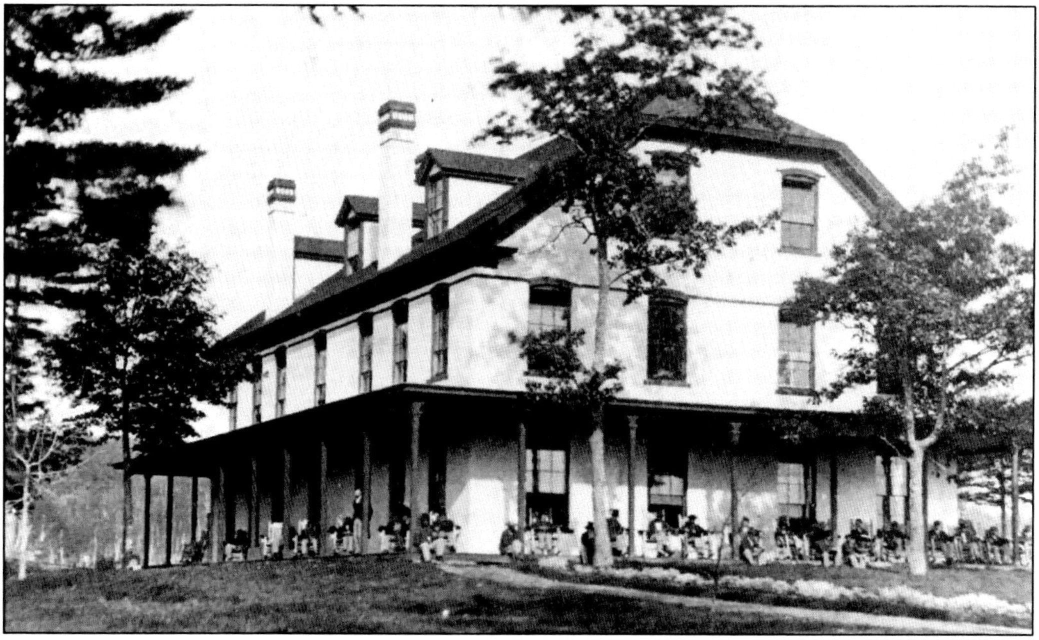

The first hospital at Togus was located in the barracks. By 1878, the increased demand for medical services had resulted in the construction of this two-and-a-half-story brick hospital for veterans "who are in such condition physically as to require nursing and a particular diet." A surrounding porch was lined with rocking chairs for patients to relax in.

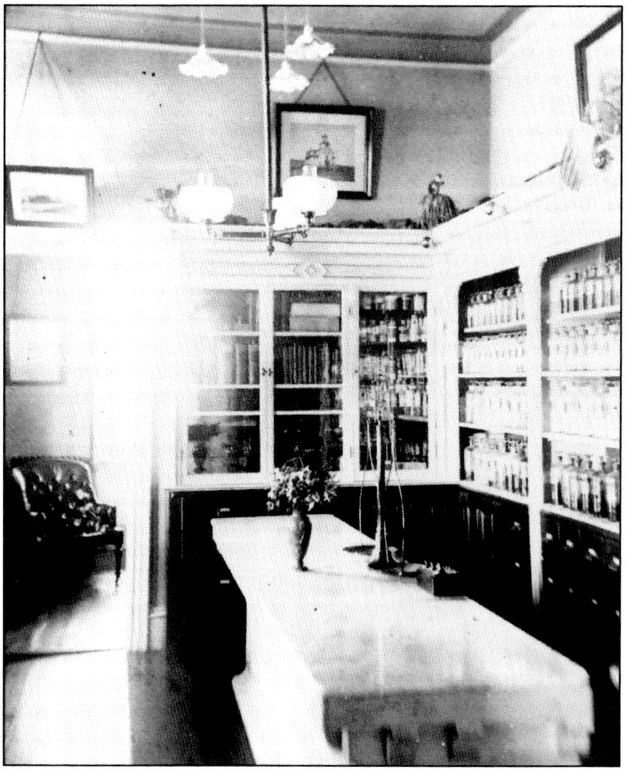

Within the hospital building was the dispensary, where the Togus medical staff maintained a large array of drugs and medicines in neat rows of glass bottles. Shelves were also provided to house a small medical library.

During the hospital's first year of operation in 1878 and 1879, 256 patients spent time in wards such as this one. The new wards were described as "large and airy; perfect means for heating and ventilating were adopted, as well as such other hygienic measures as would conduce to the comfort and happiness of patients."

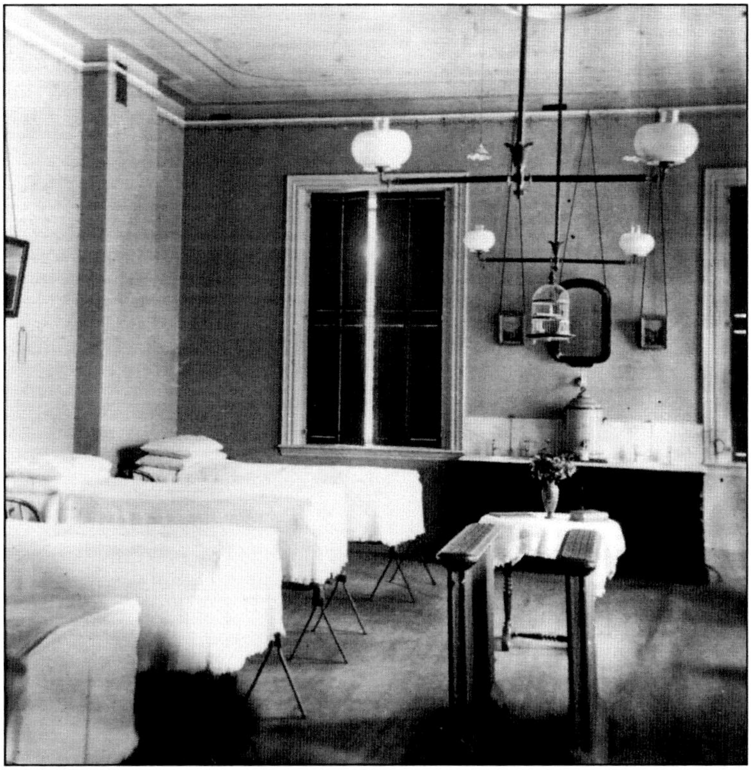

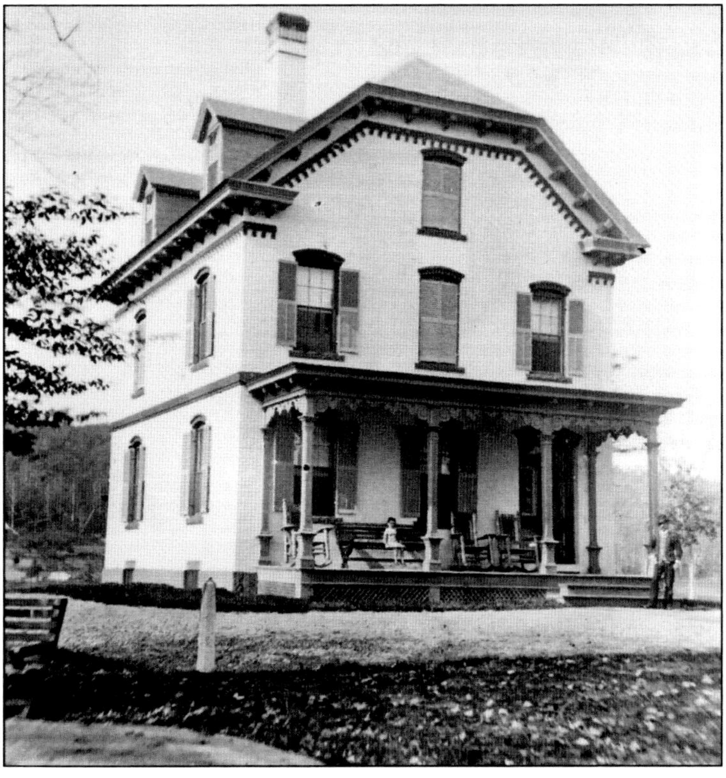

Prior to 1878, the surgeon lived in the main barracks. That year, Togus built this Italianate brick surgeon's residence near the hospital. By the early 1900s, the house had become the chaplain's home.

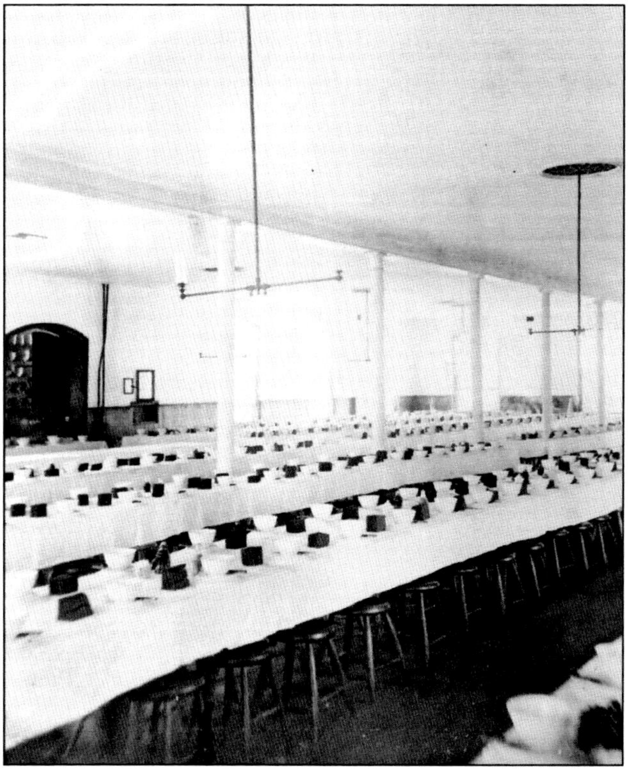

Each day, the veterans were summoned to breakfast, dinner, and supper by a bugle call. Rows of long tables covered with white tablecloths filled the spacious dining hall. Seating consisted of simple wooden stools.

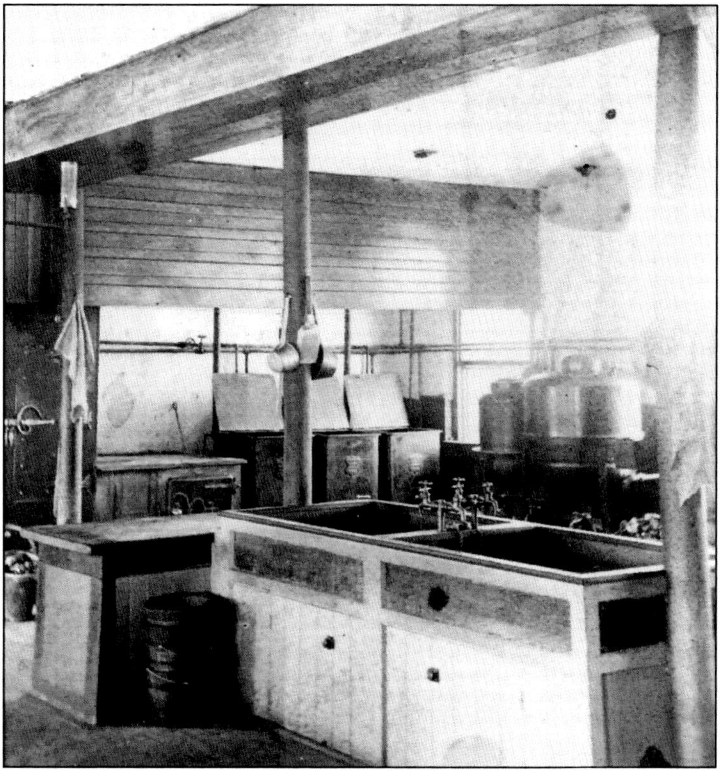

During the 1870s, the kitchen served more than 300,000 meals per year, each one costing 19¢. The main component of each meal was beef, lamb, pork, or mackerel, supplemented with produce grown by the veterans. The principal drink was coffee, of which nearly 9,000 pounds were used annually.

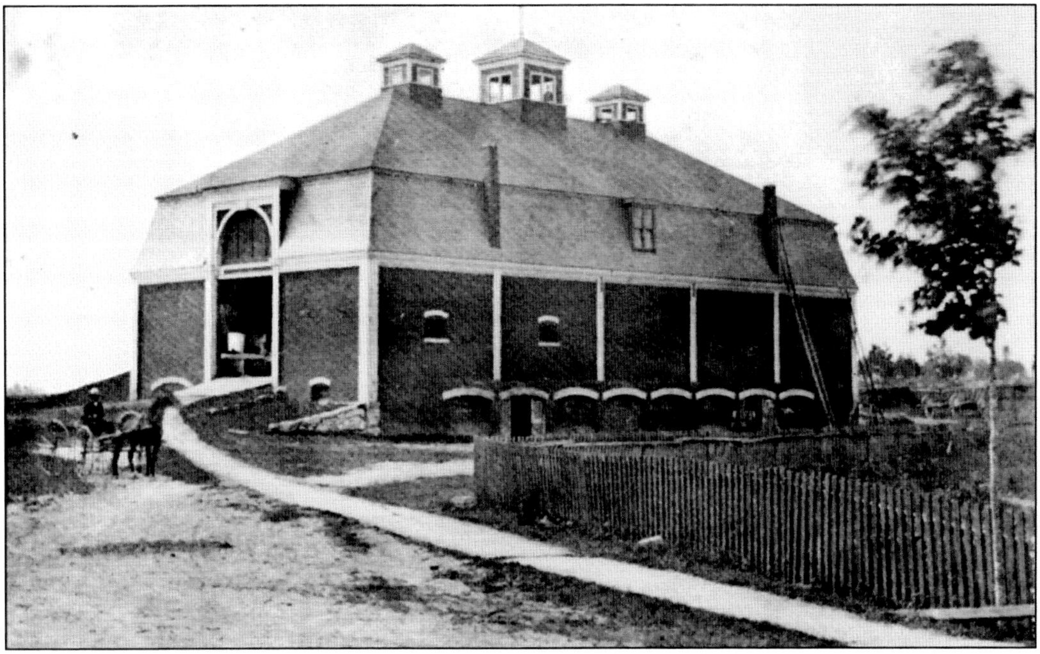

According to the 1879 guidebook, this elegant brick barn, which was constructed in 1869, "contains a goodly number of neat animals, embracing some of the best representatives of the Holstein or Dutch cattle, and Jerseys, that can be found, with specimens of improved breeds of swine and Cotswold sheep."

The veterans who lived at Togus brought with them many trades and skills. Henry Bailey titled this photograph "Catamaran built by Mr. Adams at Soldiers Home, Togus." A catamaran is a sailing vessel with twin hulls side by side.

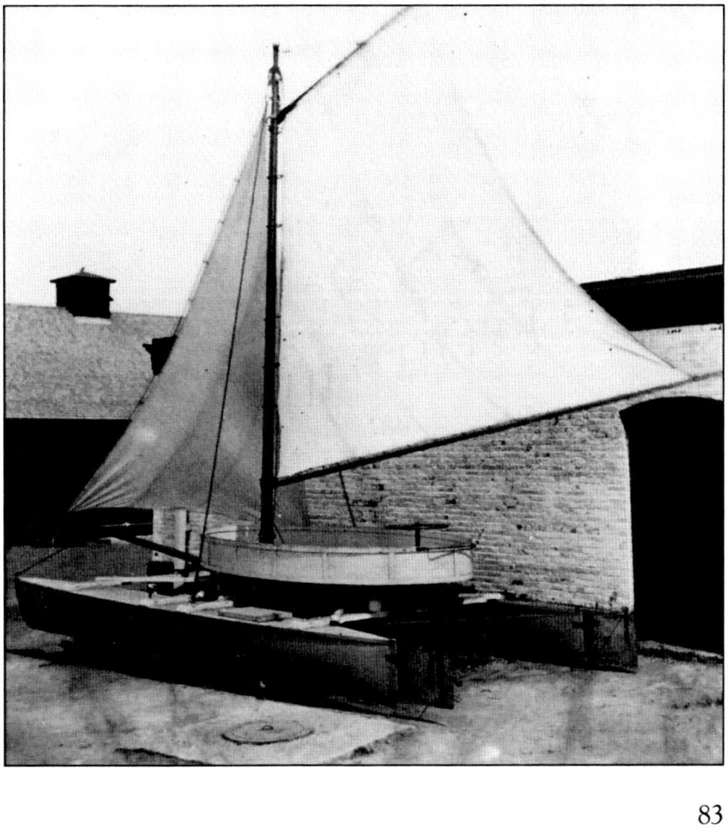

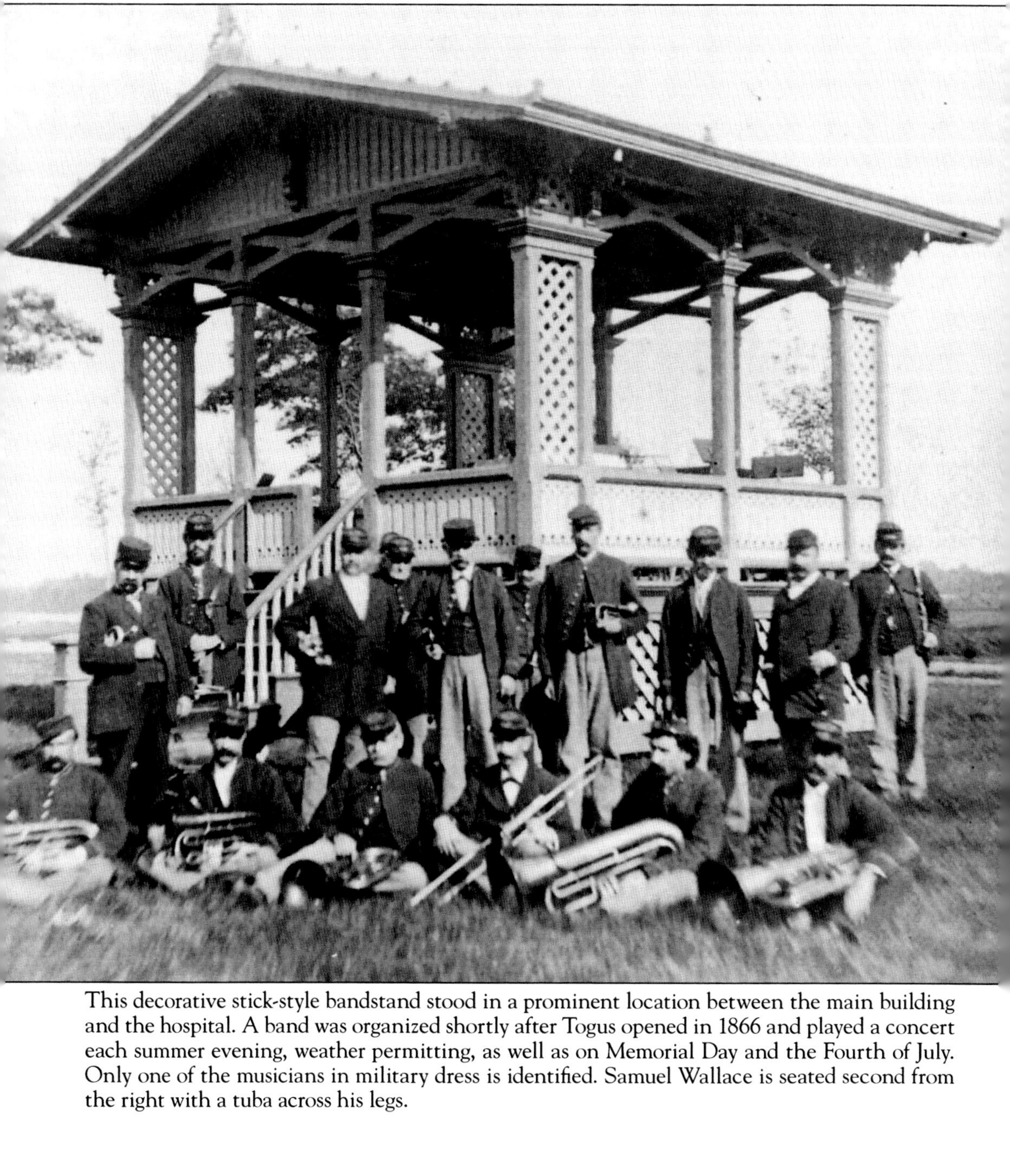

This decorative stick-style bandstand stood in a prominent location between the main building and the hospital. A band was organized shortly after Togus opened in 1866 and played a concert each summer evening, weather permitting, as well as on Memorial Day and the Fourth of July. Only one of the musicians in military dress is identified. Samuel Wallace is seated second from the right with a tuba across his legs.

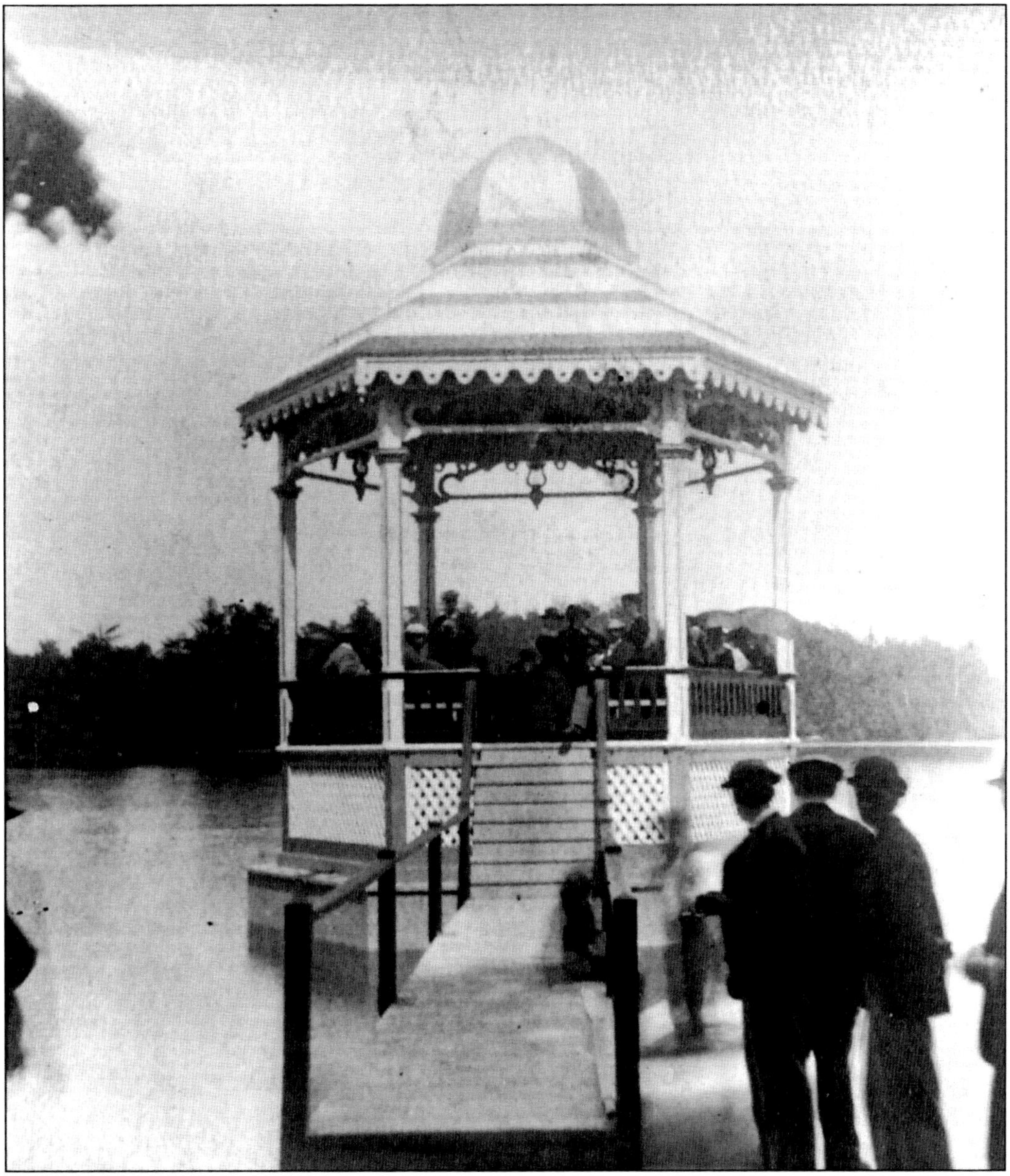

Drawing water from Greely Pond, the Togus reservoir covered an acre and contained nearly 2.5 million gallons of water. The reservoir's scenic qualities could be enjoyed from this octagonal gazebo, an ornamental island reached by a short bridge across the water.

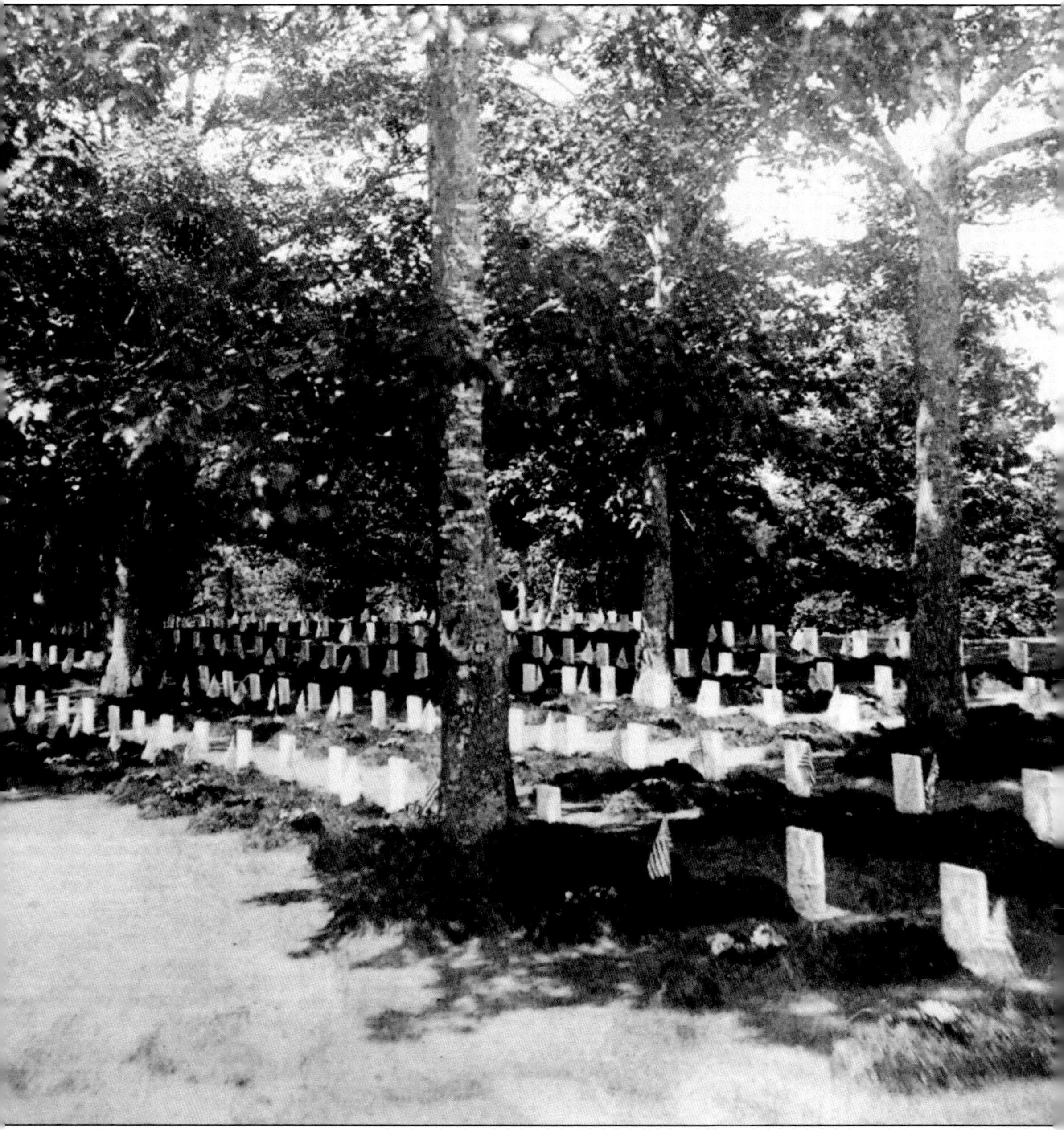

By 1879, 194 veterans had been buried in the Togus cemetery, which was located on a wooded hill overlooking the veterans' home. As a guidebook that year described the cemetery, "The graves are all arranged in regular lines, and each one is marked by a headstone giving the age, company, regiment, and state of the deceased."

Eight

SURROUNDING TOWNS

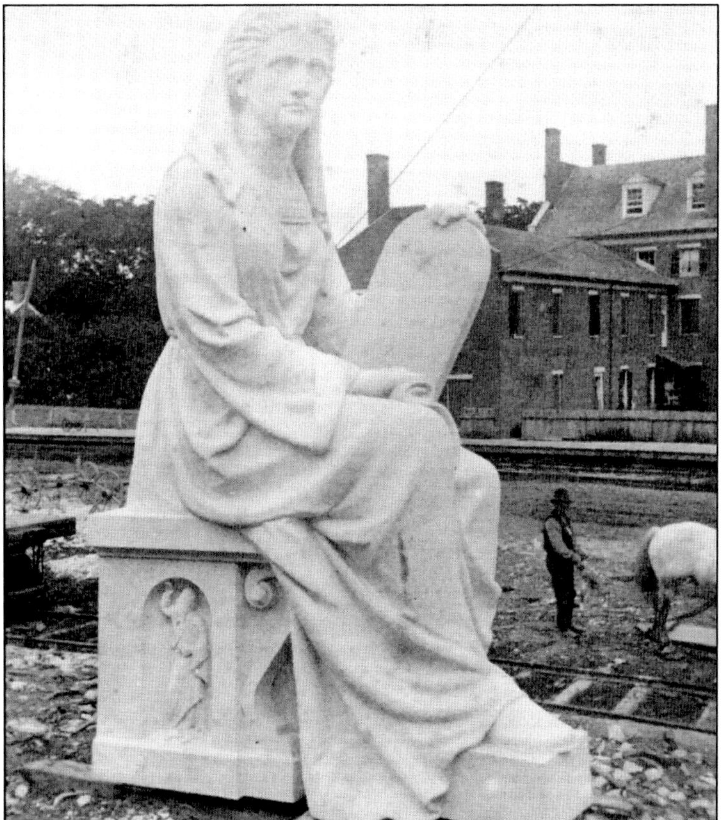

The Hallowell Granite Company provided the granite and carved the figures for the Pilgrim Monument, which was erected in Plymouth, Massachusetts, in the 1870s. Designed by Boston architect Hammett Billings, the monument featured a colossal statue of Faith accompanied by four seated figures, including Morality, shown here in the yard of the Hallowell Granite Company with the Hallowell House hotel at Second and Winthrop Streets in the background.

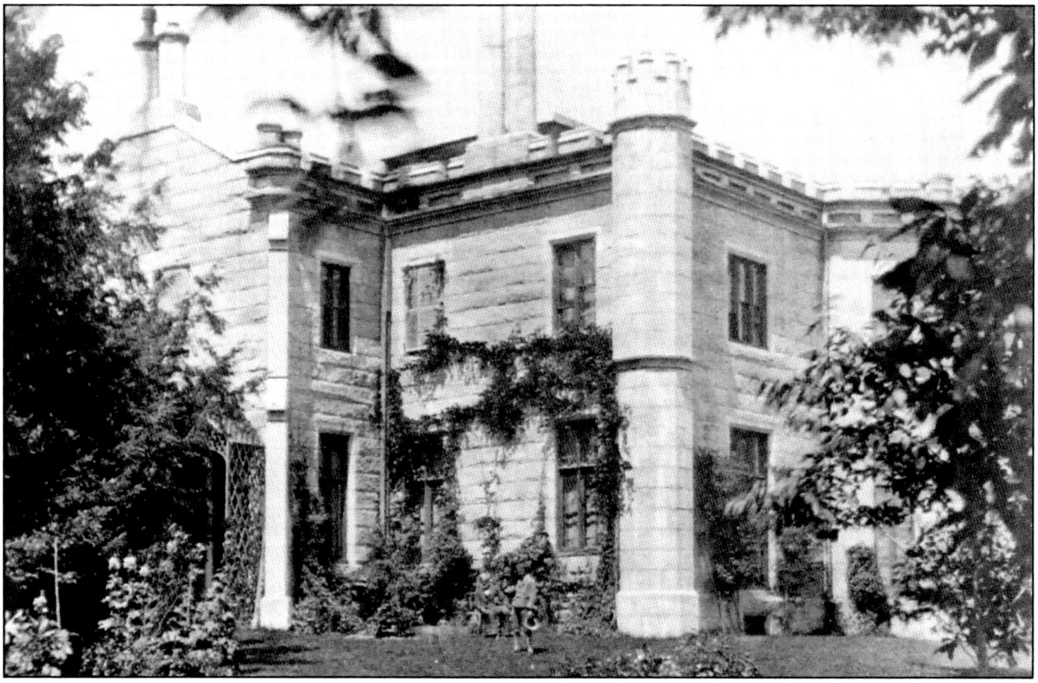

Robert Hallowell Gardiner I worked tirelessly from 1803 until his death in 1864 to transform Gardiner from a frontier outpost to an industrial community. Between 1835 and 1837, Gardiner built Oaklands, a granite Gothic Revival country house overlooking the Kennebec River. English-born architect Richard Upjohn of Boston designed this impressive residence.

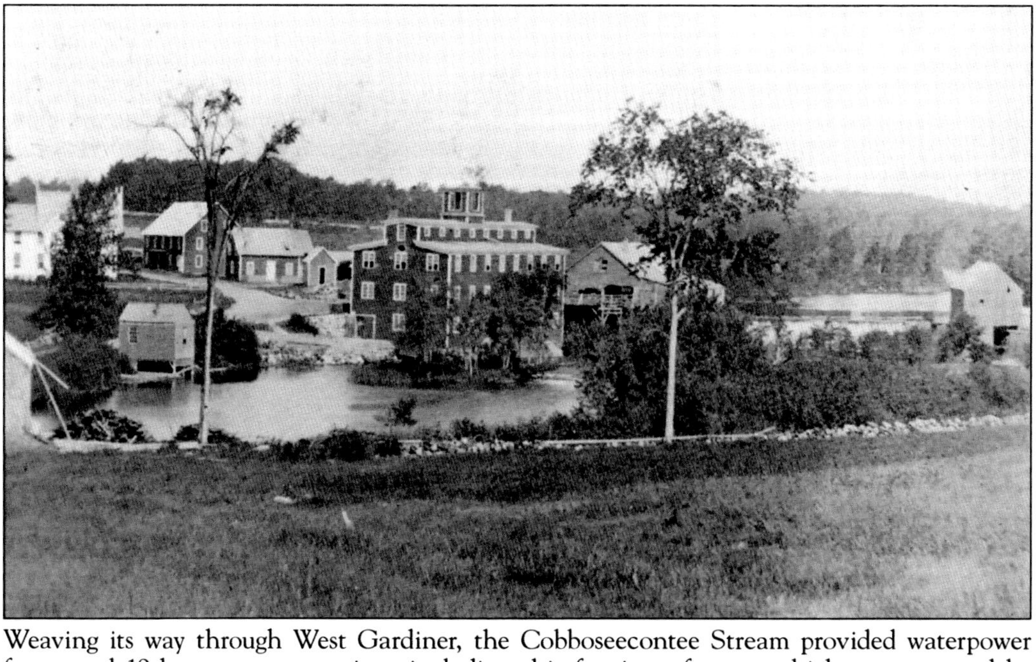

Weaving its way through West Gardiner, the Cobboseecontee Stream provided waterpower for several 19th-century enterprises, including this furniture factory, which was operated by Prentiss M. Fogler of Augusta from 1873 to 1879. P. M. Fogler and Company produced beds, tables, and lumber.

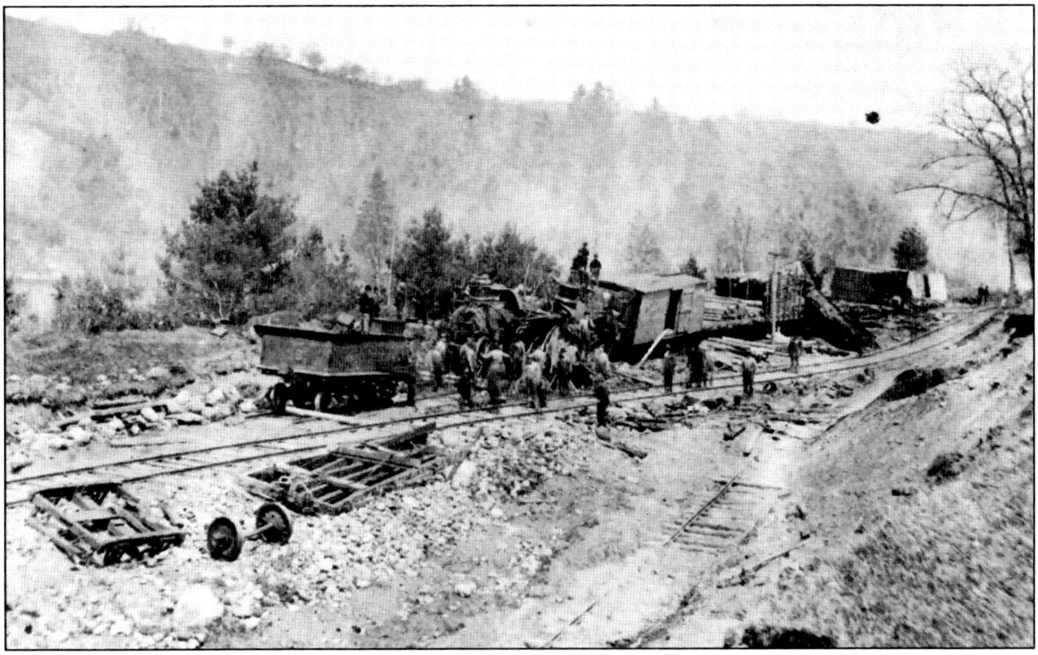

On May 18, 1883, the Maine Central Railroad experienced a major train wreck on the line between Augusta and Winslow. The next day, the *Kennebec Journal* reported, "At 11:55 a.m., the regular freight train, No. 28, from up river collided at Brown's landing in Vassalboro with an engine running wild." Both engineers lost their lives along with a fireman.

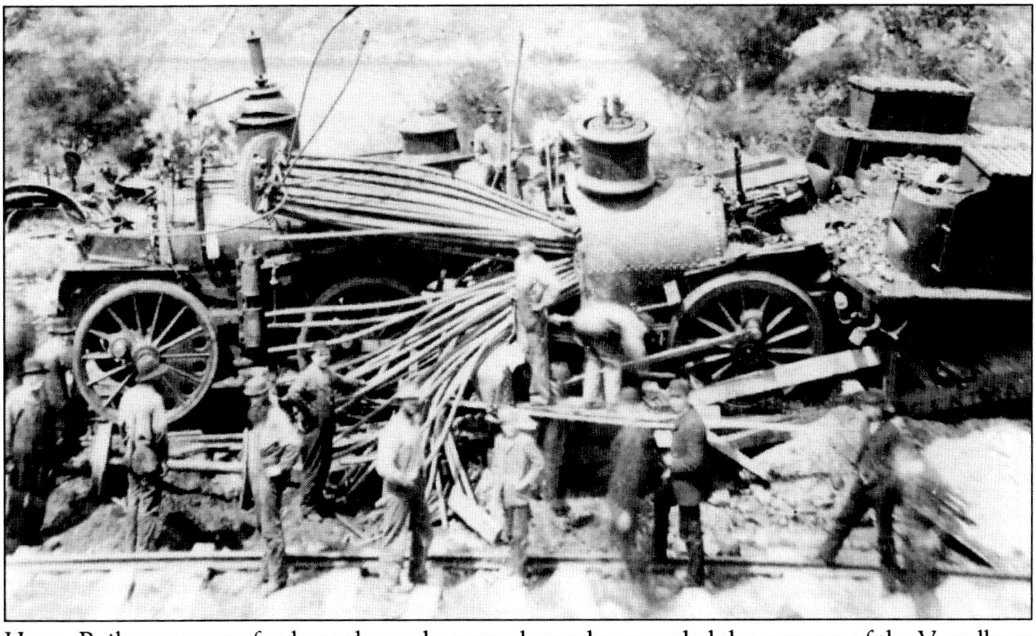

Henry Bailey was one of at least three photographers who recorded the carnage of the Vassalboro train wreck. Calling the scene "fearful," the May 19, 1883, *Kennebec Journal* noted, "The freight train consisted of 29 cars, 15 of which were wrecked. The car next to the engineer was loaded with gravel, and crashing forward, forced itself beneath the tender, which rested on top of the car."

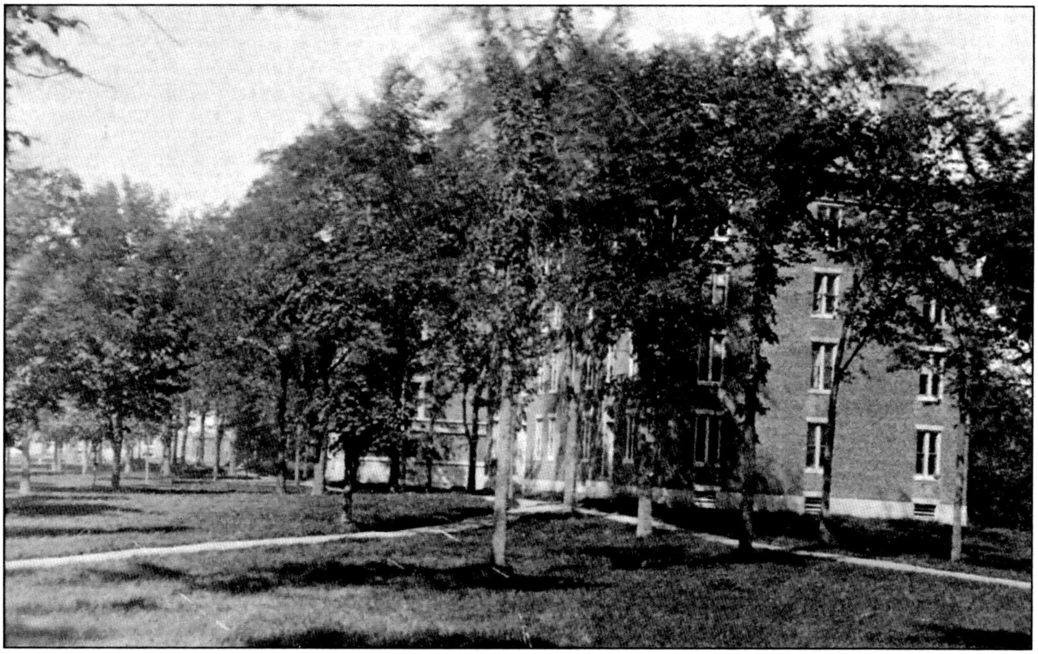

Recitation Hall (center) and South College (right) appear in this view of the old Colby College campus, located on the Kennebec River north of downtown Waterville. Founded by Baptists in 1813, the Maine Literary and Theological Institution became Waterville College in 1821, Colby University in 1867, and Colby College in 1899.

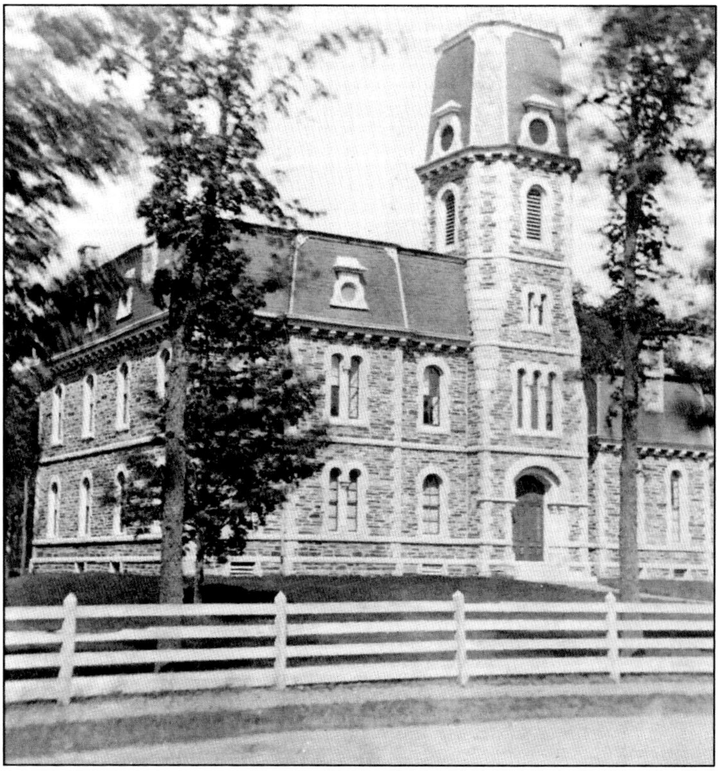

A prominent landmark on the old Colby campus in Waterville was Memorial Hall, a stately mansard-roofed building designed by Alexander Esty of Boston. Built of local rubblestone between 1867 and 1869, the hall contained a marble sculpture honoring the college's Civil War dead while also serving as the library and chapel. Vacated for the new campus in 1952, Memorial Hall and other old campus buildings were demolished in the 1960s.

Built in the Federal style in 1826 by Joseph Packard of Readfield, the First Baptist Church at Elm and Park Streets in Waterville was extensively remodeled to its Victorian appearance in 1875 from designs by Portland architect Francis H. Fassett. The Reverend Samuel F. Smith, author of *America*, served as the pastor of this church from 1834 to 1842.

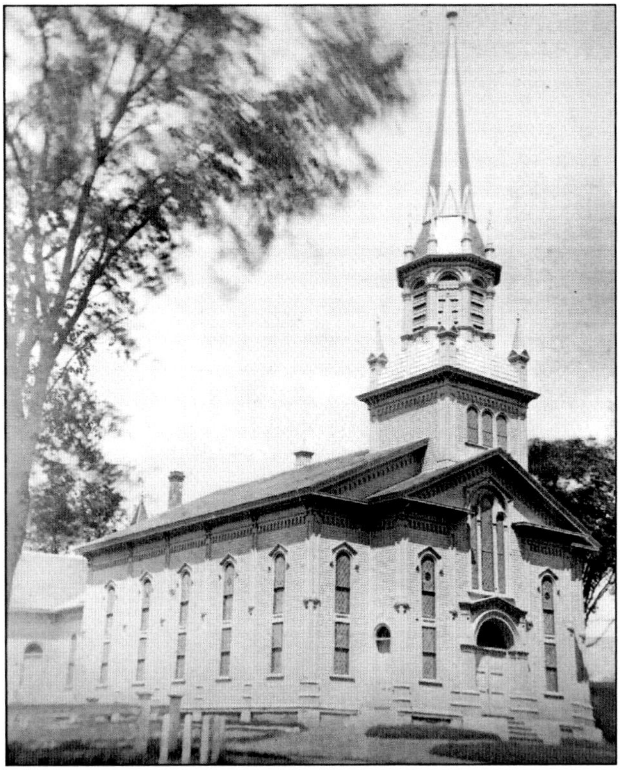

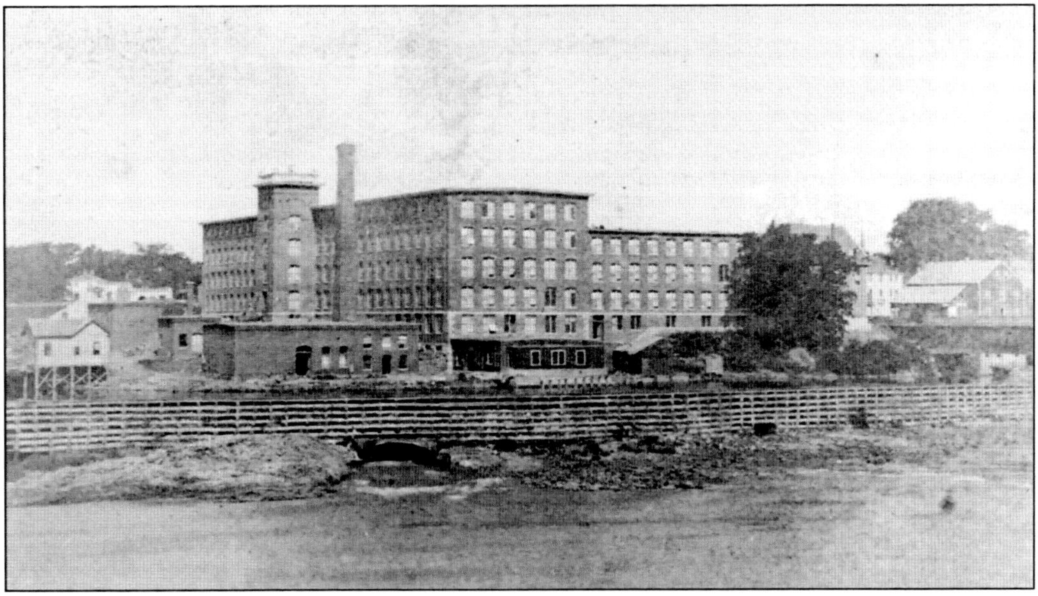

The textile industry came to Waterville on a large scale between 1873 and 1875 with the construction of the first of the Lockwood Mills, which was powered by the Kennebec River. This massive brick Italianate-style factory was planned and constructed by Amos D. Lockwood, a prominent mill engineer and developer. A second mill was added in 1881 and 1882 and a third in 1883. The complex became the Hathaway Shirt Factory in the 20th century and is now the focus of a major adaptive reuse project.

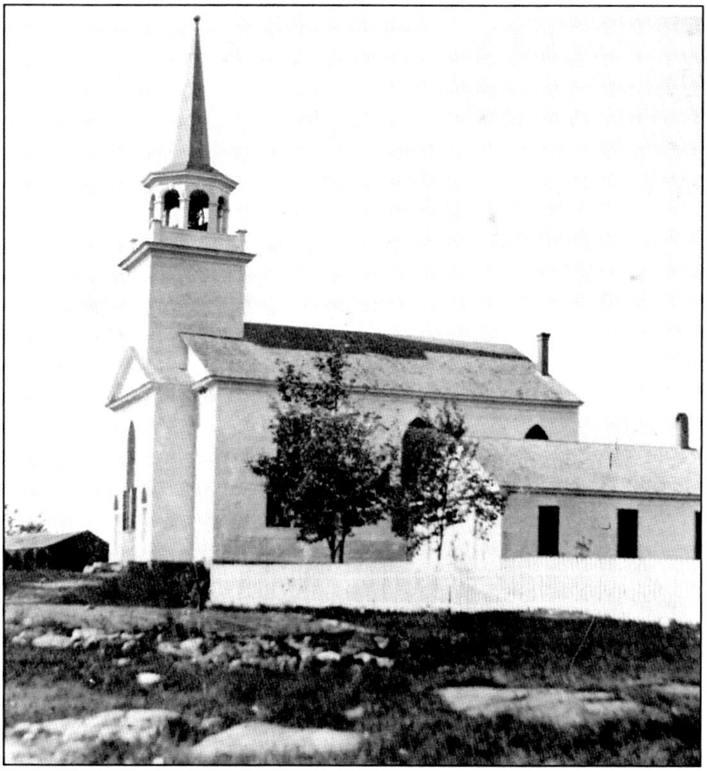

For 175 years, the East Winthrop Baptist Church has been a landmark on the road between Augusta and Winthrop. Dedicated on November 10, 1823, this Federal-style meetinghouse features Gothic Revival pointed arch doorways and windows typical of Maine church architecture of the 1820s and 1830s. The vestry at right was added in 1869.

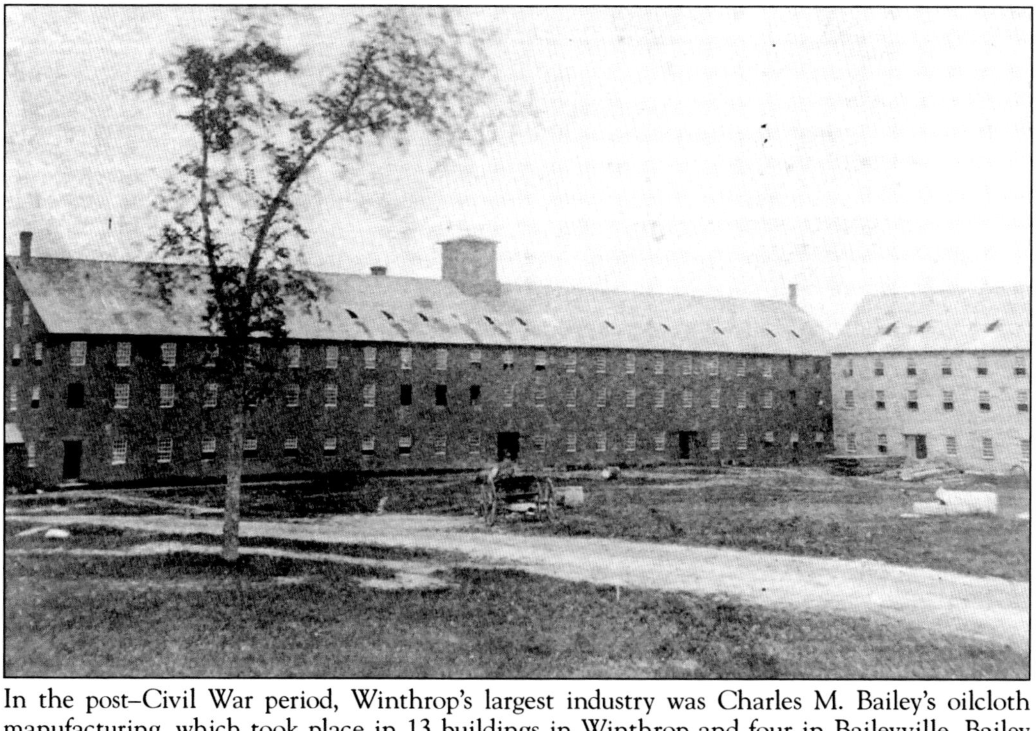

In the post–Civil War period, Winthrop's largest industry was Charles M. Bailey's oilcloth manufacturing, which took place in 13 buildings in Winthrop and four in Baileyville. Bailey employed 200 people in factories, such as these two in Winthrop.

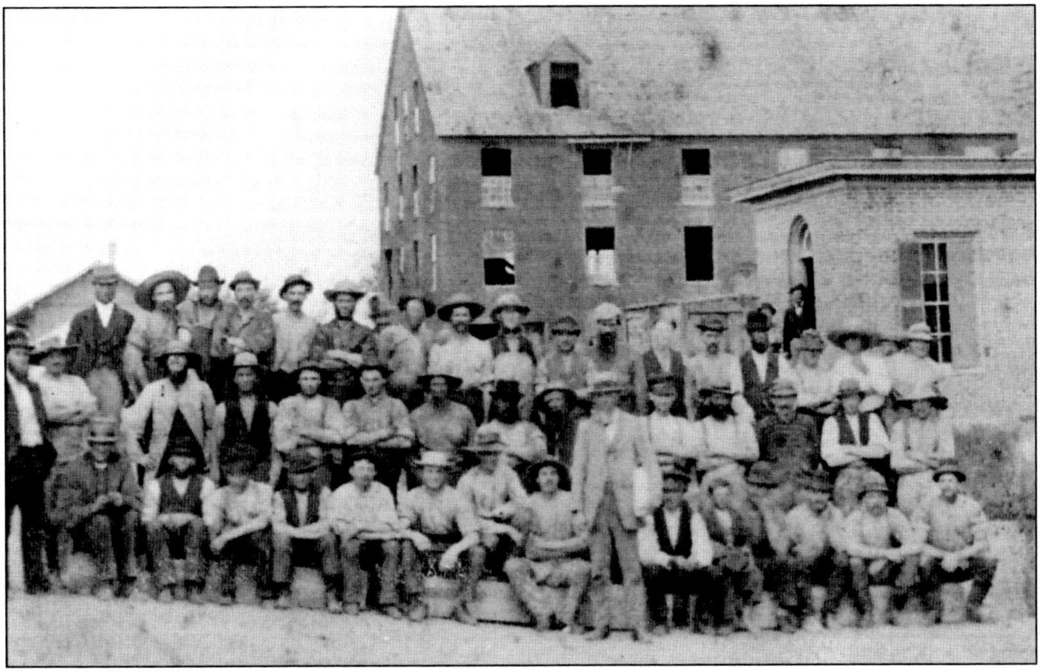

An industrious Quaker businessman, Bailey stands in front of a crew at one of his oilcloth factories in Winthrop. Bailey's dress clothes and broad straw hat are in contrast to the shirtsleeves of his employees, who produced as many as 1,800 oilcloths a week.

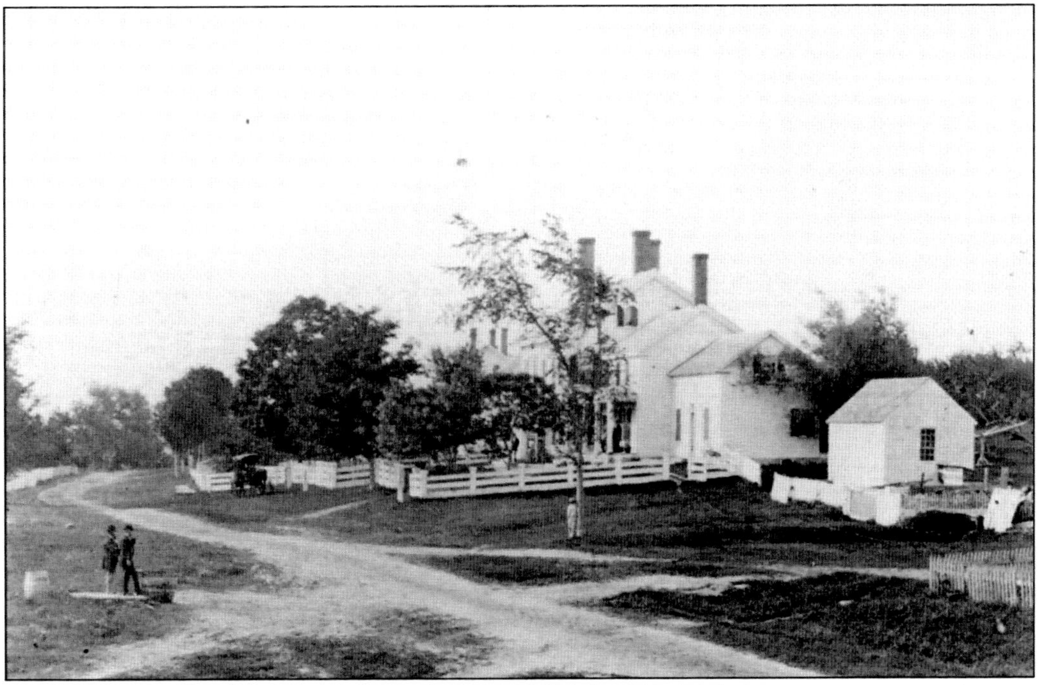

Born in the Baileyville section of Winthrop in 1817, Moses Bailey became a major manufacturer of oilcloth, partnering at times in this enterprise with his brother Charles. Moses was living in this home in Baileyville at the time of his death in 1882.

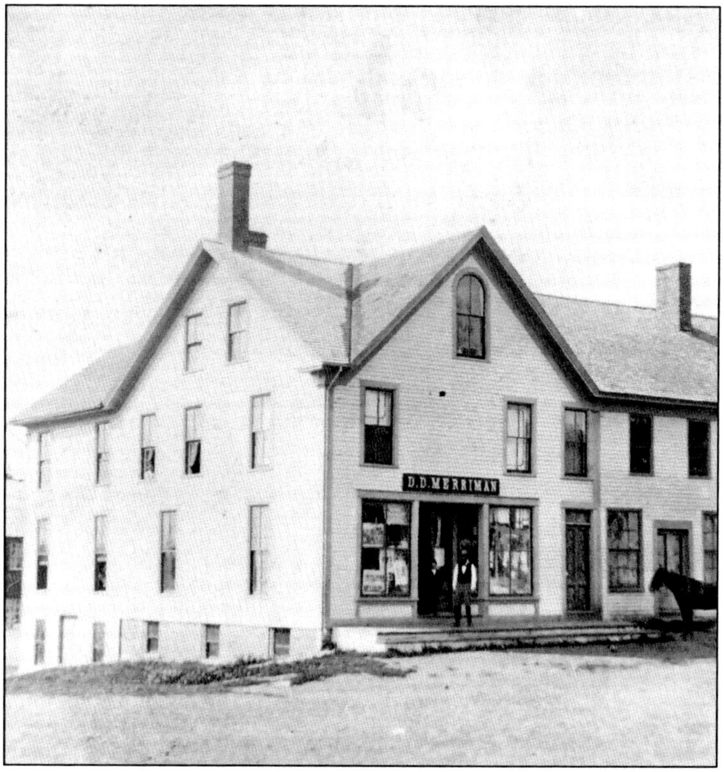

Readfield thrived as an agricultural community with Readfield Corner as its primary village. The corner's main street featured several commercial buildings, including this one that housed the dry goods business established by D. D. Merriman in 1872.

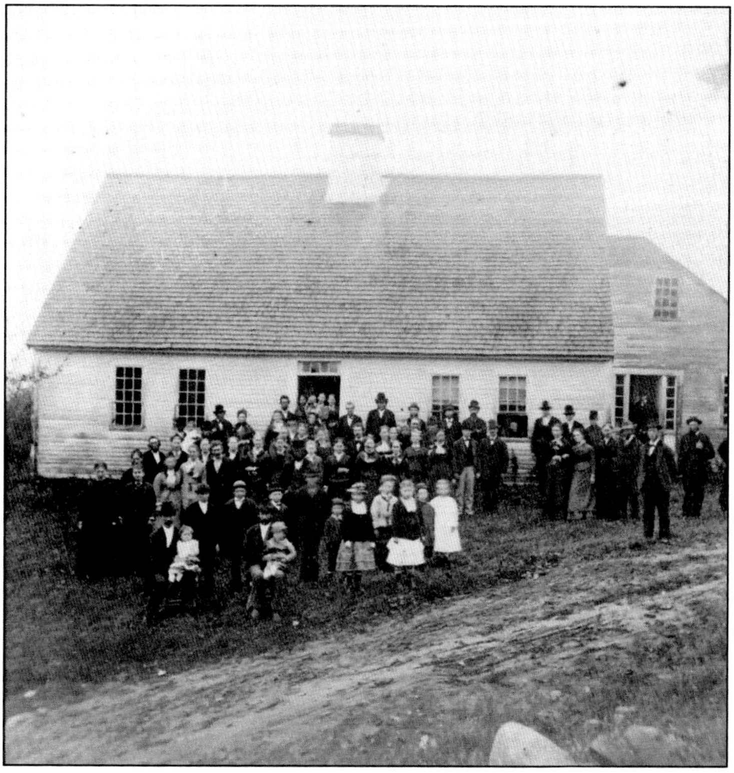

Family members held a reunion at Susan Clark's home on Hampshire Hill in New Sharon to mark her 101st year in 1877. Clark peers from the right window of the modest central-chimneyed cape where she spent 82 of the 102 years of her life.

Nine

SUMMER RETREATS

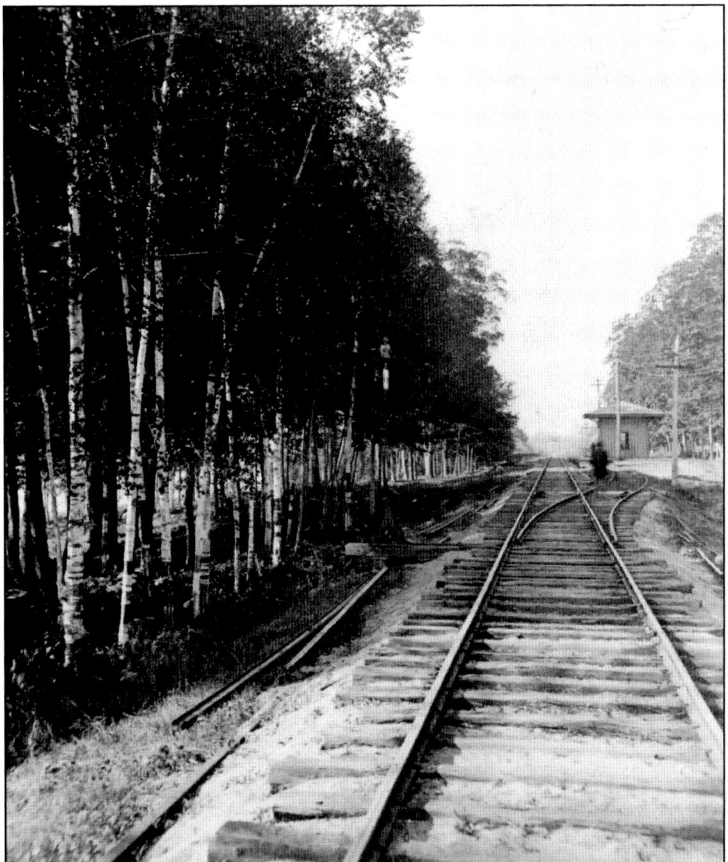

After the Civil War, attending a religious campground became a common summer experience for many Maine residents. Here the tracks of the Maine Central Railroad pass through Lakeside, a Seventh-Day Adventist camp started on Snow Pond in North Belgrade in 1880. The railroad station is at the right.

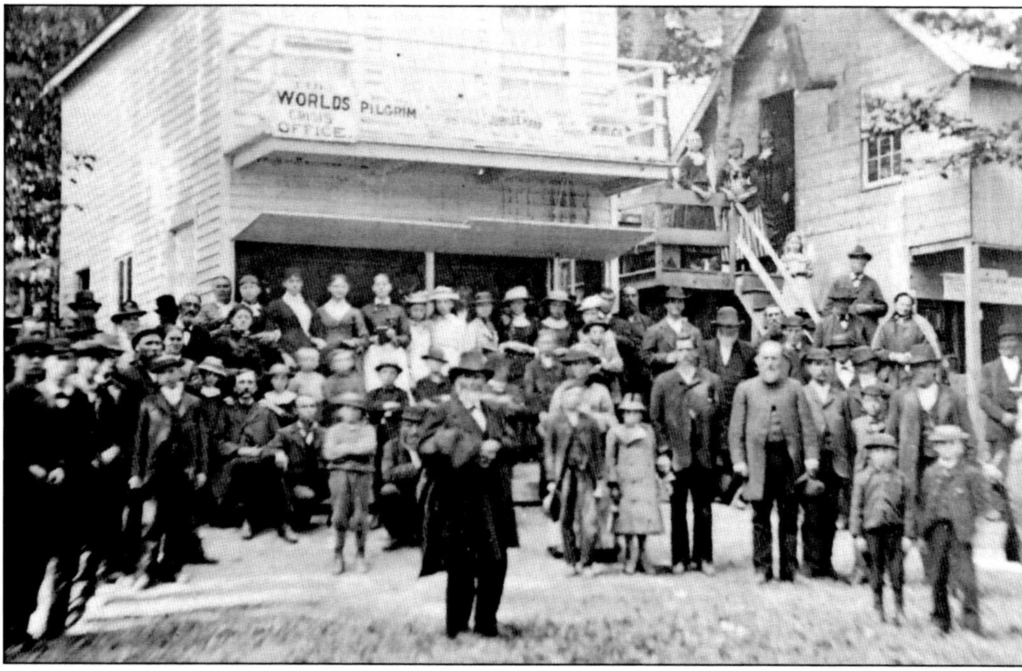

Located in a grove of hardwood trees on the western shore of Snow Pond, Lakeside consisted of 40 cottages, numerous tents, and several religious buildings such as the Worlds Crisis Office, shown here.

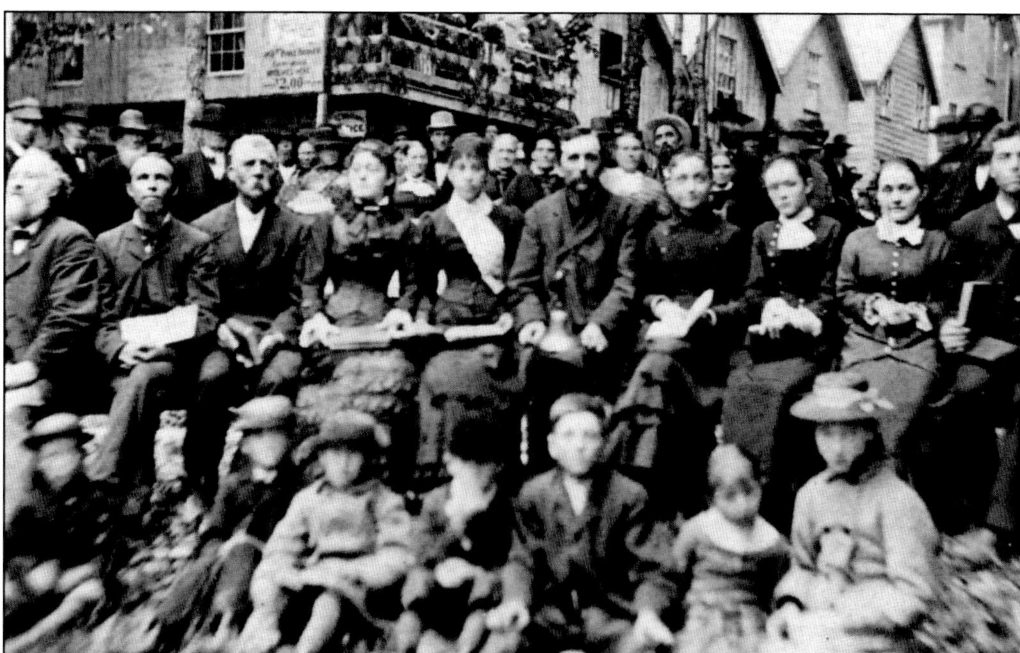

Men, women, and children of all ages were attracted to the camp meetings at Lakeside. Amid a backdrop of trees and cottages, a row of well-dressed Adventists are seated, holding prayer books and hymnals as they wait for the man in the center with the bell on his lap to signal the beginning of a service.

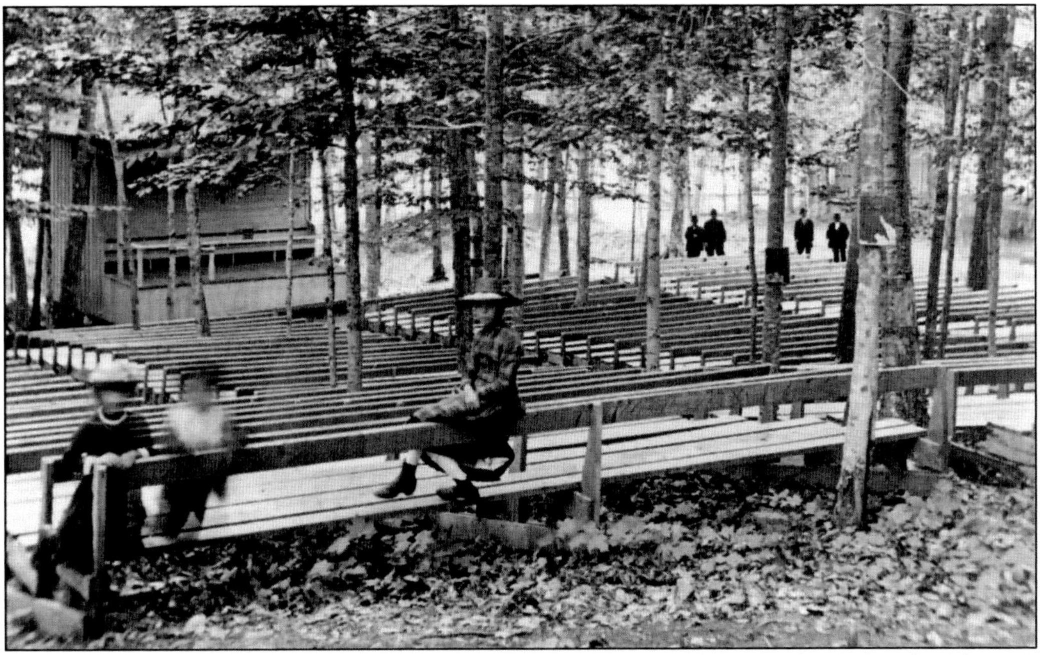

Lakeside's open-air camp meetings were held in this amphitheater of wooden benches. A contemporary visitor noted that "facing the speaker's stand are seats enough for a large multitude, on gently rising ground, so that persons in the rear can easily hear and see." For evening services and in stormy weather, the Adventists worshiped in a large canvas tent.

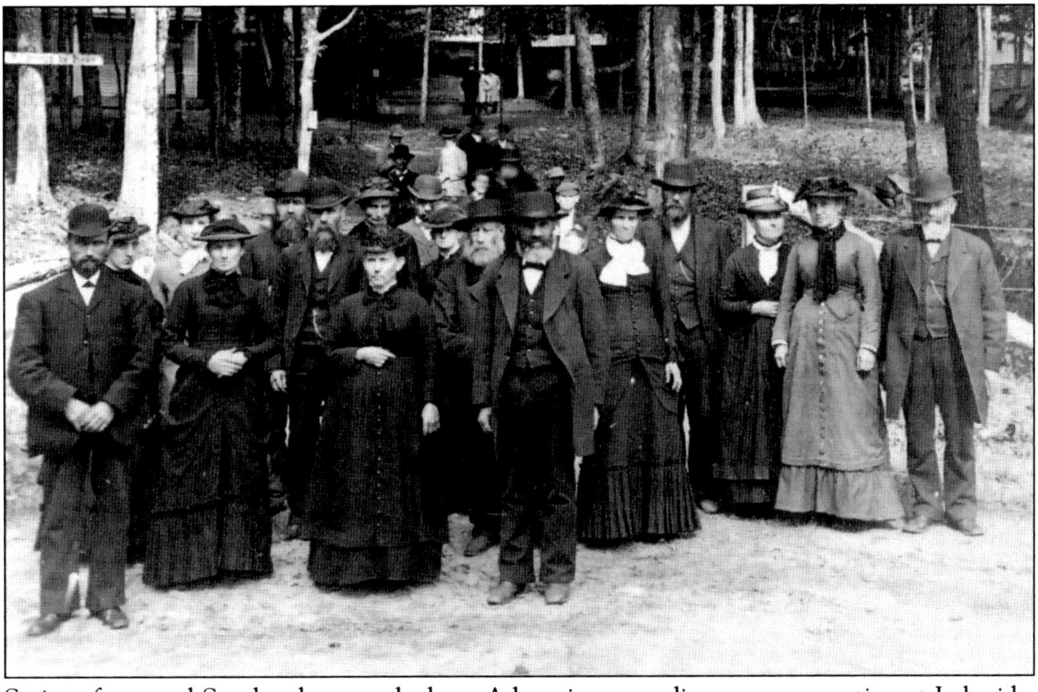

Serious faces and Sunday dress mark these Adventists attending a camp meeting at Lakeside. No matter how hot the summer heat or how rustic the setting, Victorian mores dictated formal attire for such occasions.

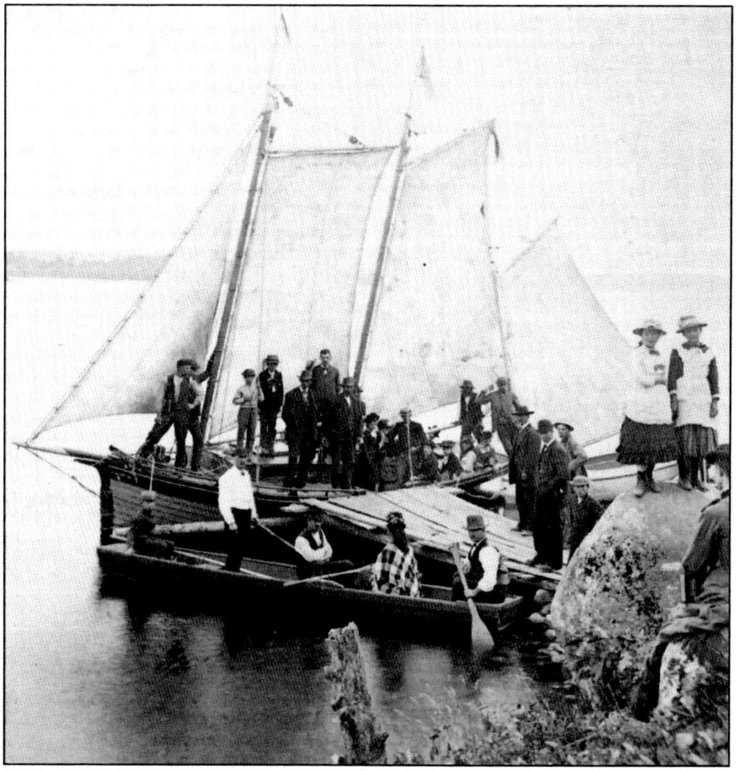

This photograph indicates that the Lakeside campground had its lighter moments. A rowboat and a sailboat provide recreational opportunities on Snow Pond.

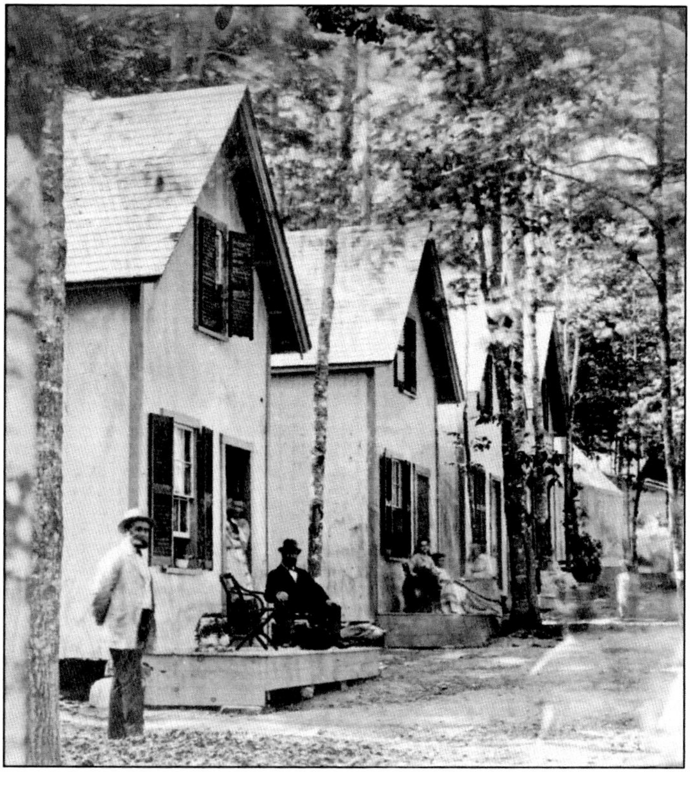

This row of small wooden cottages was part of a popular Methodist campground started in 1868 on the Kennebec River in Richmond by the Kennebec Valley Camp Meeting Association. Each summer, as many as 3,000 people gathered for outdoor services, staying in tents and cottages.

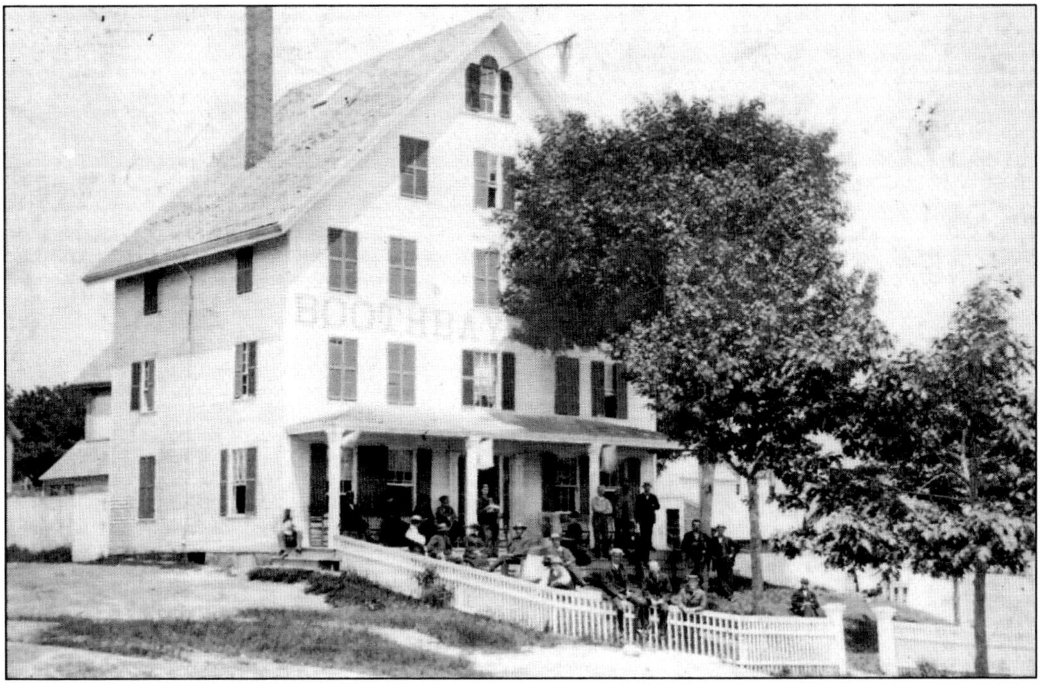

While Boothbay Harbor served as the center for a network of summer colonies frequented by Augusta residents, the town had several hotels of its own, including the Boothbay House, which remained open year-round. Starting as an inn in the 1790s, this famous hostelry closed in 1959.

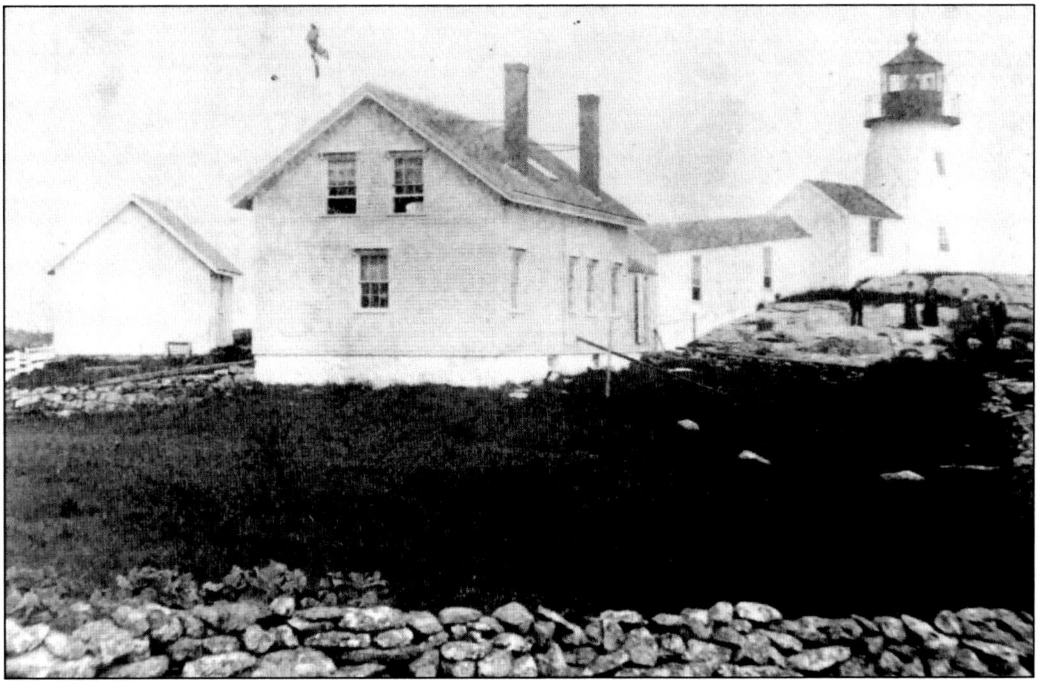

The stone tower of Burnt Island Lighthouse was constructed in 1821 as a navigational aid for vessels entering and leaving Boothbay Harbor. The keeper's house was added in 1857. Burnt Island is now administered by the Maine Department of Marine Resources.

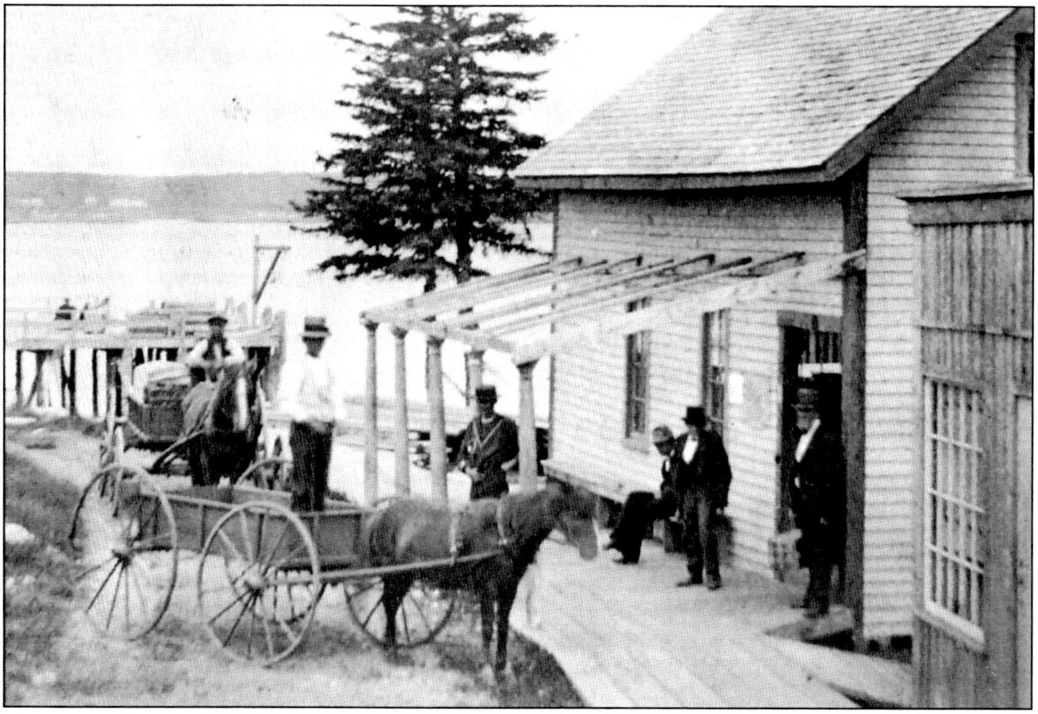

Visitors to Squirrel Island in Boothbay Harbor landed at the dock and followed the boardwalk past the store to the cottages and other amenities of the area's largest summer colony. J. B. Ham and Nelson Dingby Jr. of Lewiston purchased the island in 1870 and served the next year as president and treasurer of the Squirrel Island Association, which was formed to promote a resort community for central Maine families.

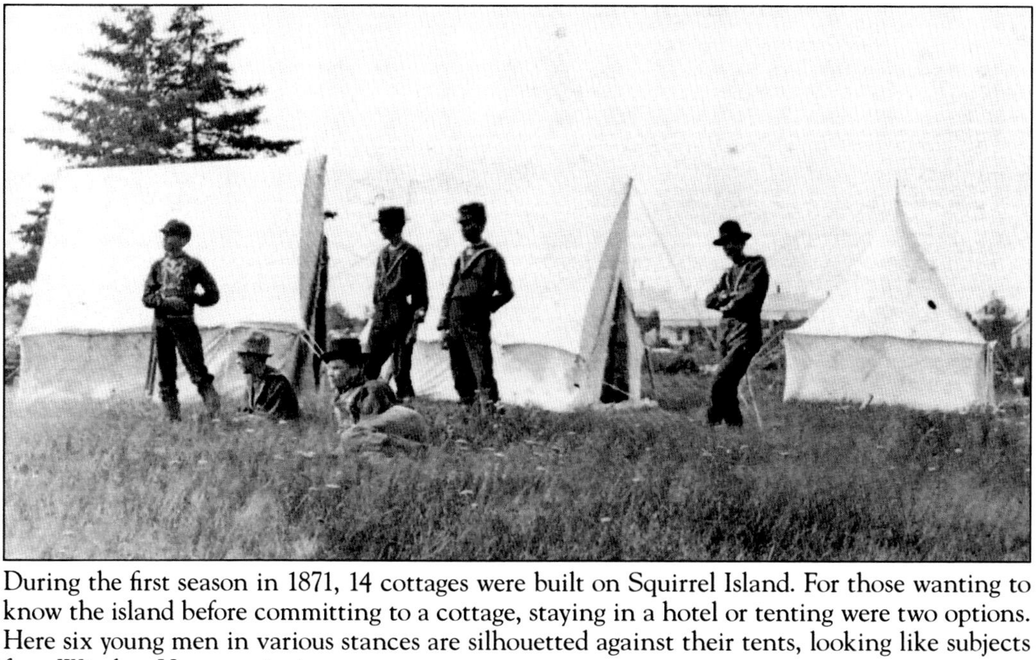

During the first season in 1871, 14 cottages were built on Squirrel Island. For those wanting to know the island before committing to a cottage, staying in a hotel or tenting were two options. Here six young men in various stances are silhouetted against their tents, looking like subjects for a Winslow Homer painting.

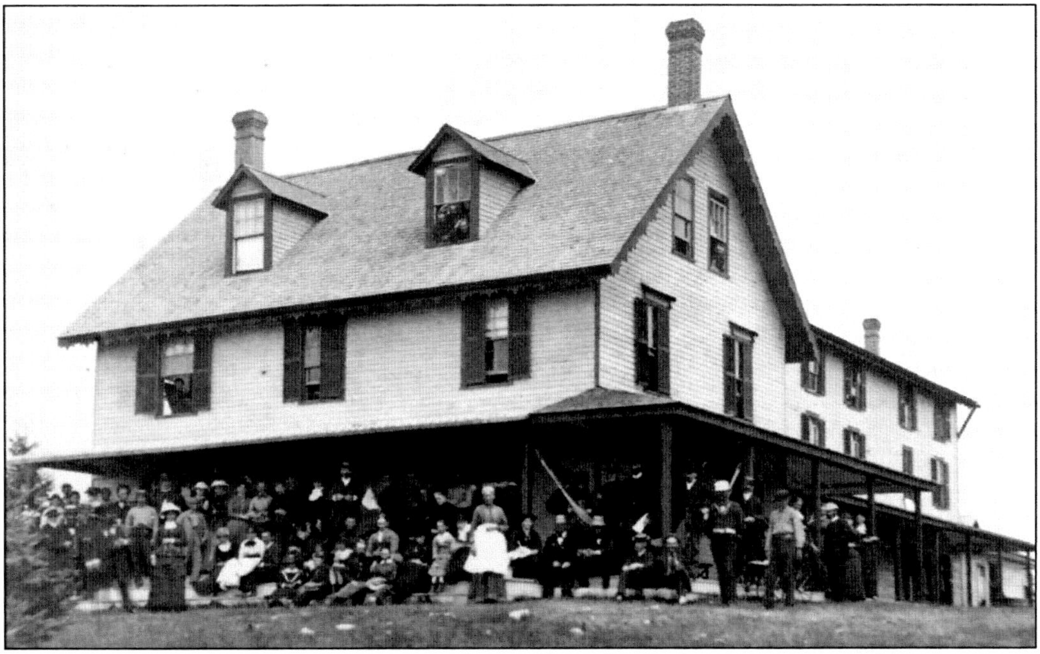

Brothers Martin Van Buren Chase and Ethan Allen Chase of Augusta acquired lot 27 in 1871 for its prominent location and built the Chase House to accommodate Squirrel Island visitors. When the Chase House burned in 1893, it was replaced in 1894 and 1895 by the Hotel Eastern, soon renamed the Squirrel Inn.

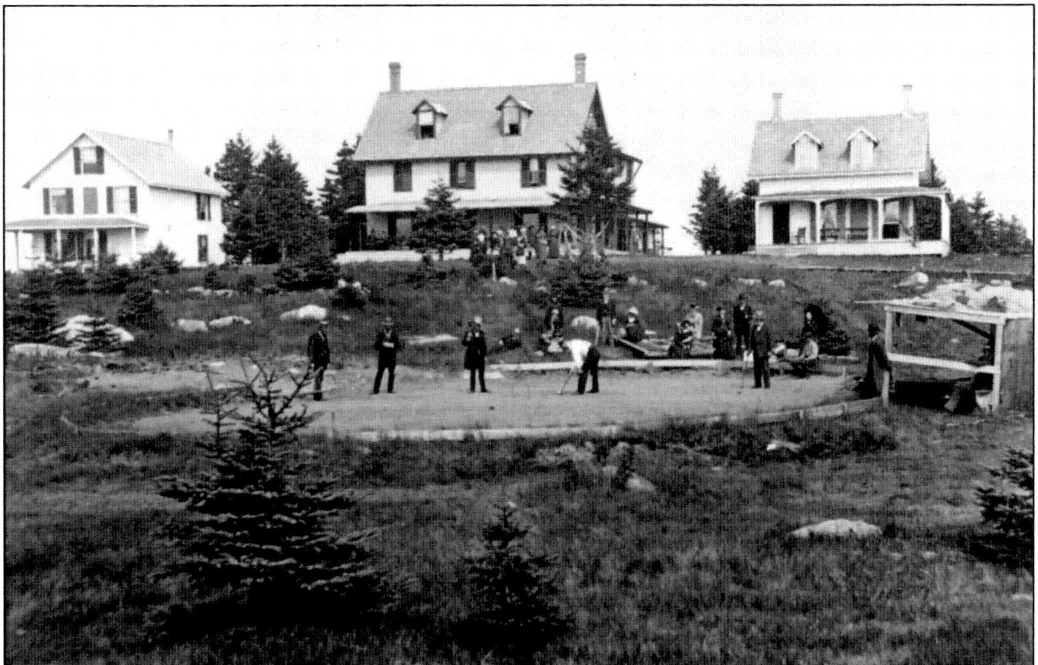

Five men play croquet in front of the Chase House. As M. F. Sweetser observed of Squirrel Island in 1883, "Families mingle in a pleasant and decorous democracy, on the croquet, archery, and tennis grounds, or along the lovely beaches, or on the yachts which skim the adjacent seas."

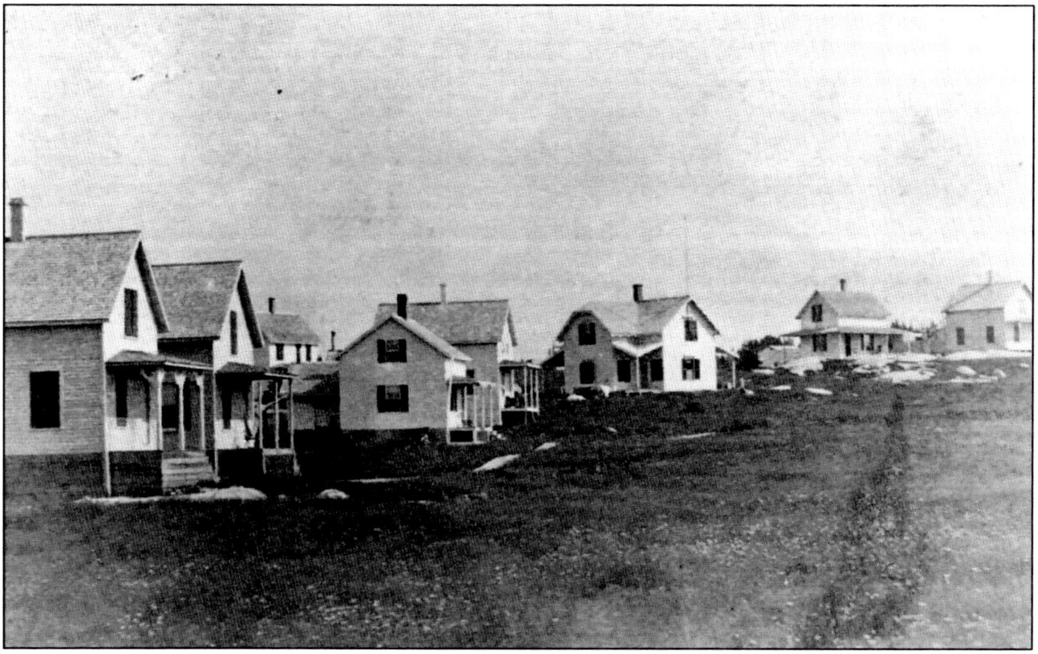

Between 1871 and 1895, 108 cottages were built on Squirrel Island, many of them by Bath contractor James E. Haley. Most of these cottages were constructed for families from the Lewiston-Auburn and Augusta-Gardiner areas.

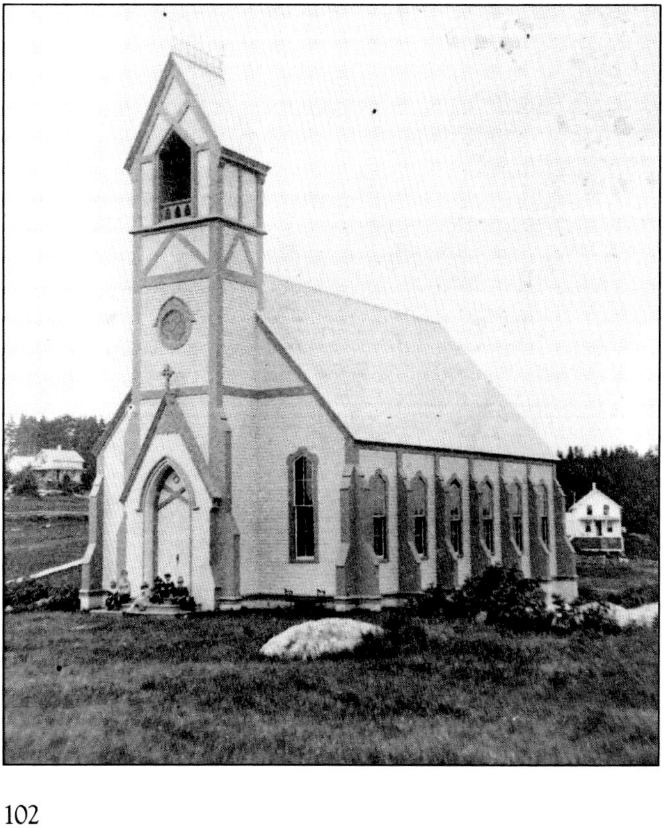

Construction on the Squirrel Island Chapel, designed by William H. Stevens and George M. Coombs of Lewiston to seat 300, began in the fall of 1879, and the chapel was ready for services the following summer. An 1880 description called the chapel "a little poem in Gothic carpentry" and claimed that it gave "our summer city an air of ecclesiastical propriety."

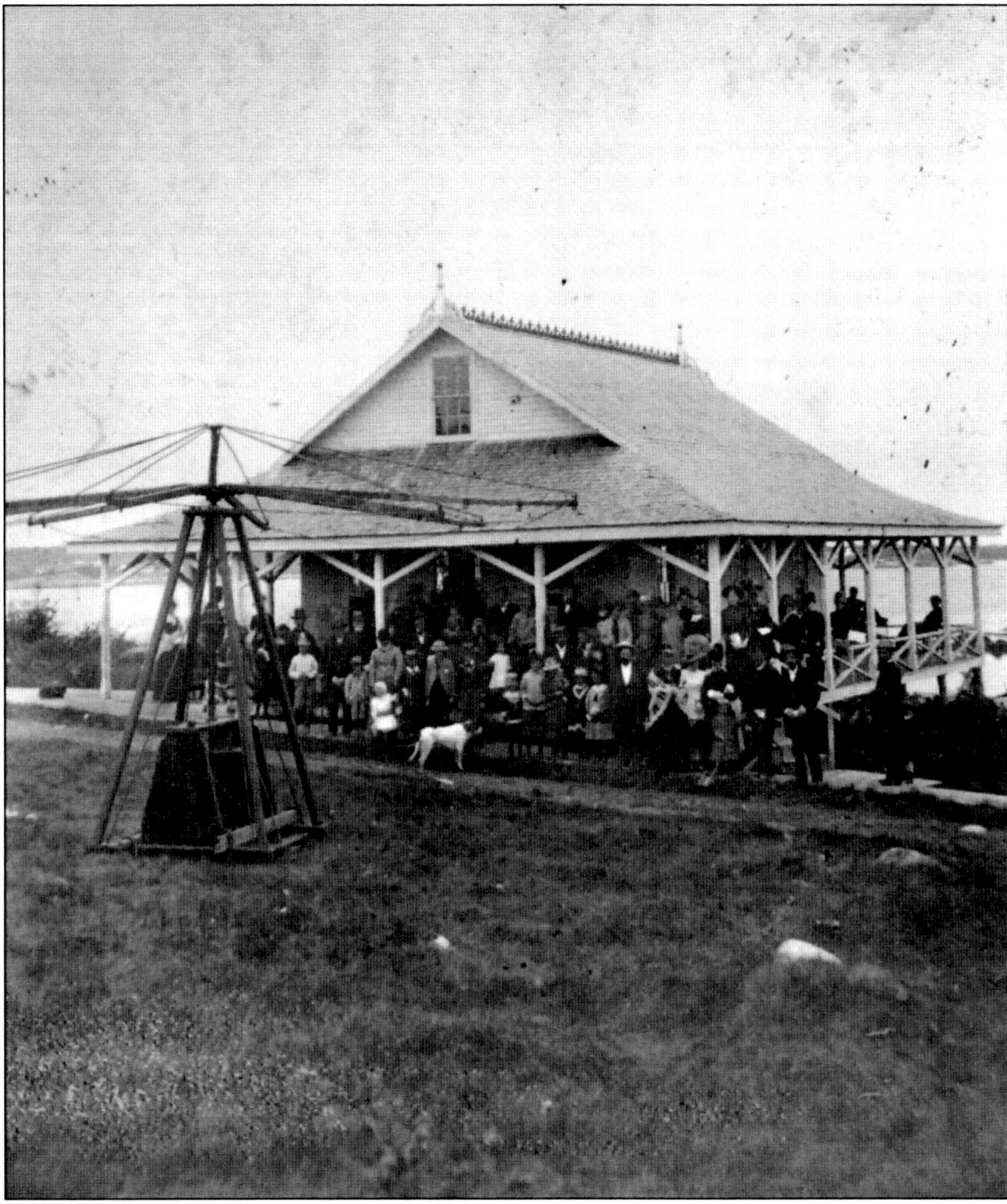

Squirrel Island residents and visitors gather on the porch of the Reading Room with a primitive merry-go-round in the foreground. Built in 1877 from designs by William H. Stevens of Lewiston, the Reading Room served as a library, natural history museum, and post office for the growing summer community. Today the building still houses the post office as well as the island's historical collections.

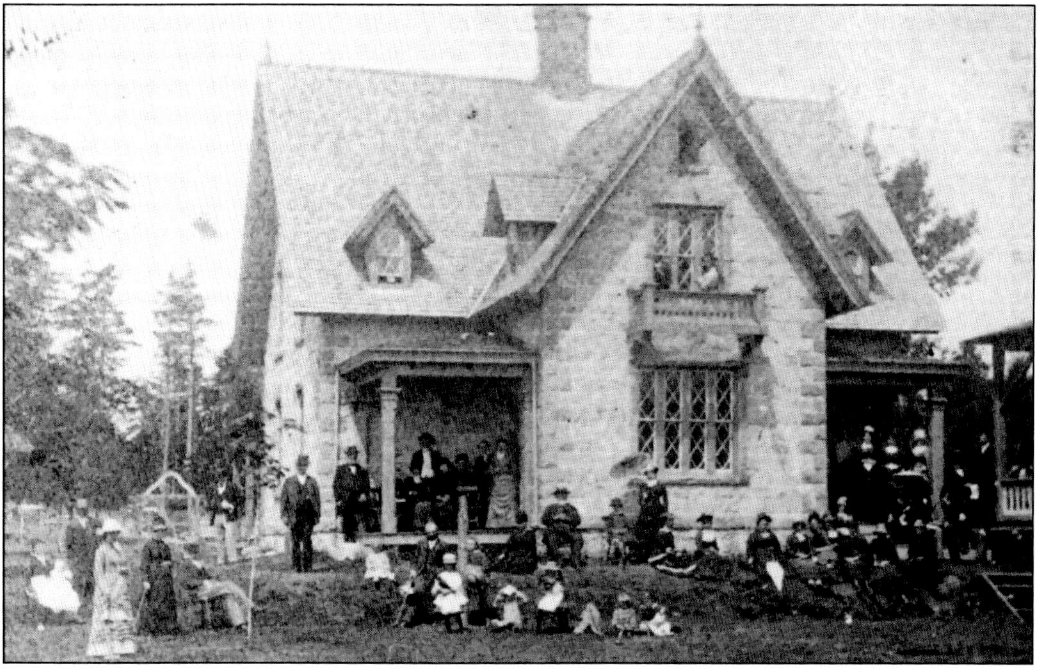

Rosewood Cottage was built on Mouse Island in Boothbay Harbor in 1864 as a stone Gothic Revival summerhouse for Alexander Johnston of Wiscasset. After only two years, Johnston sold the cottage, which became a summer boardinghouse in 1869. A period brochure described the accommodations as "15 rooms, a large fireplace in its parlor, around which guests gather for quiet and rest or evening games."

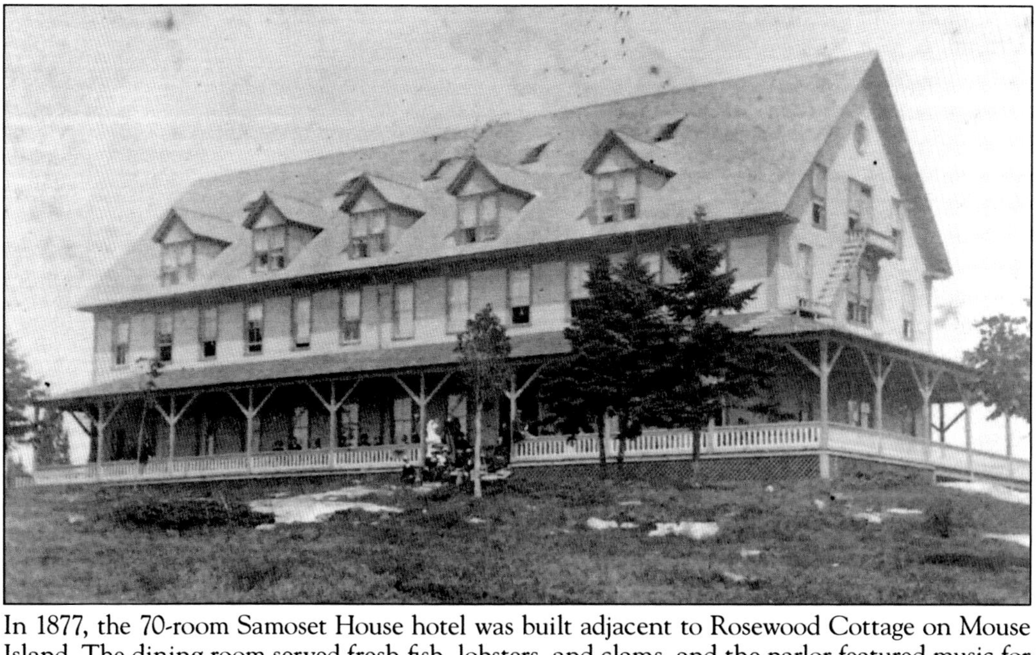

In 1877, the 70-room Samoset House hotel was built adjacent to Rosewood Cottage on Mouse Island. The dining room served fresh fish, lobsters, and clams, and the parlor featured music for dancing. The Samoset House met the fate of many wooden hotels when it burned in the summer of 1913.

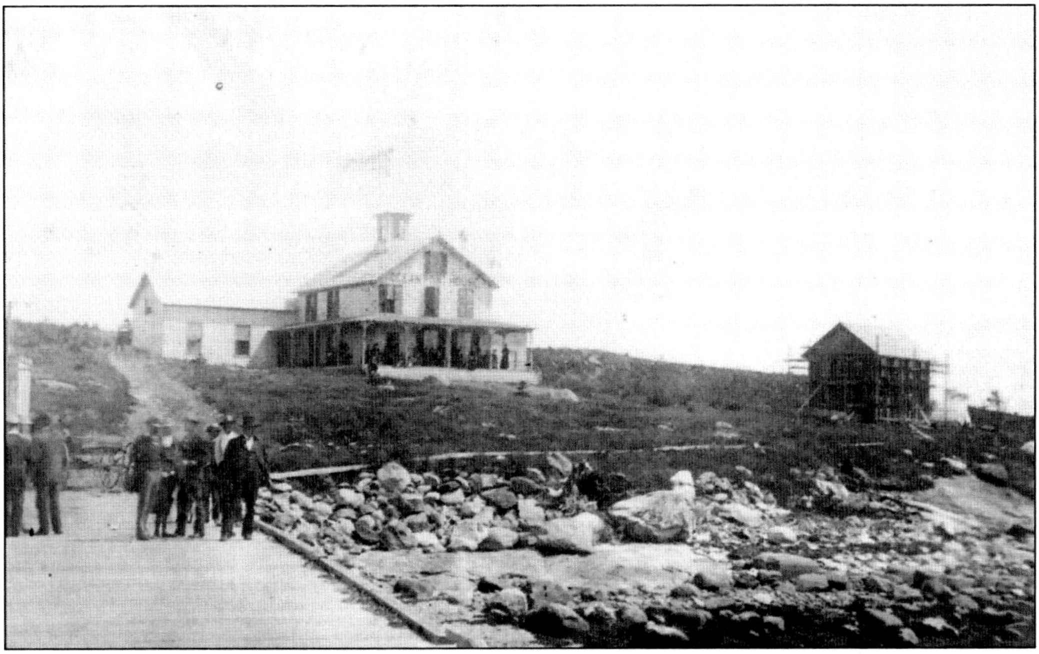

Boothbay Harbor summer retreats were popular with Augusta residents, and the Ocean Point House was no exception. Dr. L. J. Crooker of Augusta started the resort by erecting the Ocean Point House in 1876. By 1879, this summer hotel was surrounded by 20 cottages, most of them built by capital city families. One such cottage is seen under construction on the right.

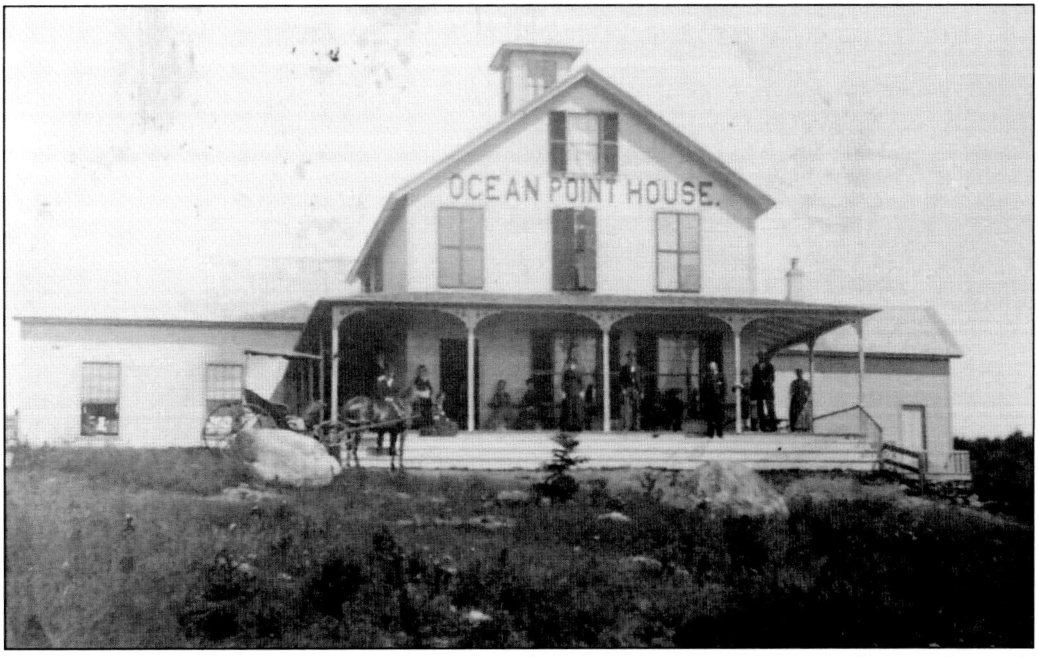

The veranda of the Ocean Point House provided a panoramic view of Monhegan, Squirrel, Damariscotta, Fisherman, and Ram Islands. The hotel table was well stocked with mackerel, cunners, and codfish, as well as milk and berries. Located seven miles from Boothbay Harbor, Ocean Point was promoted by Crooker for three decades.

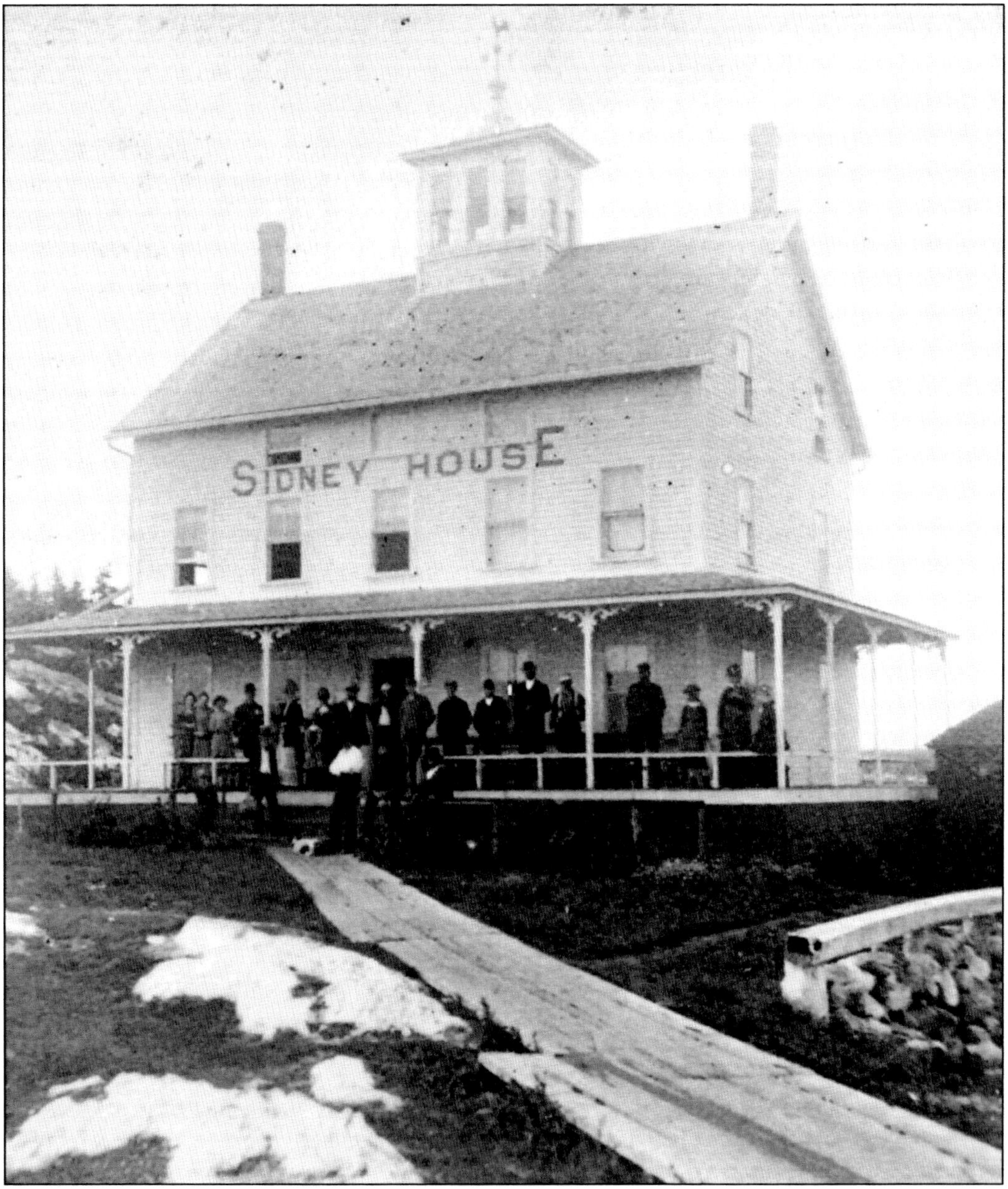

Capitol Island in Boothbay Harbor was founded by Charles A. White of Gardiner as a summer resort for families from Augusta, Hallowell, and Gardiner. The first building was the Sidney House, built in 1878 and operated as a summer hotel by "King" John Sidney, a colorful character described as having "all the vices of tame civilization."

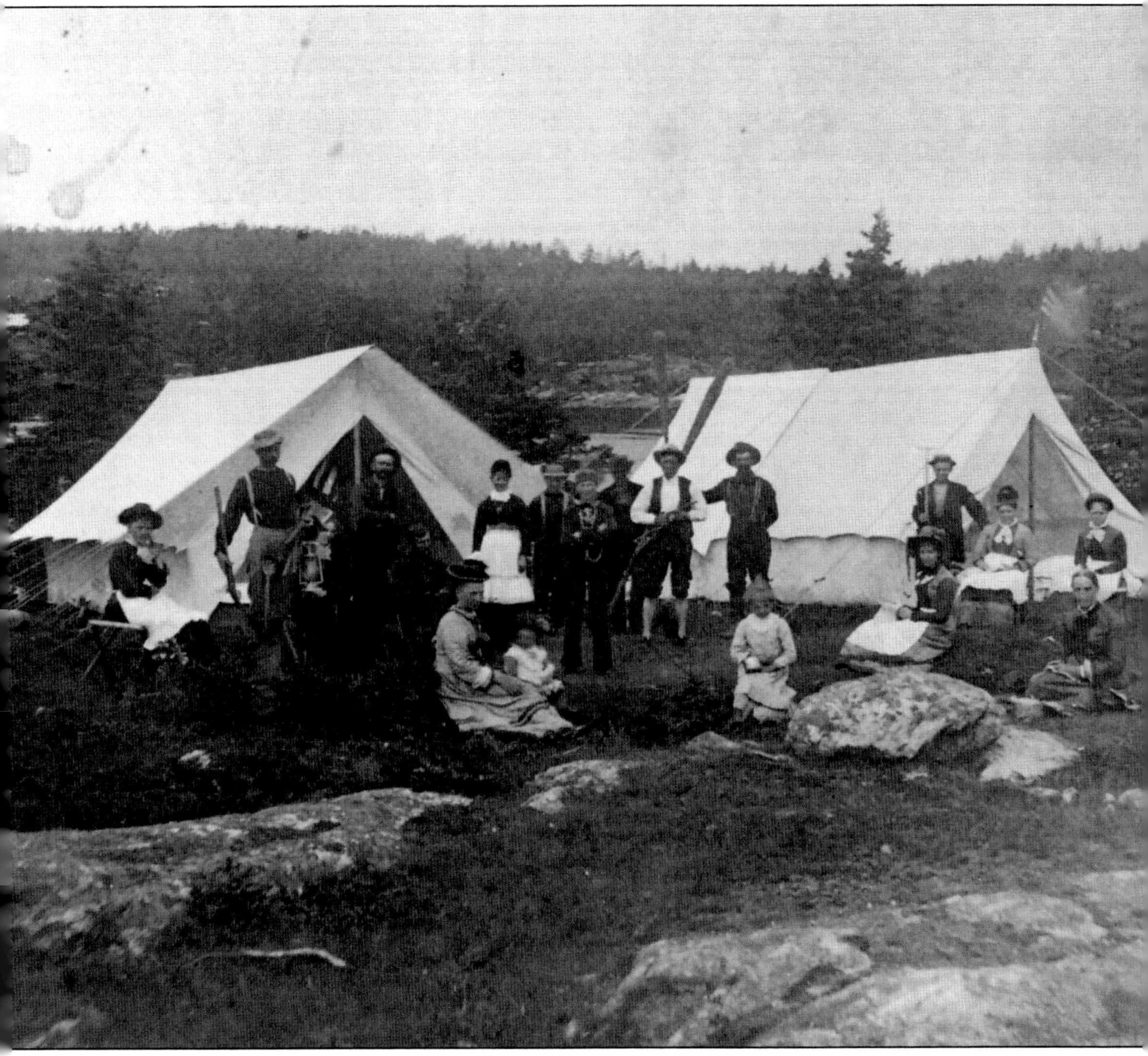

Kennebec Valley families often spent a season tenting on Capitol Island before deciding to build a summer cottage there. By 1896, the island numbered 23 cottages in addition to the Sidney House.

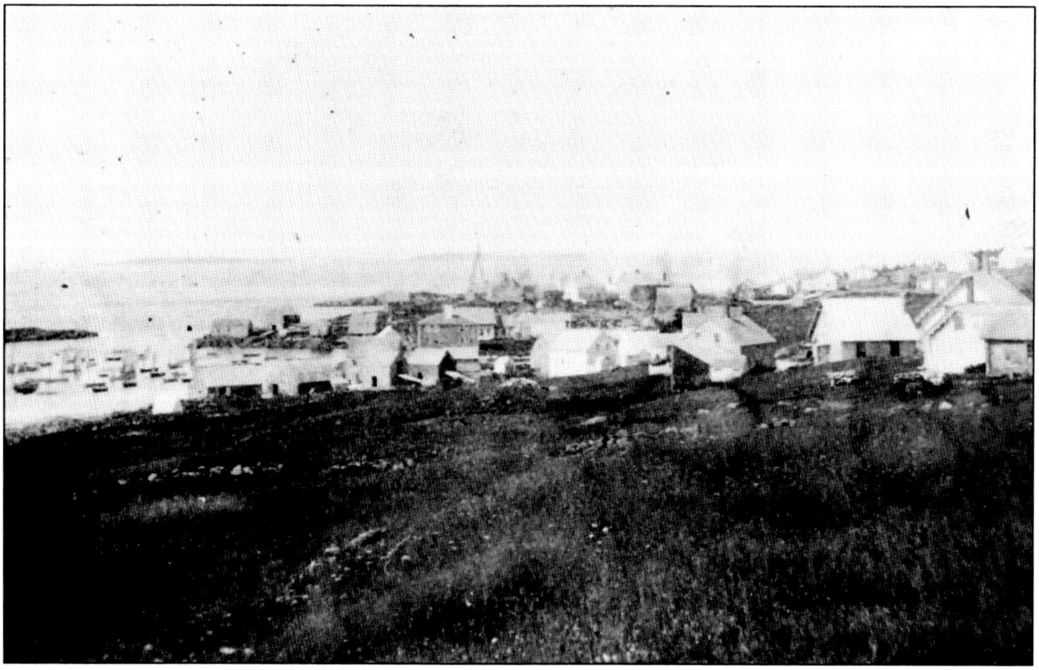

When Henry Bailey photographed Monhegan Island's harbor and village in the 1880s, this long-established fishing community, located 10 miles offshore, was evolving into a destination for artists and summer visitors. All three activities remain vital parts of the island to this day.

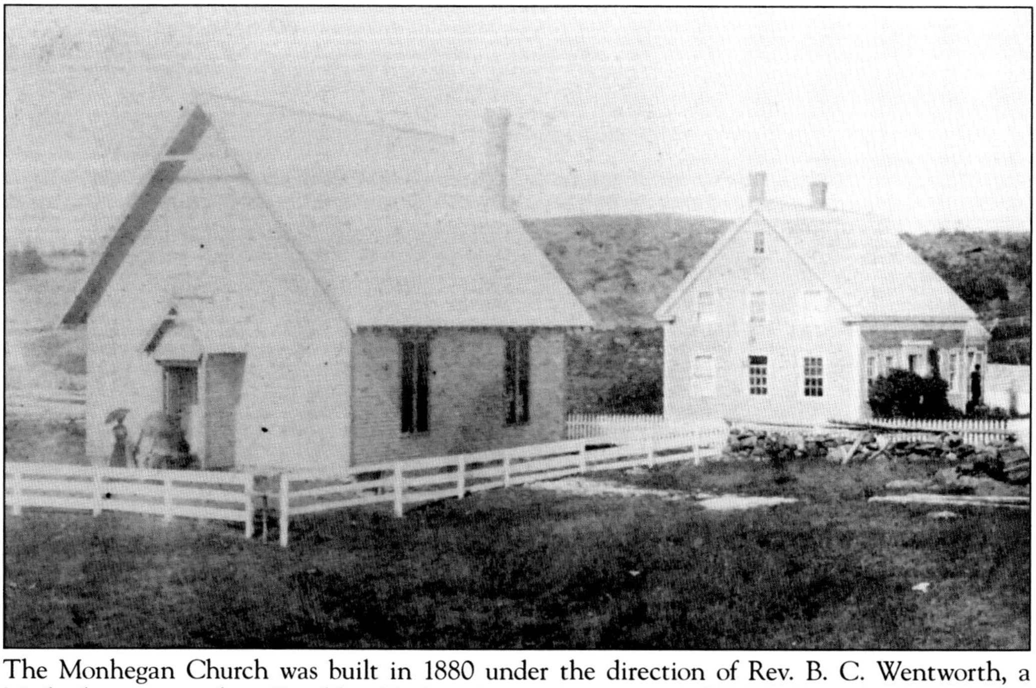

The Monhegan Church was built in 1880 under the direction of Rev. B. C. Wentworth, a Methodist minister from Boothbay Harbor. A corner tower was added in the early 20th century. At the right is Sarah Albee's boardinghouse, which was open to summer visitors by 1877. The Monhegan House hotel now occupies the site.

Tourists gather in front of and atop the Monhegan Lighthouse on Lighthouse Hill, the highest point on Monhegan Island. This handsome granite tower was built in 1850 from designs by Alexander Parris of Boston to replace the original stone structure, which began operation in 1824.

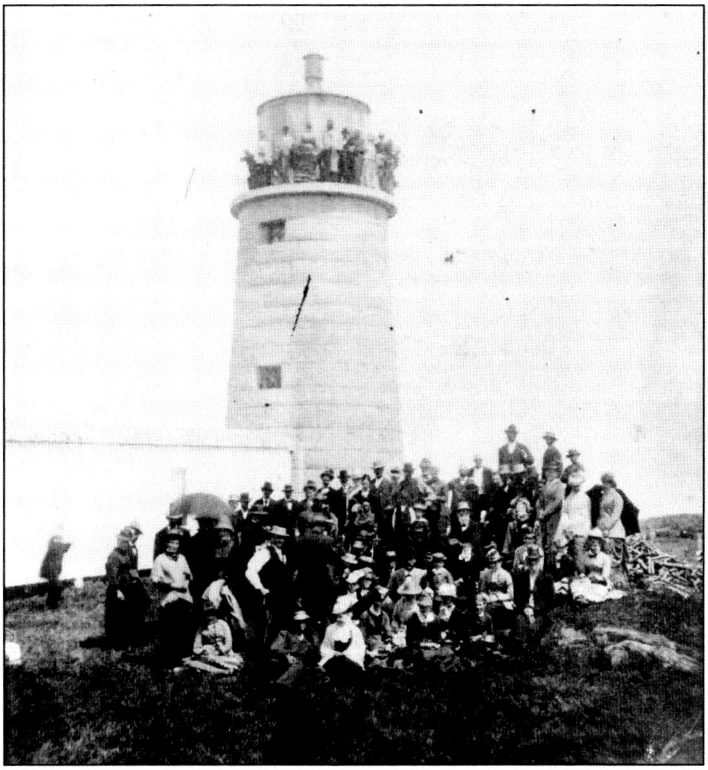

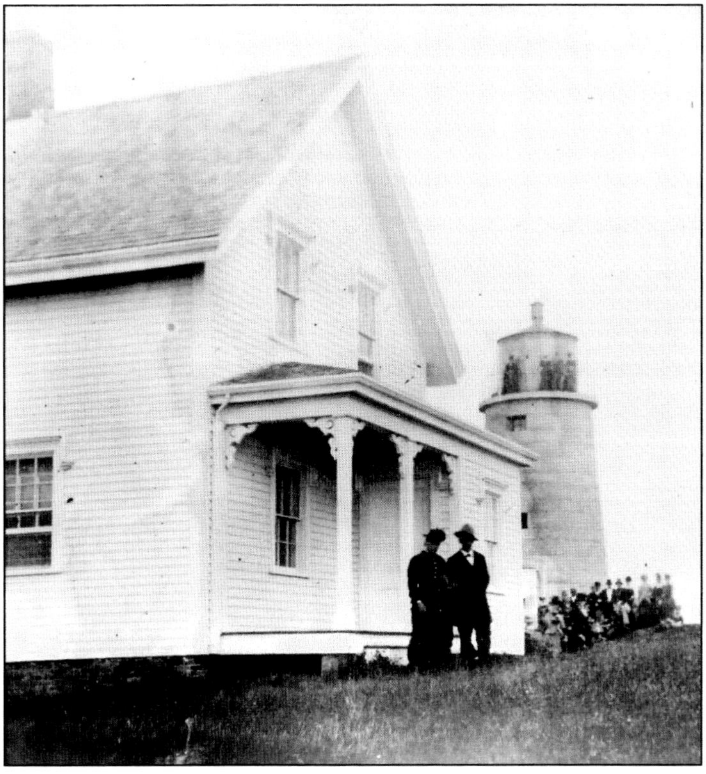

The Monhegan Lighthouse keeper's house was built in 1875 and now contains the Monhegan Museum's displays of the island's history and natural history. The lighthouse complex includes a recent reconstruction of the 1857 assistant keeper's house, which provides gallery space to show the museum's outstanding art collection.

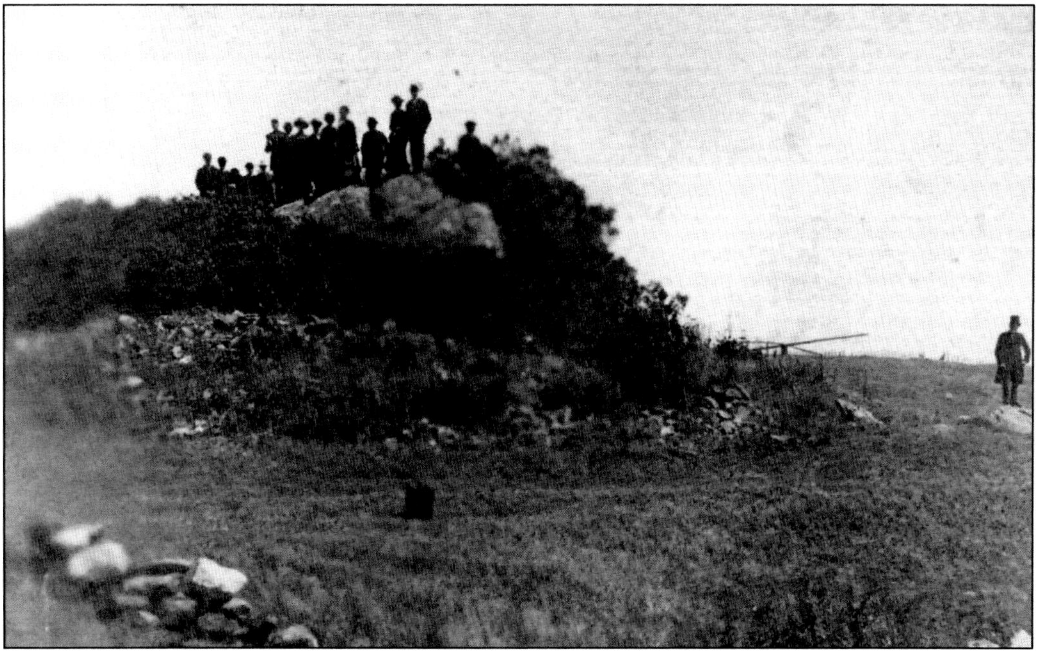

At the tip of the Bristol peninsula is Pemaquid, a site of a settlement established in the 1620s and fortified in 1677, 1692, and 1729. In the post–Civil War period, the site of these forts became a tourist attraction, and summer visitors posed for the photographer atop the Fort Rock, which had been incorporated into the 1692 and 1729 installations.

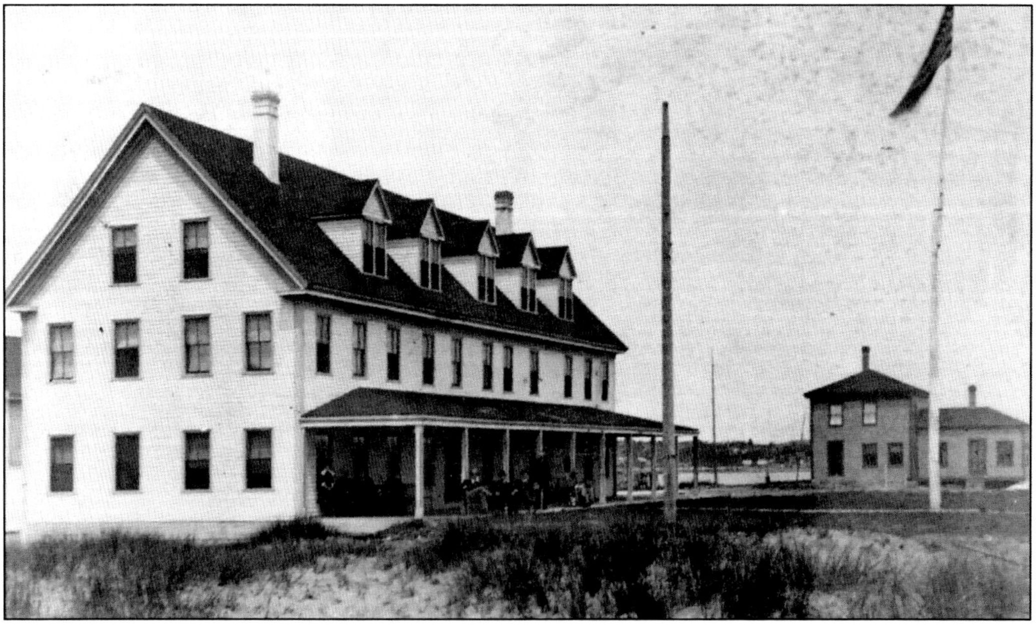

Located at the mouth of the Kennebec River, Popham Beach developed as a popular summer resort after the Civil War. A prime attraction of the Eureka House, later the Riverside, was its location on a broad sandy beach just south of Fort Popham. An 1888 tourist brochure noted that "the fine beach affords excellent bathing facilities, while the constant stream of vessels passing up and down the river adds an interesting feature."

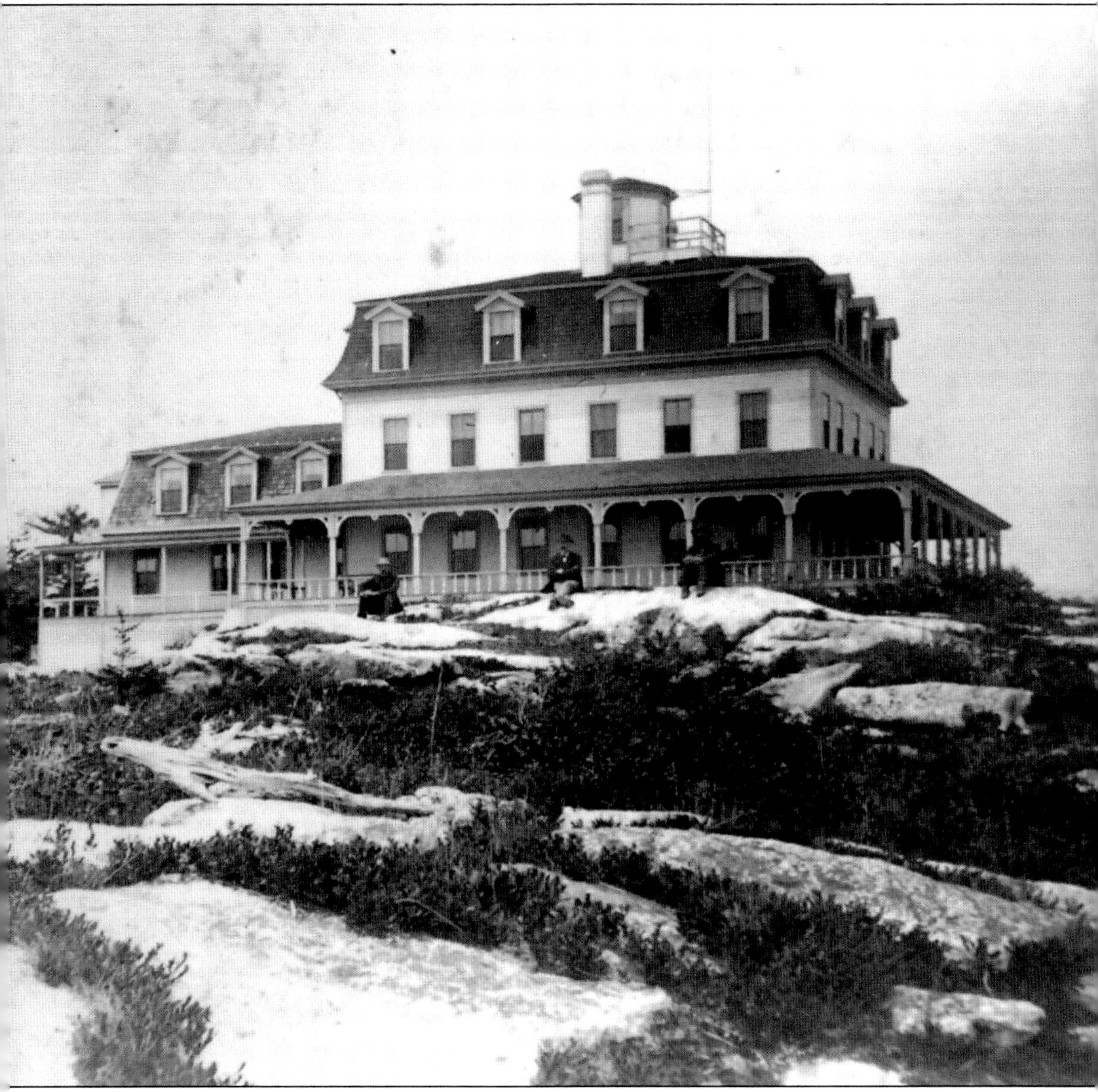

A quarter of a mile from the Eureka House was the Ocean View House, later the Rockledge, located on a bluff 100 feet above Popham Beach. Its commanding view of the beach, the river, and the ocean attracted summer visitors to the extent that a 36-room annex was opened in 1888.

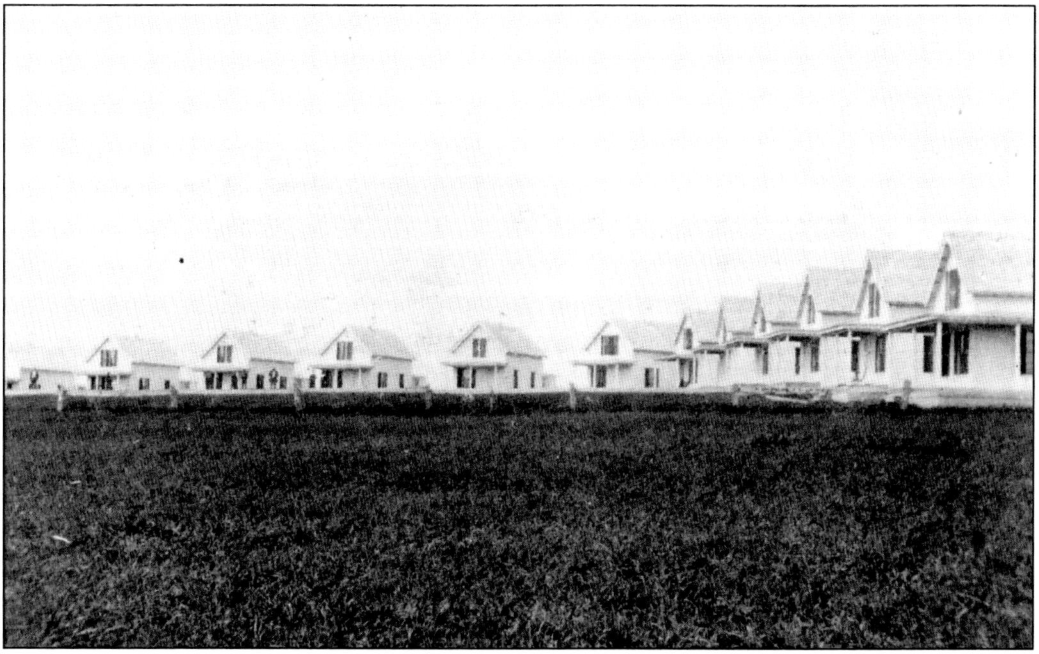

In 1876, five businessmen from Lewiston and Auburn founded the Auburn Colony in South Harpswell as a summer retreat for family and friends to enjoy "society, health, and recreation." By the spring of 1877, Charles Greenleaf and Company of Lewiston had completed the construction of 20 identical 17-by-30-foot cottages.

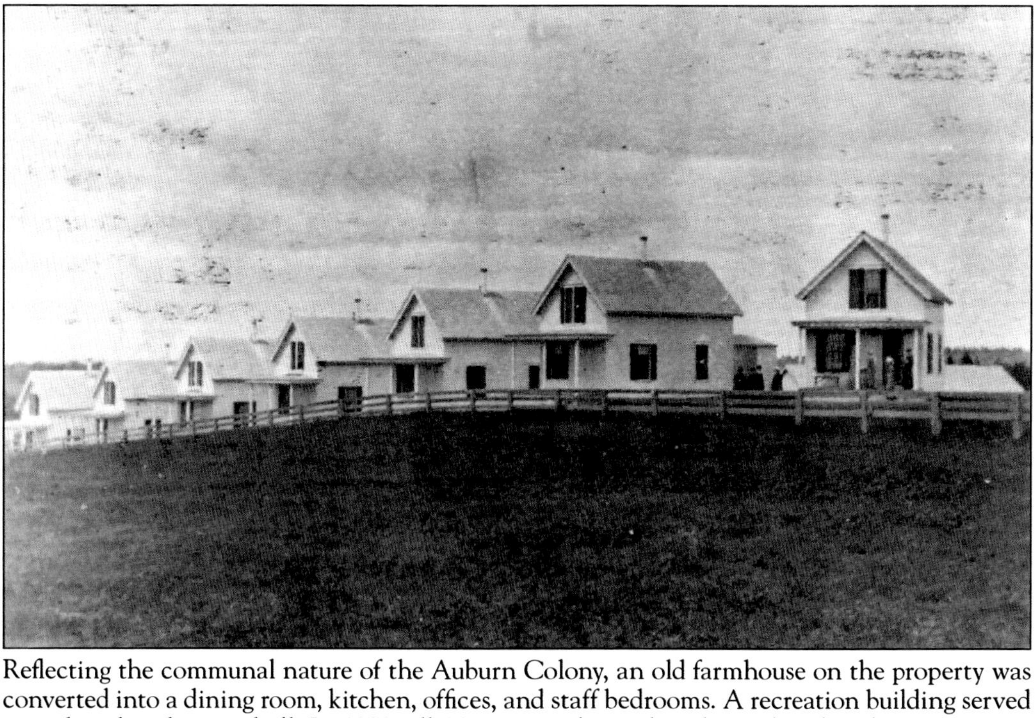

Reflecting the communal nature of the Auburn Colony, an old farmhouse on the property was converted into a dining room, kitchen, offices, and staff bedrooms. A recreation building served as a chapel and music hall. In 1899, all 20 cottages burned, to be replaced with 14 new ones by 1901.

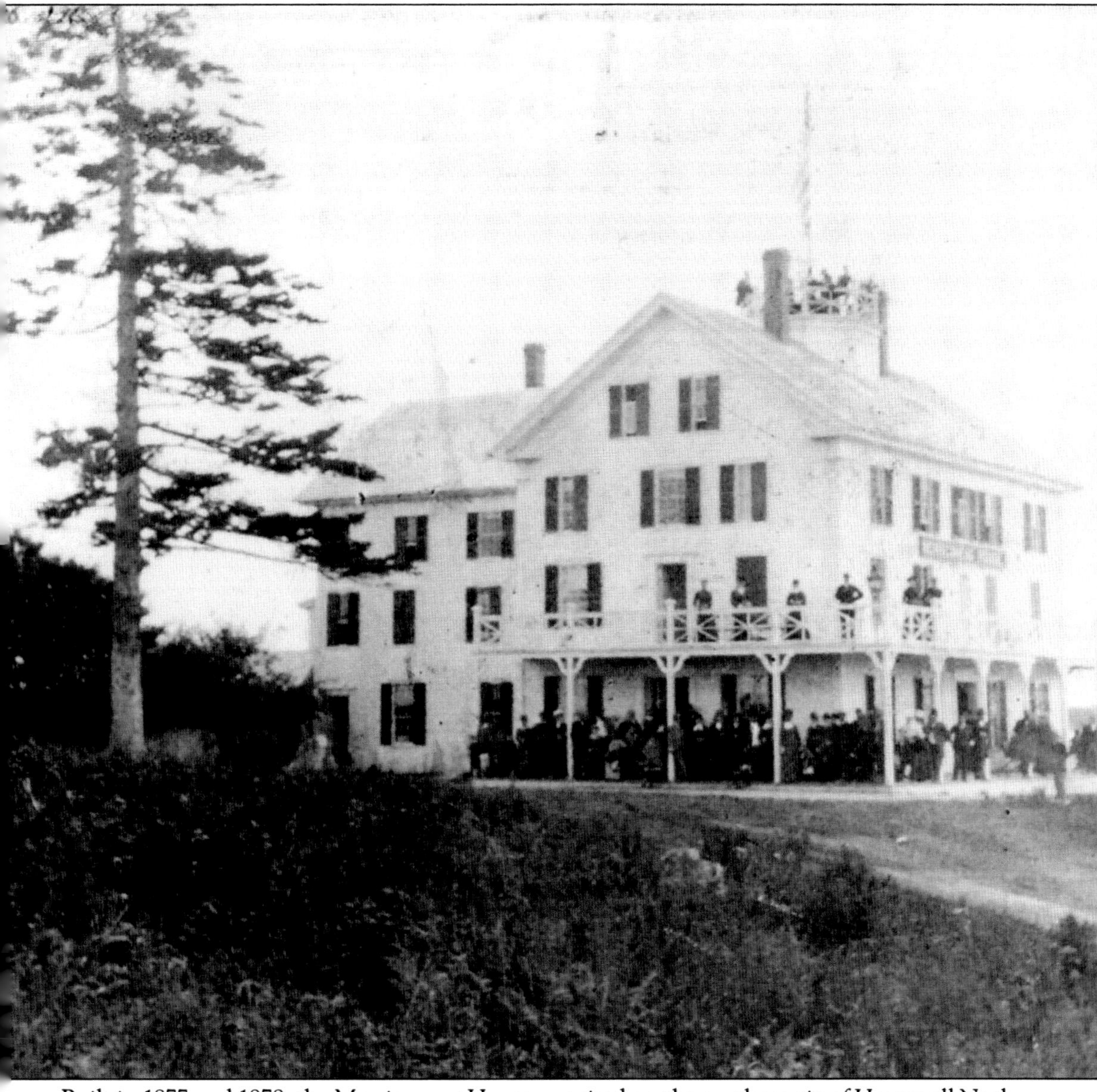

Built in 1877 and 1878, the Merriconeag House was sited on the southern tip of Harpswell Neck. This summer hotel operated for more than 50 years before going through a period of closure that led to its demolition in 1952.

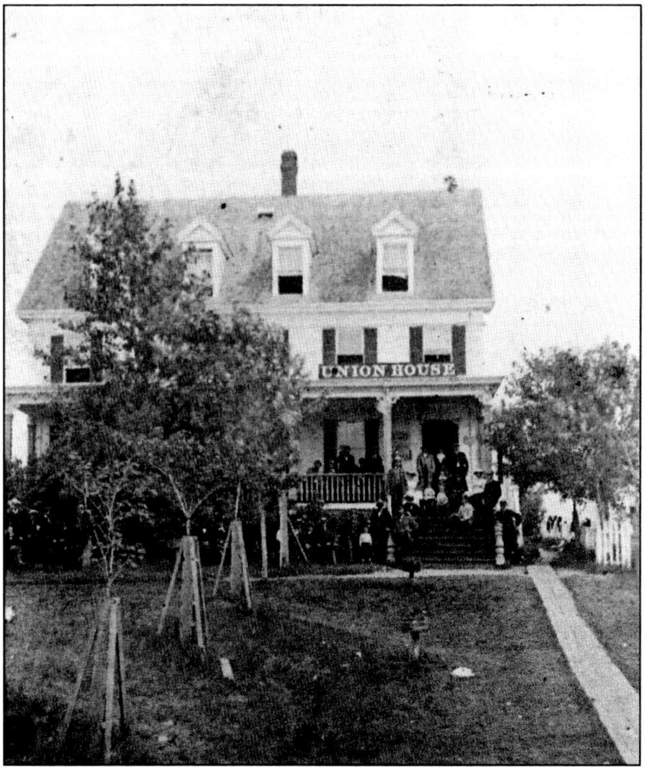

As Portland's most populated island, Peaks Island attracted vacationers as early as 1851, the year that William and Eliza Jones are believed to have opened the Union House as a summer hotel at Jones Landing. Favored by Canadian visitors, the Union House was famous for its fish chowders.

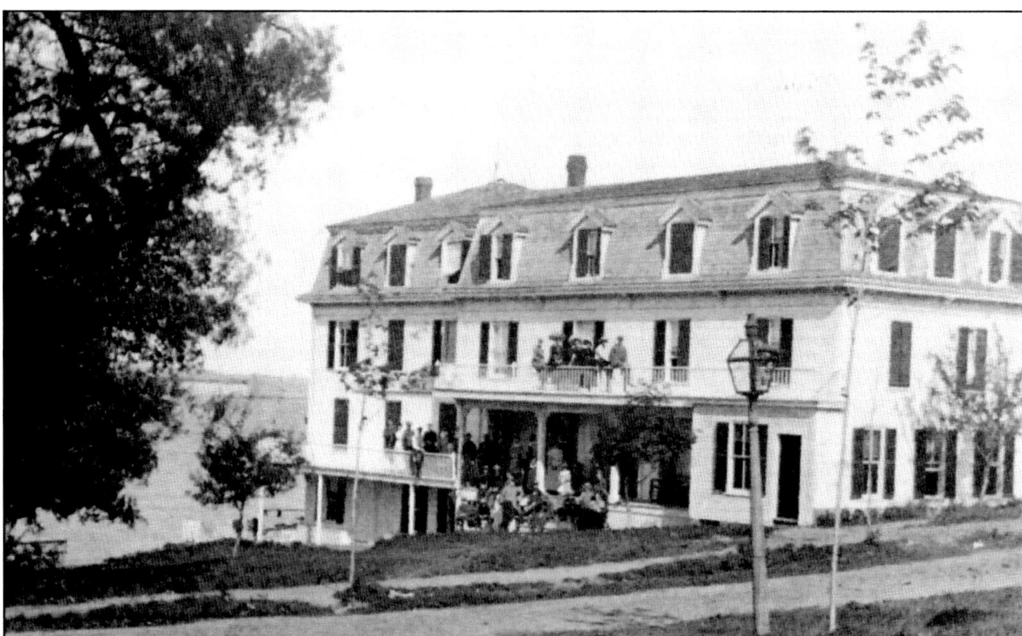

Reflecting Peaks Island's growing appeal as a summer resort after the Civil War, John T. Sterling established the Bayview House near the Union House in 1872. Four years later, Edward H. Elwell noted, "This house stands high on the bank above the shore and commands a fine view of the harbor and the city."

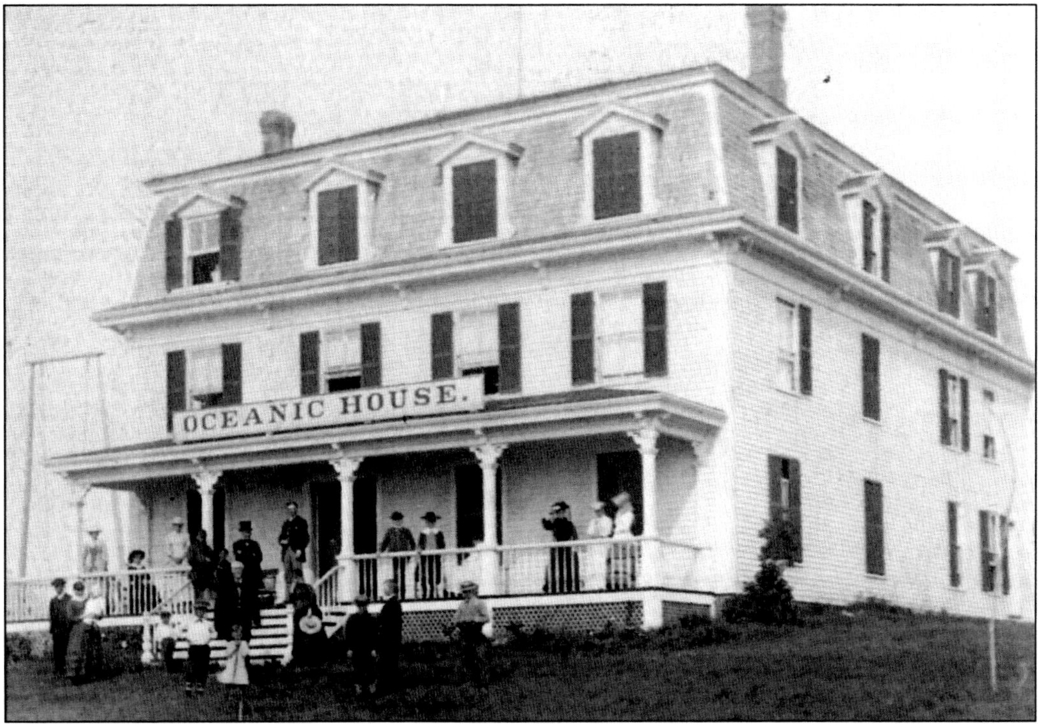

Robert T. Sterling built the Oceanic House at Trefethen's Landing on Peaks Island in 1874. An 1884 brochure noted that "on the elevation known as Beacon Hill stands the Oceanic House, one of the largest, most retired and popular summer resorts on the island."

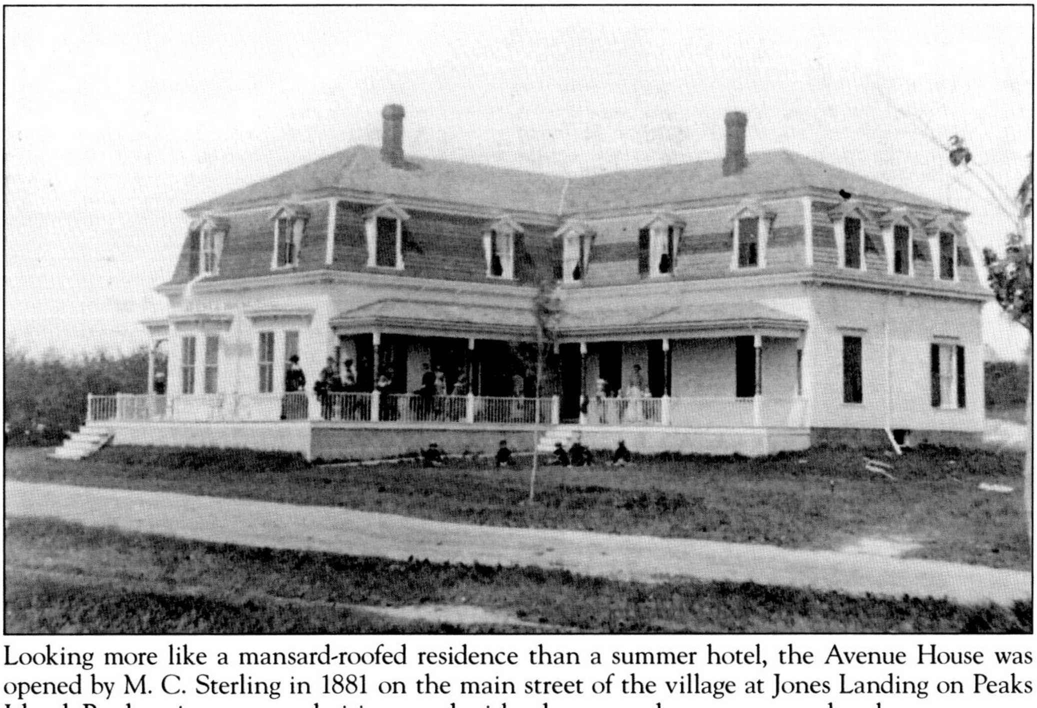

Looking more like a mansard-roofed residence than a summer hotel, the Avenue House was opened by M. C. Sterling in 1881 on the main street of the village at Jones Landing on Peaks Island. By that time, seasonal visitors to the island supported seven summer hotels.

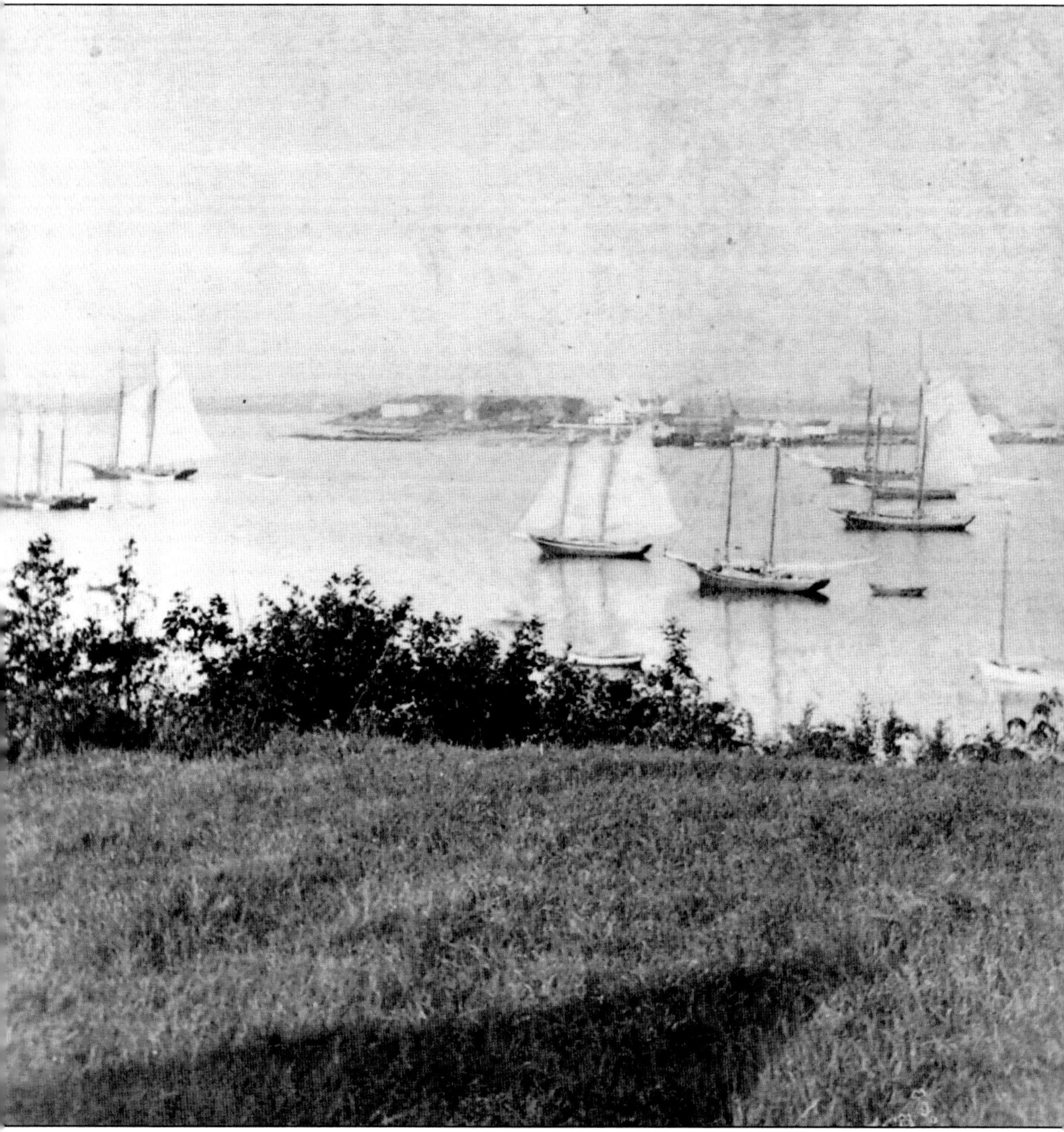

Fishing schooners lie at anchor with others under sail in this view looking from Jones Landing on Peaks Island to House Island. There a wooden blockhouse that was built in 1808 was replaced during the Civil War by a massive granite installation known as Fort Scammel, appearing in this picture on the left side of the island.

Ten

HENRY BAILEY AND HIS FAMILY

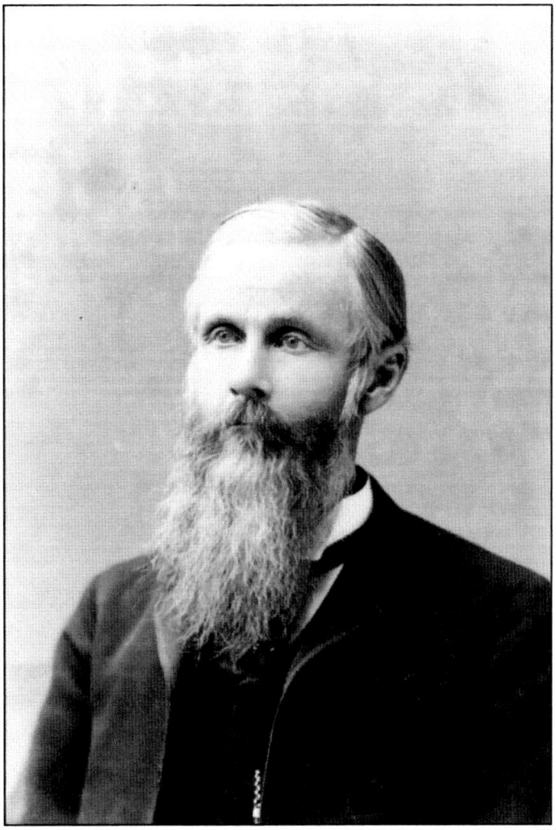

Henry Bailey was photographed in his early 60s by fellow photographer George F. McIntosh, who had a studio in Gardiner in the 1880s. (Hawkins collection.)

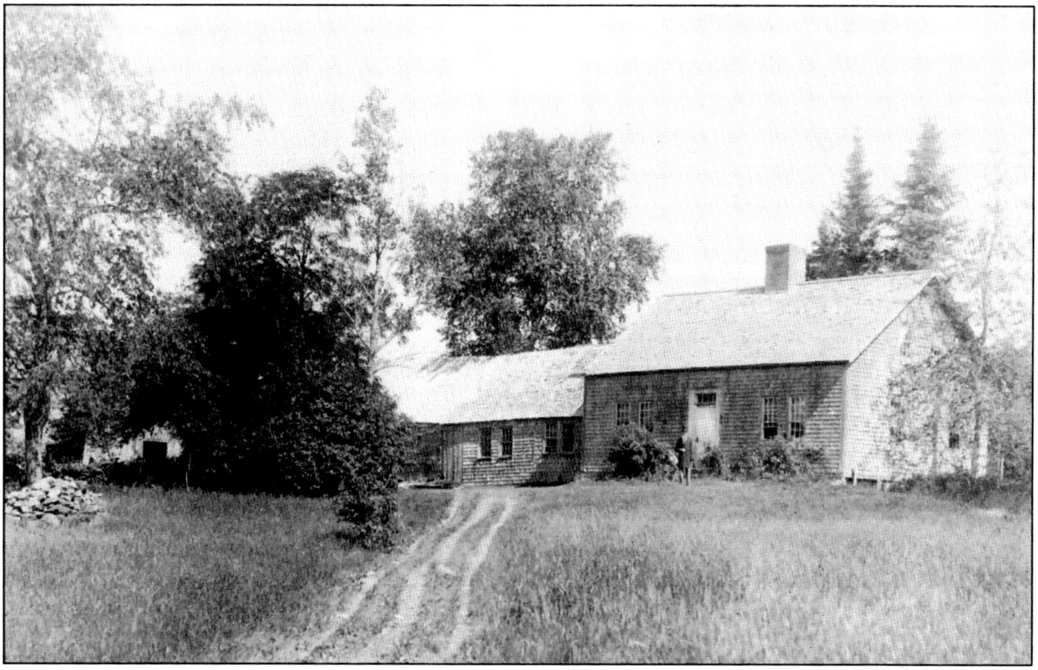

Henry Bailey was born in this West Gardiner farmhouse in 1822, the youngest of Timothy and Betsy Bailey's nine children. Raised in a Quaker household, young Bailey worked as a shoemaker from the 1840s through the 1860s. (Hawkins collection.)

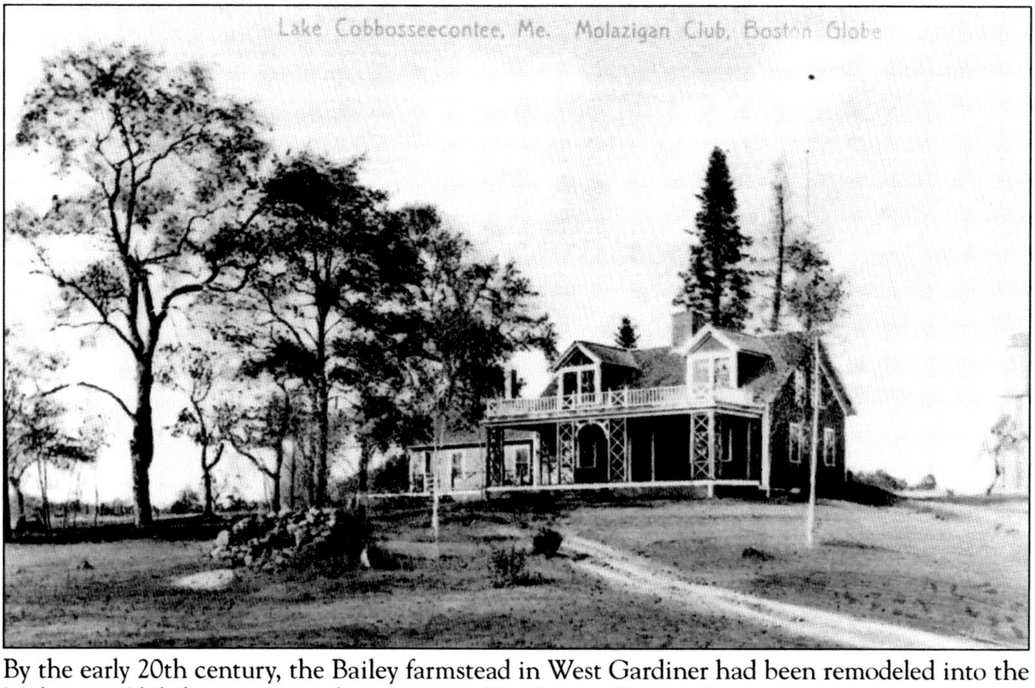

By the early 20th century, the Bailey farmstead in West Gardiner had been remodeled into the Molazigan Club for sportsmen from Boston. (Hawkins collection.)

This ambrotype portrait of Bailey probably dates from about 1858, the year the adjoining picture of brother-in-law Augustus F. Morse was taken. Morse instructed Bailey in photography. (Hawkins collection.)

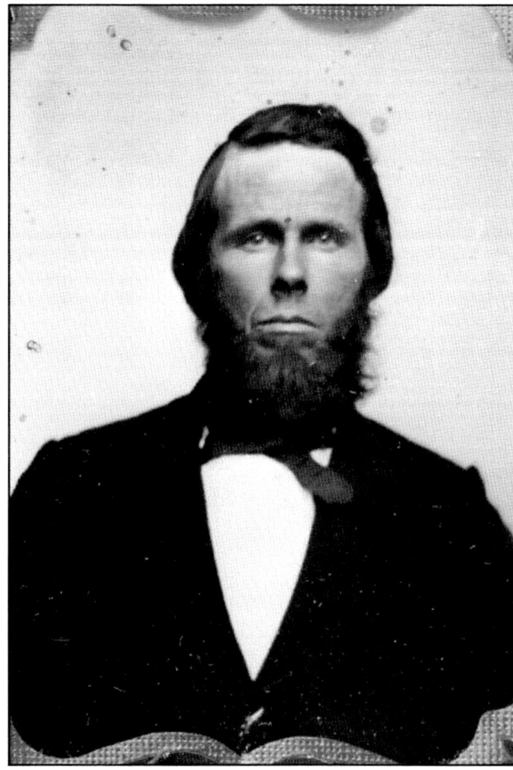

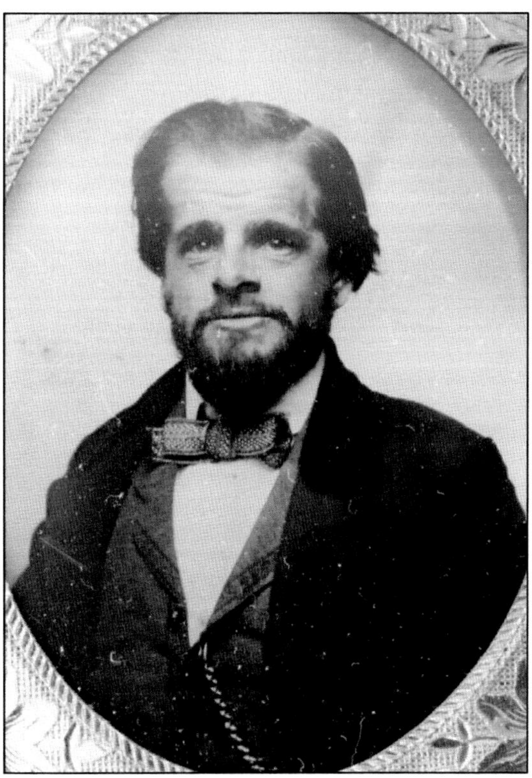

Born in Bowdoinham in 1835, Morse operated a photography studio at Water and Union Streets in Hallowell from the 1860s to the 1880s and then ran a store at the same location. He died in 1925. (Hawkins collection.)

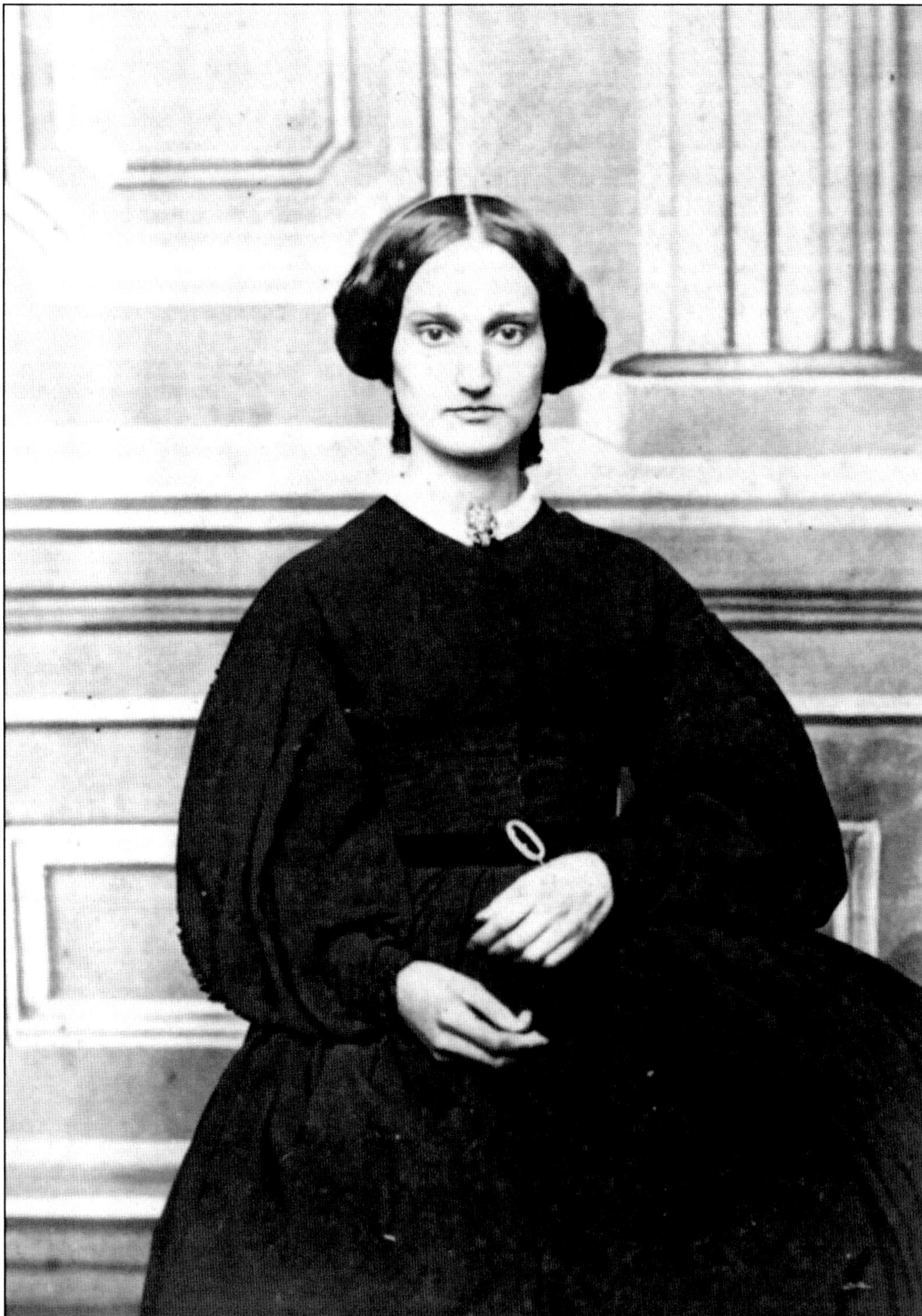

In 1856, Henry Bailey married Elmyra Gray of Hallowell on her 16th birthday. She died at the age of 27 in 1867. (Hawkins collection.)

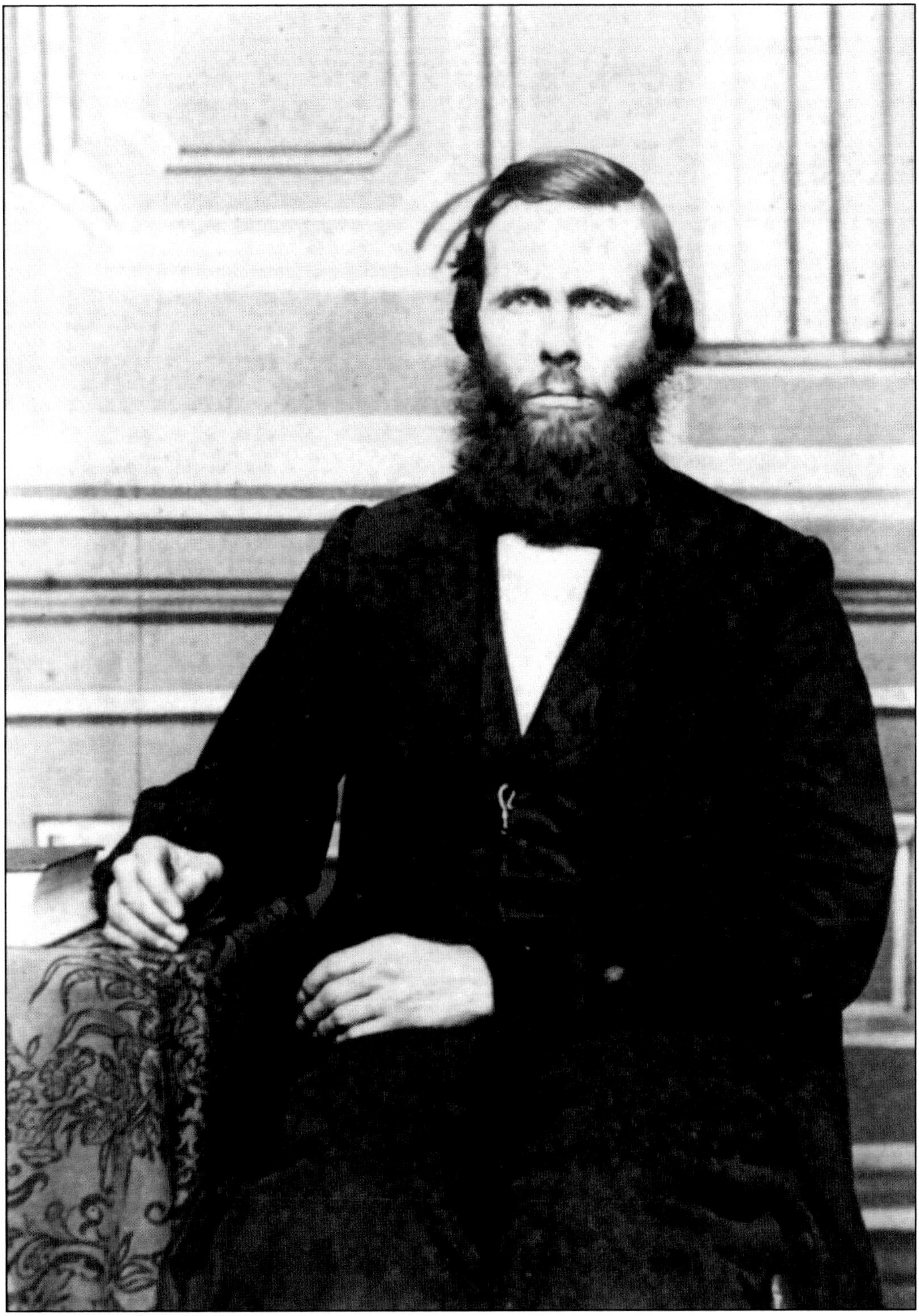

Bailey's brother-in-law Augustus F. Morse took this pair of formal studio portraits of Bailey and his wife, Elmyra, in 1862. (Hawkins collection.)

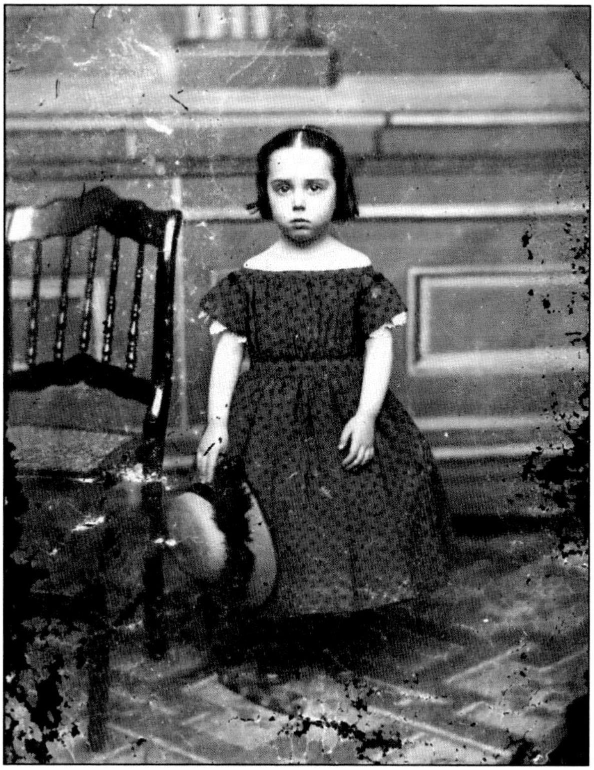

Henry and Elmyra Bailey's first daughter was Etta, who was born in 1858 and died in 1940. She married Elbridge Richards, a motorman for the Augusta, Gardiner, and Winthrop Street Railway. (Hawkins collection.)

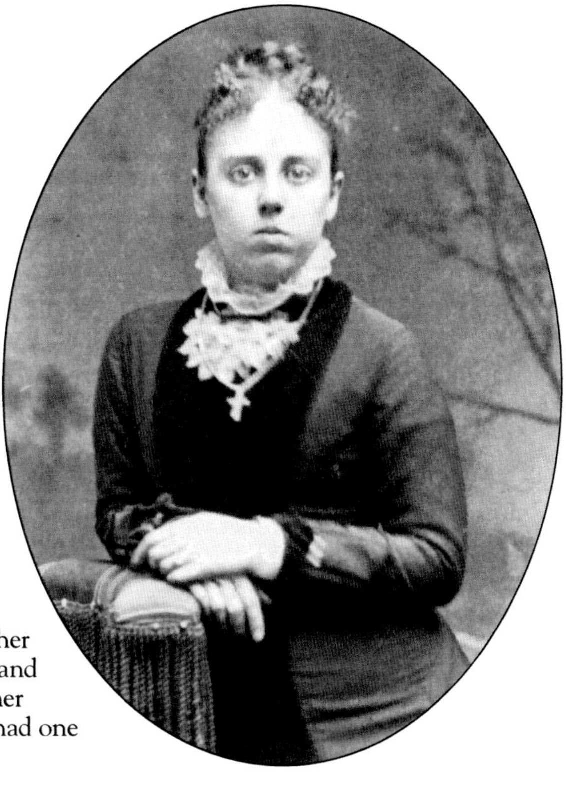

Seen here as a young woman, Etta assisted her father, Henry Bailey, with his photography and became an accomplished photographer in her own right. She and her husband, Elbridge, had one daughter. (Hawkins collection.)

The Baileys' second daughter was Eunice, who was born in 1864 and lived until 1955. She married Charles Shorey, the superintendent of the harness shop at the Maine State Prison in Thomaston. (Hawkins collection.)

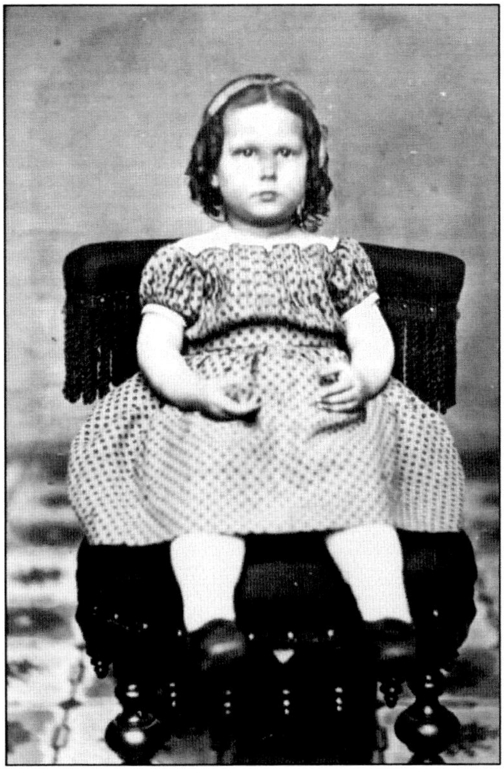

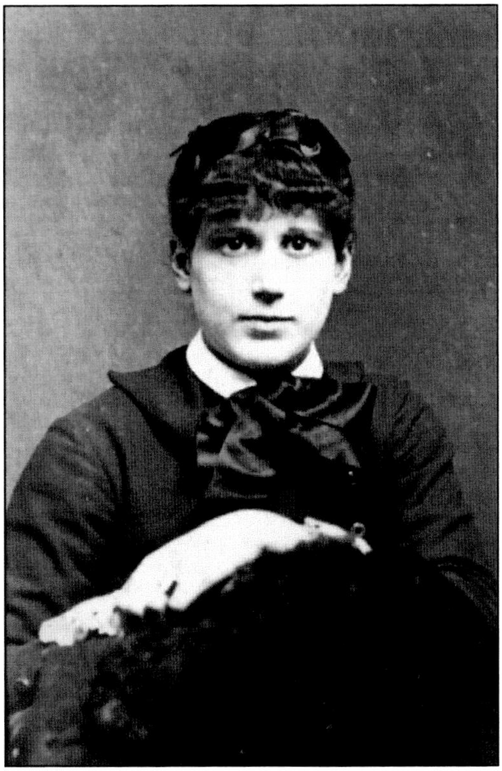

A youthful Eunice looks directly into the camera. She and her husband, Charles, had five children, four girls and a boy. (Hawkins collection.)

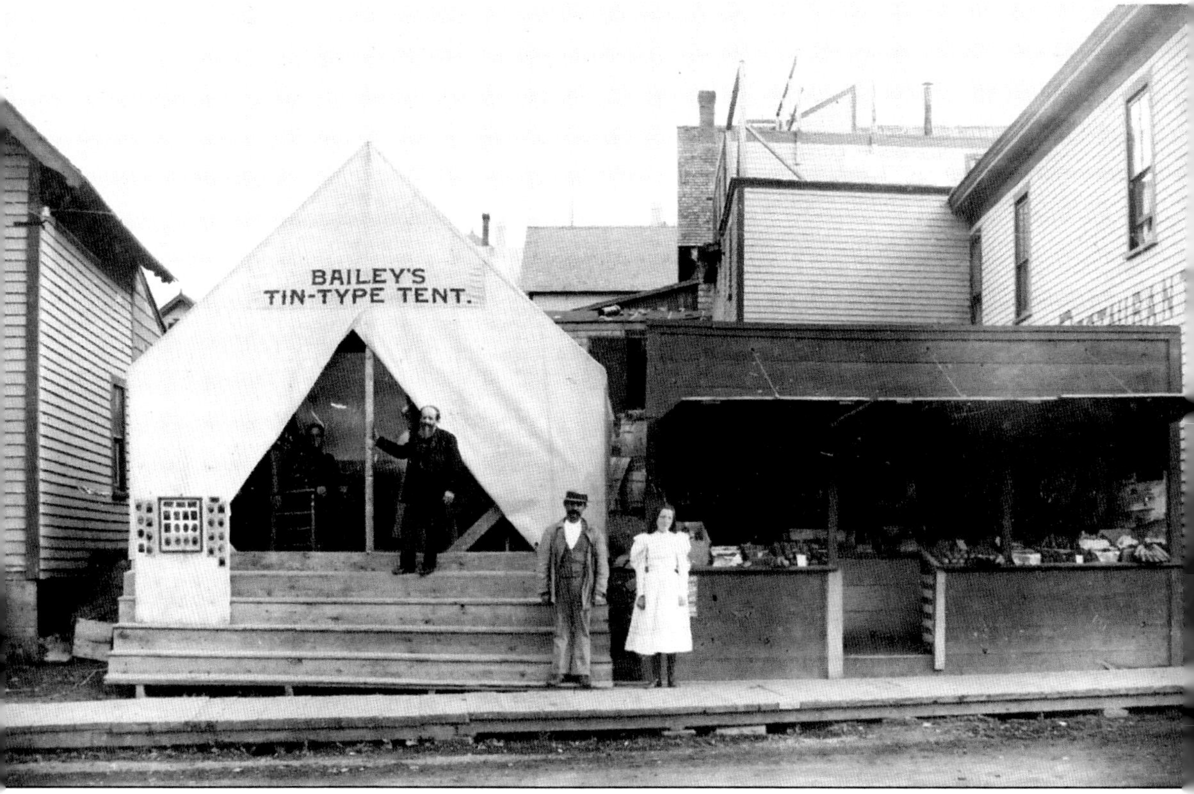

From 1885 until his death in 1894, Henry Bailey took tintype portraits of summer visitors in this tent in downtown Bar Harbor. Bailey was assisted by his brother-in-law Augustus F. Morse, shown standing on the steps, and his daughter Etta Bailey Richards, who is seated in the tent. (Hawkins collection.)

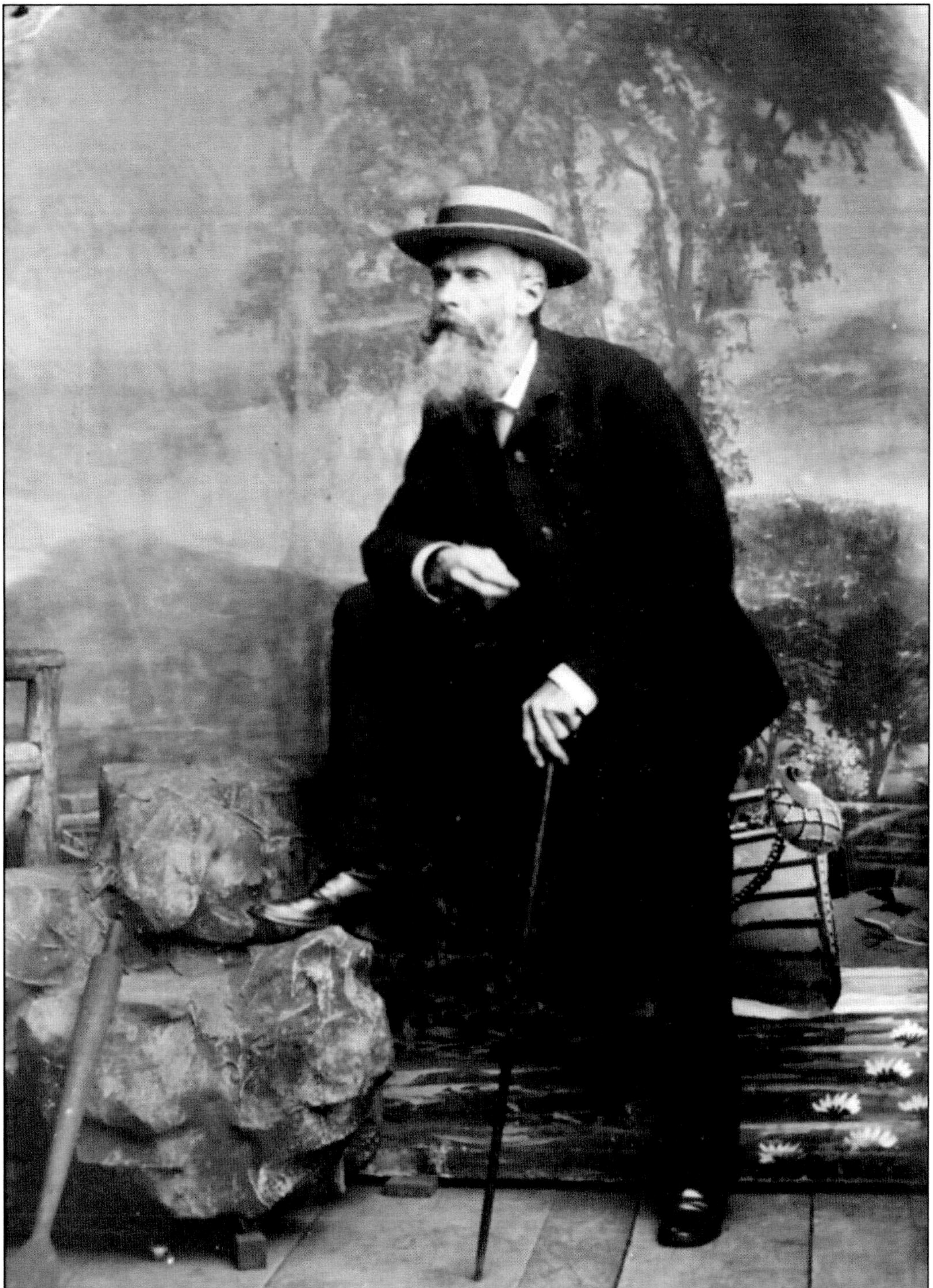

This tintype of Bailey in old age was taken against a painted backdrop and studio props in his Bar Harbor photography tent. (Hawkins collection.)

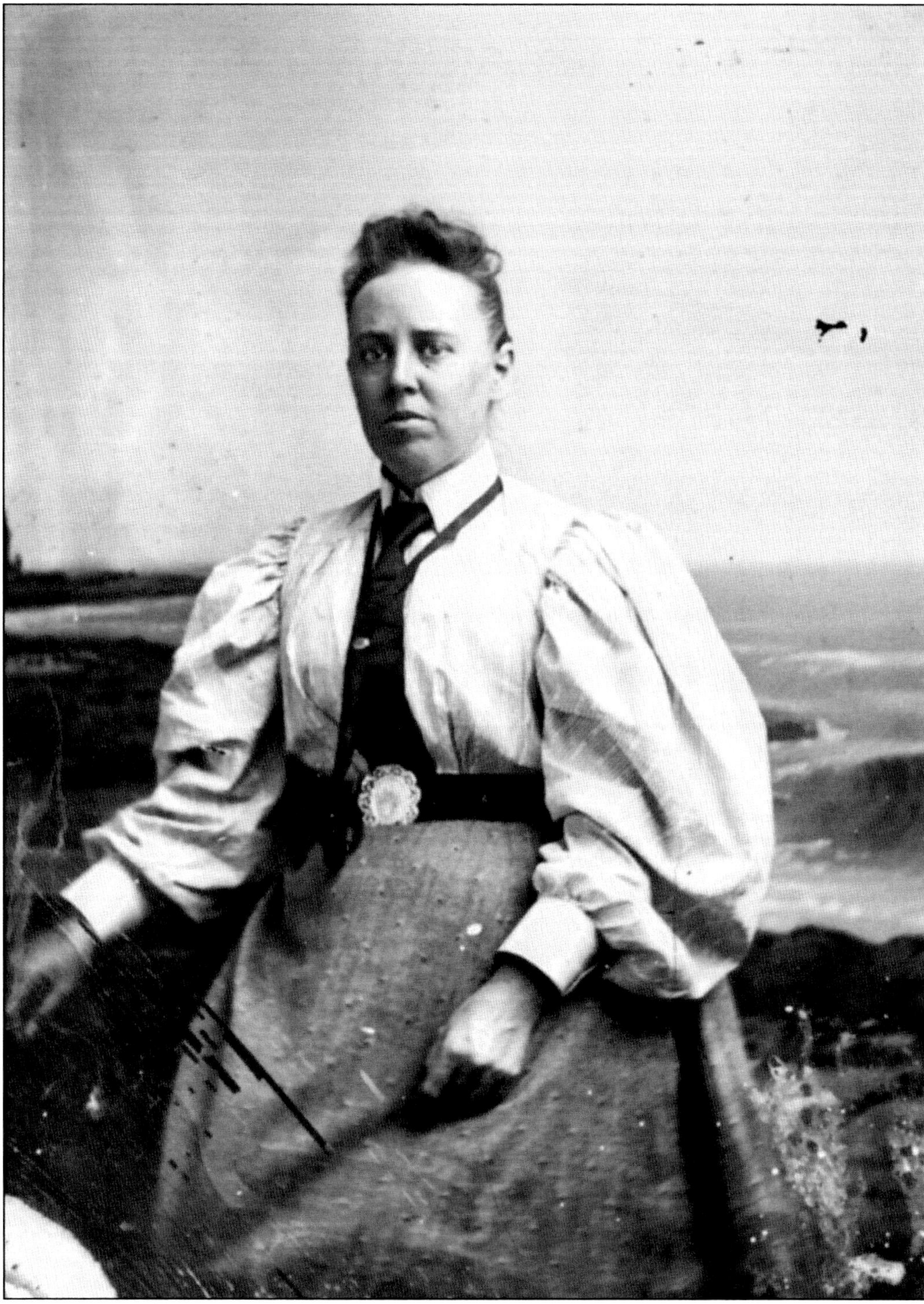

Etta Bailey Richards poses for a tintype portrait in front of a coastal painted backdrop in her father's Bar Harbor photography tent. (Hawkins collection.)

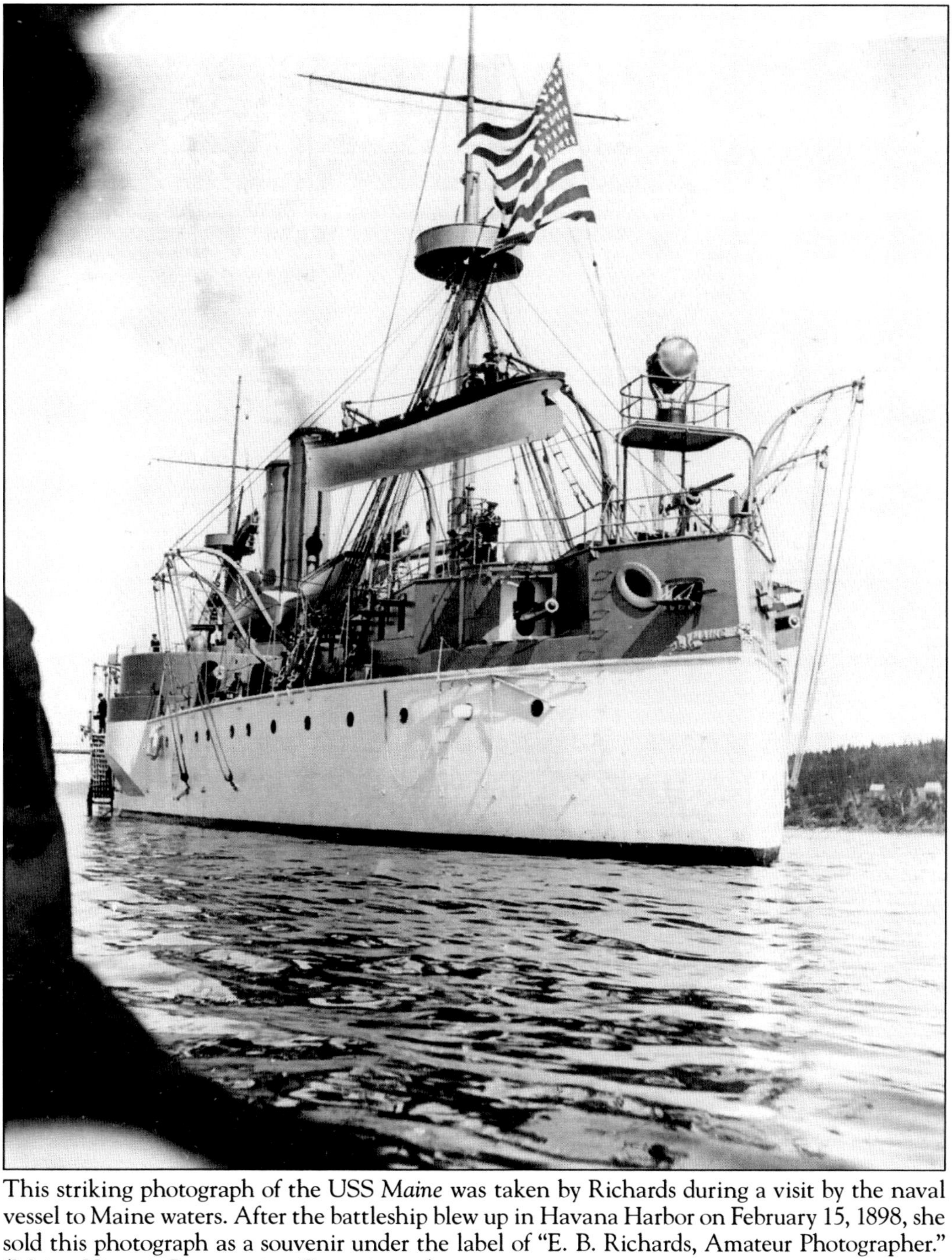

This striking photograph of the USS *Maine* was taken by Richards during a visit by the naval vessel to Maine waters. After the battleship blew up in Havana Harbor on February 15, 1898, she sold this photograph as a souvenir under the label of "E. B. Richards, Amateur Photographer." (Maine Historic Preservation Commission.)

Consistent with our mission to preserve history on a local level, this book was printed in South Carolina on American-made paper and manufactured entirely in the United States. Products carrying the accredited Forest Stewardship Council (FSC) label are printed on 100 percent FSC-certified paper.

MADE IN THE USA